Critical Perspectives on the Internet

Critical Perspectives on the Internet

Edited by
Greg Elmer

ROWMAN & LITTLEFIELD PUBLISHERS, INC.
Lanham • Boulder • New York • Oxford

ROWMAN & LITTLEFIELD PUBLISHERS, INC.

Published in the United States of America
by Rowman & Littlefield Publishers, Inc.
A Member of the Rowman & Littlefield Publishing Group
4720 Boston Way, Lanham, Maryland 20706
www.rowmanlittlefield.com

P.O. Box 317, Oxford, OX2 9RU, United Kingdom

British Library Cataloguing in Publication Information Available

Library of Congress Cataloging-in-Publication Data Available

ISBN 0-7425-1131-6 (cloth : alk. paper)
ISBN 0-7425-1132-4 (pbk. : alk. paper)

Printed in the United States of America

♾™ The paper used in this publication meets the minimum requirements of
American National Standard for Information Sciences—Permanence of Paper
for Printed Library Materials, ANSI/NISO Z39.48-1992.

Dedicated to my parents
Christopher and Carol Elmer

Contents

Preface: A Critical Primer for the Internet   ix
   Greg Elmer

Acknowledgments   xiii

Part I: Critical Introductions

1   Disorganizing the "New Technology"   3
   David Sholle

2   A Critical History of the Internet   27
   Brian Martin Murphy

Part II: Net Architecture

3   The Case of Web Browser Cookies: Enabling/Disabling
   Convenience and Relevance on the Web   49
   Greg Elmer

4   Surfing for Knowledge in the Information Society   63
   Richard Rogers and Andrés Zelman

Part III: Rethinking Net Communities

5   The Myth of the Unmarked Net Speaker   89
   Alice Crawford

6   Digitizing and Globalizing Indigenous Voices: The Zapatista
   Movement   105
   Donna M. Kowal

Part IV: Globalization and Governance

7   **E-Capital and the Many-Headed Hydra**   129
    Nick Dyer-Witheford

8   **Convergence Policy: It's Not What You Dance, It's the Way
    You Dance It**   165
    Marcus Breen

9   **Internet Globalization and the Political Economy of
    Infrastructure**   183
    Bram Dov Abramson

Index   203

About the Contributors   215

Preface: A Critical Primer for the Internet

Greg Elmer

While the contributions to this collection each bring unique, and sometimes contrasting arguments, taken as a whole I believe they provide an expansive—though in no way comprehensive—introduction to critical approaches to the Internet. For the close reader, this collection's contribution to Internet criticism can begin to be gleaned from the subtitles of the book's four postintroductory sections: "Critical Introductions," "Net Architecture," "Rethinking Net Communities," and "Globalization and Governance." Such headings are, however, quite porous, as many of the book's articles could just as easily be reclassified under titles such as Privacy, Identity, Net Rhetoric, Architecture, Resistance, etc. Moving beyond these headings, this introduction will attempt to provide a brief outline or primer for critical approaches to the Internet. With the help of the book's authors, their ideas, and words, these introductory thoughts will highlight some key underlying problematics, arguments, and topics that critical approaches have typically addressed in the past and will no doubt need to revisit in the not too distant future.

In the present tense at least there seem to be two connected arguments that frame many critical studies of the Internet. The first is a refutation of the claim that the Internet—or the emerging "information society" in general—represents a revolutionary era.[1] Such claims have formed the basis for a certain social discourse which Alice Crawford's chapter dubs "techno-populist rhetoric." Other authors both here and elsewhere have also referred to this approach as cyber-hype, cyber-libertarianism, new media boosterism, or cyber-promotion. Chief proponents of this approach from both corporate and government spheres include Bill Gates (as arguably chief benefactor of the Internet), and Al Gore (as its chief political "inventor").[2] It is often argued that the most revolutionary aspect of the Net is its ability to bypass the need for a broker or middleman. The Internet, in other words, "dis-intermediates" relationships by seemingly giving individuals the ability—and power—to directly communicate and otherwise transact with other individuals (Patelis 2000). Consequently, the techno-populist approach argues for a pluralist definition of the Net where, Alice Crawford notes, old social hierarchies are seemingly "flattened."

Secondly, and inherently tied to these broader social, political, and economic discourses, is of course the technology of the Internet itself. Thus, in an attempt to directly respond to techno-populists, David Sholle asks the question in the first chapter of the book, what's so "new" about new media such as the Internet? One answer consistently offered by both boosters and critics of the Net focuses on the hypertextual architecture of the Web, in particular, and the decentered network of the Internet in general. However, what remains to be widely articulated, from a critical perspective, is exactly how a theoretically nonsequential, multiauthored, and decentered medium has changed as a result of the widespread use of commercial Web browsers, Internet Service Providers (such as AOL), and an ongoing process of Net "portalization" (the growth of one stop—or more aptly, first stop—shopping and search sites such as Yahoo, Excite, MSN, etc.). One might be simply tempted to conclude that such largely commercial changes to the Internet have provided users packaged, customized, or personalized content that subtly—or more explicitly—discourages nomadic browsing or other more radical challenges to established norms and rules of ordering, classifying, and distributing knowledge and property. However, what strikes me as particularly encouraging about this collection is that many of its contributors, particularly Rogers and Zelman, Murphy, and Dyer-Witheford, in addition to detailing the process of Internet corporatization and portalization, have also questioned how the Internet's many fissures, cracks, crevasses, and sometimes gaping holes have offered radical possibilities for the critical computing community, everyday users, WTO protester, Zapatista, etc. The case of online music swapping program Napster and a host of other peer-to-peer file sharing networks provides perhaps the most obvious and widespread example of how individual users can use the underlying architecture of the Internet to challenge established media industries.[3]

Thus as a network of personal computers, routers, specialized networks, and larger institutional servers, employing a host of different protocols, programs, and standards, the Internet has often been used to tactically and effectively disrupt established online and offline social and political relationships (see, for example, Donna Kowal's discussion of the Zapatistas in Mexico). However, so as not to generally conclude that such examples offer a pluralist definition of the Internet, as the techno-populist approach clearly argues, the critical perspectives brought forward in this book rigorously investigate, historically, empirically, and theoretically the broader social, technological, and political factors that both facilitate or restrict challenges to dominant power structures such as the Mexican government or the music recording industry. Clearly the degree to which users are able or encouraged to harness some of the more decentered, pluralistic, antihierarchical, and otherwise anarchic possibilities of the Web is heavily dependent upon their PC-Net literacy (including their knowledge of mainstream software or access to specialized software and user communities), their PC hardware and peripherals (including sufficient modem speed and dedicated servers for more large scale political efforts), and their Internet Service Provider (as many ISPs forbid, or technologically limit through firewalls or surveillance methods, various forms of "subversive" computing).

Accordingly, the book's chapters implicitly incorporate one or many of these mitigating factors of Internet use within their broader arguments. For instance, from an empirical standpoint, Richard Rogers and Andrés Zelman's chapter discusses specialized research software that can map public debate on the Web. By mapping the interconnected hyperlinks of online interests, the authors offer a politically dynamic view of the social life of issues on the Web. What's more, such "issue networks" also provide a stark contrast to the dominant portal approach of Yahoo, Excite, MSN, and others who simply provide suggestions for possible paths based upon "cool stuff," associative reasoning (keyword searches), or most popular user hits (cf. The Lycos 50).[4] By contrast, from both theoretical and historical perspectives, Nick Dyer-Witheford and Brian Martin Murphy's chapters argue that critical challenges to dominant Internet politics and policies are the result of strategic interventions from multiple user communities using disparate technologies. Thus, while discussing quite different subject matter, Brian Murphy and Greg Elmer both make the case for an everyday, user-centered approach to the study of the Internet—one that investigates the impact of online user policies and software privacy preferences. As a complementary perspective to Murphy and Elmer, Alice Crawford, and to a lesser extent Richard Rogers and Andrés Zelman, offer compelling critiques of the "dis-embodied" online user and Internet as online community-town hall, both central propositions of early influential studies of computer-mediated communication (see especially Rheingold 1993).

Lastly, Bram Dov Abramson's comprehensive and exceptionally lucid discussion of the complex technological infrastructure of the Net adds a helpful global, regional, and national context to the discussion of Internet users, technologies, and histories. In an era where past neoconservative privatization plans have begun to haunt railway passengers in Britain or almost all Californians on the power grid, Marcus Breen's broader political and cultural discussion of the role of the state in forging Internet policy and regulation also seems to be particularly germane—as do all critical perspectives that attempt to bring to life networks of—and for—radical social change.

NOTES

1. For an excellent critique of so-called "revolutionary" technologies see Dyer-Witheford's *Cyber-Marx* (1999), specifically chapter two.

2. Cf. Phil Agre (2000).

3. David Garcia and Geert Lovink refer to this potentially subversive element of the Internet as an example of "Tactical Media."

4. http://50.lycos.com.

BIBLIOGRAPHY

Agre, Phil. 2000. "Who Invented 'Invented'?: Tracing the Real Story of the 'Al Gore Invented the Internet' Hoax." *Read Rock Eater Digest*. Online at http://commons. somewhere.com/rre/2000/RRE.Al.Gore.and.the.Inte1.html.

Dyer-Witheford, Nick. 1999. *Cyber-Marx: Cycles and Circuits of Struggle in High-Technology Capitalism*. Urbana: University of Illinois Press.

Elmer, Greg. 2001. "Hypertext on the Web: The Beginning and End of Web Pathology." *Space and Culture*, 10.

Garcia, David, and Geert Lovink. The ABC of Tactical Media. Online at www.waag. org/tmn/frabc.html, accessed June 2001.

Patelis, Korinna. 2000. "E-Mediation by America Online." Pp. 49–63 in *Preferred Placement: Knowledge Politics on the Web*. Ed. Richard Rogers. Maastricht: Jan Van Eyck Akademie Editions.

Rheingold, Howard. 1993. *The Virtual Community*. Reading, Mass.: Addison-Wesley.

Acknowledgments

I've always found the terms "collection," "reader," or "edited book" to be woefully inadequate in describing this particular formatting of words, ideas, arguments, and authors. This project was the culmination of much more than collecting, reading, and editing manuscripts. To obtain the prerequisite inertia for this project, intellectual and critical energy was harnessed from many a source over the years. I'd like to particularly thank Briankle Chang, Bram Abramson, Jonathan Sterne, Jody Berland, Thomas Swiss, Brian M. Murphy, Steve Jones, Rob Shields, Ken Hillis, Fred Turner, Mark Andrejevic, David Lyon, Elfriede Fursich, Michael Keith, Marilyn Matelski, Katya Haskins, and Dana Mastro for their inspiring research, ongoing counsel and support, encouraging comments, and engaging conversations. For a holistic education in new media criticism, programming, and design I'd like to thank Richard Rogers, Noortje Marres, and others working with the Govcom.org Foundation in Budapest and Amsterdam.

The book of course would not have come together without the contributors and the initial encouragement and later understanding (and patience) of Brenda Hadenfeldt, acquisition editor at Rowman & Littlefield. Thanks to James Steinberg for the efficient preparation of the book's index. First rate editorial assistance was provided by Ryan Ellis, my increasingly sought-after research assistant at Boston College. For institutional support and research funding from Boston College I'd like to recognize the many contributions of my chair Dale Herbeck, my department's administrative assistant Mary Saunders, and Deans Joseph Quinn and Michael Smyer. For love, support, pride, and perspective, Paula and Keegan.

I

CRITICAL INTRODUCTIONS

1

Disorganizing
the "New Technology"

David Sholle

The air today is saturated with discussions of the revolutionary implications of new media technologies. Academics, politicians, corporate public relations agents, various digirati, and all manner of "spinners" are racing to proclaim just how revolutionary these new technologies are. The personal computer, digital media production, MP3s, the Internet , and the Web are all seen as the inevitable result of technological progress that will bring (or has already brought) sweeping changes to our society, political system, economy, and our very consciousness. This chapter will explore the problems associated with this conceptualization of technology and will then address the question of what exactly is "new" about new technology. This question centers on the argument over whether this technology will be an agent of freedom or an instrument of control. Will new media technologies break down barriers, increase access, and allow individuals to freely create, or will they assist in creating new hierarchies and new methods of institutional control? The aim of this chapter is to analyze the place that new media technology has in changing our social institutions and our way of representing and practicing in the world.

WHAT IS TECHNOLOGY?

What is technology? This is not really a common question. In everyday life we are prone to simply accept technology as it is; our knowledge of technology is simply our knowledge of its use. The everyday definition of technology is that it is that realm of objects or devices that we call machines or tools. Within contemporary culture, technology is particularly marketed in a way that leads us to add the word "advanced" to this definition and the most "advanced" technology is thought to be the one that will do the most for us. In other words, technology is usually seen in the light of the most "advanced" results of scientific and technological development. Now, when viewed as simply objects, technologies are divorced from the scientific labor that produced them, and they are disconnected from the historical circumstances of particular cultures, economic systems, and political decisions. The result of these disconnections is a popular stance toward technology that can be characterized as one of "amazement."

"Advancing" Technology

In today's society, which appears so driven by images of advancing technology, the most common view of the significance of technology is that it is simply inevitable. Louis Rosseto expresses the utopian side of this—technology as salvation, as the motor of all change. As he expresses it, "Everything is changing: you, your family, your education, your neighborhood, your job, your government, your relation to 'the others.'"[1] Jacques Ellul, on the other hand, expresses the dystopian side—technology as runaway machine, robbing the human of its place in bringing about change. As he puts it, "technique is artificial, autonomous, self-determining, and independent of all human intervention."[2] For utopians such as Rosetto, new technology is a source of freedom— an open, democratic space that will extend the potential of all to creative (and lucrative) activities. For dystopians such as Ellul, new technology is a source of control—enabling the extension of corporate and state surveillance and management into more and more areas of both public and private life. As opposite as these views are they indicate a set of common traits that dominates discussion of technology today.

Utopians and dystopians both express some variant of what has been called technological determinism—that technology on its own determines the shape of human history and consciousness. Thus, McLuhan claimed that "today computers hold out the promise of a means of instant translation of any code or language into any other code or language. The computer, in short, promises by technology a Pentecostal condition of universal understanding and Unity."[3] Ellul goes so far as to claim that technology is "independent of all human intervention." We see this discourse today in both corporate advertisements for e-business and in government initiatives for the development of information networks. The utopians and dystopians both emphasize the inevitability and autonomy of technology. Rosetto gleefully announces that "everything is changing," chiming in with those who view technology as a runaway force that must be joined "else it pass us by." In this rhetoric, technology is autonomous of the social; it is as if technology, once constructed, becomes an automatic process that humans must obey.

Another common trait, expressed most clearly by McLuhan, is that technology forms and affects human consciousness and human relationships. He claimed that with the computer, "The next step would seem to be, not to translate, but to by-pass languages in favour of a general cosmic consciousness. . . . The condition of 'weightlessness' that biologists say promises a physical immortality, may be paralleled by the condition of speechlessness that could confer a perpetuity of collective harmony and peace."[4] Rosetto's *Wired* magazine rhetoric, with its militant updating of McLuhan's notions of a network-consciousness, is a prime source of this. The claim here is that human practices will move to virtual reality where the physical aspects of actual conduct become archaic markers of the former "meat" world. These all-encompassing transformations of consciousness are often invested with a type of religious significance. Here, technology becomes the salvific force that will bring never-ending peace and harmony (or at least make one's business run smoothly). In a Xerox ad, characters who look like the Greek gods hover over a screen through which they see humans hopelessly trying to do business without the benefit of the newest technology. The gods intervene with Promethean fire in the form of various cyber-tech equipment. We are left to the "'fate'" of technology which is, itself, a force of nature.

Thus, finally, this discourse ambiguously interprets technology's relation to the natural and organic. As Rosetto puts it, "Electric technology is bringing about social changes so profound that their only parallel is probably the discovery of fire."[5] Thus, information technologies are linked to the natural element "fire," and it is crucial here that both the computer and fire are "discovered." Likewise, McLuhan linked computers to the biological, a move again taken up by *Wired* magazine in its equation of the bit with the secret of life. On the other hand, the dystopians (like Ellul) see technology as an artificial intrusion into the natural realm. Here, "the milieu" of machine is seen as a replacement of the natural world, but ironically it is just as much a natural force. Thus technology, when seen as a conditioning machine, becomes an autonomous external force that is equal to nature.

As a result, technology is seen as a self-contained sphere—the artificial, physical machine. It is this aspect of the dominant discourse on technology that leads us to think of it as a self-existent separate realm or as a set of objects that act as an independent force in our lives. As a result, it appears that we cannot act upon technology, but rather only with it. Still, simply attacking McLuhanism or even Marxism as "technologically deterministic" leads to a political impasse—the choice between techno-utopianism and neo-Luddism.[6] A simple anti-determinism stance makes it difficult to locate any actual effects of technology. Instead, what lies behind the present discourse on technology is not a strict determinism, but rather an erasure of the social construction of technology.

In the current hyper-technological discourse, the problems resulting from the construction and use of the new technologies are framed as social in character, yet these problems are reversible through technological solutions. At the same time, the manner in which new technologies and technological thinking enter into and frame problems in a particular way is ignored. In either case, the social construction of technology is left unexamined. In these institutional discourses, how technologies develop and how they are connected to scientific labor, cultural factors, economic practices, and political decisions remain hidden from view. Ultimately, we are prone to taking a "gee whiz" view of technology, one that naturalizes the existence of the technological object.

This "technology-as-tool kit" approach would like us to view technology as benign, as an amazing array of inventions that simply drop out of the blue. As Robins and Webster put it, such a view sees technology as separate from the social: "Because so many commentators, in adopting this perspective, accept as their starting point a completed technology, they are impelled to offer the public no role other than that of consumer of the latest gadgetry. Ignoring the processes by which technology itself comes to be constituted means that one is restricted to consideration only of the likely impact the latest product will have."[7]

A Critical Theory of Technology

Instead, a critical theory of technology argues that technologies are more than a collection of tools; that they are, in fact, processes that structure the world in particular ways. As such, technologies are social, political, and cultural artifacts that are central to human action and in turn affect human action.[8] In other words, technology is the medium of daily life in modern societies. We should not see technology and the social as separate domains. This viewpoint on technology, a viewpoint that centers on its social construction, will be the basis for examining what is "new" about new technology.[9]

The automobile, as an abstract motor vehicle, is relatively neutral. But the development of it within a particular form of industrial capitalism is not. It evolves from and leads to a particular formation of social life in which transportation becomes privatized, leading to a form of culture that Raymond Williams called "mobile privatization." It is not simply the application of the technology that is biased toward certain ends; the very design of the technology is embedded in political, economic, and cultural values.

Feenberg insists that the totality (the overarching pattern of social, cultural, political, and economic practices that form the web of society) precedes the particular. The social web that defines and implements the technology is far more significant than any particular tool of technology itself. That being said, although technical devices are not the sole reason for changes in society, the spheres in which they exist do redefine the patterns of everyday life.

In *Questioning Technology*, Feenberg offers a way of looking at technological phenomena that recognizes that they are underdetermined. That is, though a given technology takes up a certain function, there is nothing inherent in the notion of technology as a functioning tool that entirely dictates its particular use. The technical principles behind a particular device are not entirely responsible for its design.[10] This is clearly evident in the case of radio technology, where the question of the radio's use in point-to-point communication versus its use in broadcasting was hotly contested, resulting in a choice to primarily develop radio as a one-way medium. Nevertheless, the use of the technology as a means of point-to-point communication persists, albeit at a smaller scale. The point is that technologies do not simply fulfill a function in meeting natural needs; rather their development is caught up in the social construction of needs. As Feenberg points out, the complex process of social construction underlying technologies is most frequently forgotten when a particular technology becomes accepted as a given regime. He states:

> Such regimes incorporate many social factors expressed by technologists in purely technical language and practices. I call those aspects of technological regimes which can best be interpreted as direct reflections of significant social values the "technical code" of the technology. *Technical codes define the object in strictly technical terms in accordance with the social meaning it has acquired.* These codes are usually invisible because, like culture itself, they appear self-evident. The telephone, the automobile, the refrigerator and a hundred other everyday devices have clear and unambiguous definitions in the dominant culture: we know exactly what they are insofar as we are acculturated members of our society. But there is nothing obvious about this. . . . Each of these objects was selected from a series of alternatives by a code reflecting specific social values.[11]

What Feenberg is claiming here is that a technology such as the computer is a product of social processes from the beginning. The particular construction of knowledge in institutions of science and engineering, the economic interests of companies, the cultural patterns of consumption, the spatial arrangements of communities and nations, the political motifs of government policies are inscribed into the technology from the very beginning.

The further implication of this process is that technologies are not fixed once and for all. There are powerful forces that may attempt to narrowly define a technology in purely technical and functional terms, so that its potential reinterpretation is steered to comport with interests of power and profit. But as Dyer-Witherford has pointed out, technologies "are often constituted by contending pressures that implant in them contradictory potentialities."[12] This is clearly the case with the Internet, a network whose roots lie in military uses, whose development shifted toward goals of democratically distributed communication through academic and hacker uses, and which is now potentially being channeled toward a for-profit broadcast model by powerful economic interests.

A critical theory of technology starts from the basis that technologies are not preordained, nor are they separable from the social contexts through which they are developed and evolve. Nevertheless, there are aspects of any technology that are material and which are not entirely socially constructed. But even granting this, we must recognize that when we claim revolutionary effects for a technology, it is not simply these material factors that we are talking about. In the end it is the social purposes behind the technology that are determinate.

WHAT IS NEW TECHNOLOGY?

The Ubiquitously New

What is "new" about new technology? To answer this question, it is first necessary to know what is meant by "new." The "new" is ubiquitously used within marketing strategies for nearly every product and service: revolutionary new formulas, unique designs, the latest models, space age designs, and so on. The average consumer is well aware of the hype attached to "new" products, but is also often unable to escape the pressure to keep up. Now, the claims for "new media" technologies go well beyond the claims traditionally made for consumer products. We are told that these technologies will change everything—the way we live, work, think, and relate to each other. The typical message we confront today is that new digital technology is a complete break from the past, that it is sweeping away the past, and that if we don't join in, we will be left behind. We don't seem to have any choice about this—technology is in control.

The idea that society is determined by technology is a very old one, but it has taken on a new twist in the so-called "information age." For centuries, human beings have used technologies as metaphors to characterize historical periods: the iron age, the industrial revolution, the steam age, the electronic sublime, the nuclear age, the space age, and now the information age. Particular technological objects are made to stand in for the general determining nature of technology. In the past, the railroads, the telegraph, the automobile, the airplane, the atom bomb, and the computer have been seen as technologies of such impact that society as a whole was transformed by them. We should note how the types of machines used to symbolize "technology" as a whole change and become the means through which we designate the new. We have a tendency to think only of the new and ignore older technologies as if the previous "revolution" was a false start or a now archaic mode (what happened to "the Nuclear Age"?). In the end we learn nothing. In fact, it is typical that the social significance of a technology only gets discussed when that technology is new. Historians have documented that the telegraph, telephone, radio, television, and cable TV were all initially received in startlingly utopian/dystopian terms. Each time, it was claimed that the technology would unite people around the world, bring about the end of war, solve the problems of education, change human consciousness. Each time, the technology's detractors made outlandish claims of impending danger and destruction. Each time, these "inventions" were incorporated into the social order, and as time passed they became understood as given and unquestioned.[13] When was the last time you heard any social commentary about the telephone?

So, what are the claims of "newness" that we should address when assessing the new media technologies? It should be clear that it cannot be anything as formulaic as a strictly technical explanation, yet it must have something to do with the technical elements themselves. If we are really to assess the "newness" of digital technologies, we must look beyond these technical elements themselves to changes that connect them to changes in social relations, values, goals, and modes of thinking.

Microprocessing, Digitization, and the Network of Networks

As already noted, throughout history various technologies have been described as bringing about revolutionary changes and have even been used to divide history into periods. As Gordon Graham notes, in 1868, Charles Francis Adams, Jr., characterized the railroads as "the most tremendous and far-reaching engine of social change which has ever blessed or cursed mankind." This statement sounds almost exactly like the claims now being made about the Internet. The question is: How exactly are these technologies transforming in their impact? Graham stipulates that we should be looking for impacts that transform "the character of personal and social life across a wide range"[14] of phenomena.

But how can we demarcate a specific device as generating these transformations? Can we really divide up the history of technology into periods defined by the invention of a specific device? In the case of the railroad, this "device" is based in the previous developments of the wheel and steam engine. In the case of the Internet, we have a technology that is dependent on such previous inventions as writing, movable type, and the microprocessor.[15] It becomes evident that there is no clear moment at which a technology is something radically new, nor is there a definite point where a new technology eradicates previous technologies. Yet, it cannot be denied that the complex of inventions, scientific knowledge, and engineering practices that coalesce into specific configurations of devices can have and have had profound effects on the social totality. But this very possibility—

that a technology can have a transformative impact—is already reliant on a complex of previous scientific, political, social, and economic structures and choices. Thus, in analyzing the "newness" of new technologies, we would be looking for evidence that these technologies contribute to changes in the configuration of space and time, the relationship of humans to nature, the structure of the family and domestic space, the relationship of workers to the labor process, the conduct of financial institutions, the configuration of cities, and shifts in the conduct of politics.

Keeping this in mind, how are these processes embodied in the current so-called information revolution? What are the primary technologies involved? Since we are looking for technological complexes that may contribute to large-scale alterations in the structure of social and cultural life, then the likely candidates will be technologies that are involved in the control of, or the interconnection of, a vast array of other types of technology. An example from the past would be the wheel, which is instrumental in transport, the pulleys and gears of machinery, the mechanisms of timepieces, and so on. Accordingly, the focus, here, will be on three broad sets of technological complexes: (1) Microprocessing, (2) Digitization, and (3) the Network of Networks. It should be noted that these are not so much devices as they are processes that consist of material and intellectual components.

Now, why microprocessing? Jerome Ravetz has characterized the microprocessor as an elemental form that functions as the control mechanism within the technological milieu of the information society.[16] It functions as a producer of control functions in the factory, as an organizer of the flow of transactions, as a monitor of labor. Thus, the microprocessor promises to profoundly affect the overall conduct of economic life. And, why digitization? The advent of digital processes—the capability of reducing complex material and intellectual processes to a common set of binary markers—is not only one of the conceptual foundations of the microprocessor, but it also contributes to a reconceptualization of the nature of knowledge and information. "Digitization" refers not to the technical construction of storage and processing operations inside the microprocessor, but rather to the processes of representation that the computer and other new media make possible. Thus, digitization affects our construction of information and knowledge and so affects our overall cultural life. And finally, why the Network of Networks? The Network of Networks refers roughly to what we call the Internet. It is not so much a technological device, but rather a technologically driven way of structuring the relationship between individuals, groups, and states. In so doing, it contributes to the reconfiguration of our relationship to space and time. As a result, it may have profound effects on how we relate to each other, our communities, and the world.

NEW TECHNOLOGIES: FREEDOM AND CONTROL

It would be impossible in one short chapter to address all of the possible changes that may be brought about by new media technologies. In fact, some of these changes, such as the claim that computers eliminate paper, are not only potentially trivial but are in themselves suspect. The paperless office has never come about. A few broad, more substantive categories of potential change are the impact on consciousness, the impact on the structure of knowledge and its acquisition, and the impact on the labor process.

Consciousness and Invisibility

The new twist in contemporary new media technologies is that, now, technology is not seen purely as an object but as an abstract notion of digitization. The new technologies themselves are kind of boring—silicon chips, video screens, and so on. They become attractive through the notion that they are "intelligent" and that they enable us to form magical virtual selves.

Past technologies, such as the steam engine, led to analogies of the machine with the human body. Machines were extensions of the arms and legs and thus were looked at in terms of their physical power. Counterposed to this, the development of new technologies has led to analogies of the machine with the human mind. For the first time, a predominant technology is based on thinking processes that very quickly have become simply identified with the processing and control of information. As a result, human qualities such as intelligence and memory are attributed to computers and in reverse, the qualities of computers such as feedback and information processing are attributed to the human brain. As Barglow points out, mechanical technologies such as the automobile assume a human agent that operates them, but information technologies seem to give rise to activities that are essentially subjectless:

> Our language indicates as much: Terms like "feedback" and "interface" describe relationships among people as if they were relationships among cybernetic processes and objects. As our lives become more involved with information technologies, we may find that these involvements call into question the notions of centered, coherent subjectivity and personal freedom what have traditionally propped up our ideals of selfhood and individuality.[17]

Ironically, the notions of selfhood and individuality are precisely the values that are being promoted as the outcome of the new media. Our slippage in the use of machine/human metaphors in descriptions of information technology indicates a fundamental antagonism that underlies the potential of the new media landscape: It is fundamentally centered on the opposition between control and freedom. This opposition is central to several key areas of argument over the revolutionary potential of the new technologies. First, the new technologies can be looked at as extensions of human consciousness. Do new technologies, as transparent interface tools, create an environment that is conducive to opening up areas of the self that enhance its freedom, or do they limit and control human activity? Second, the new technologies can be looked at in terms of how they affect the interaction of the self with the other. Do they break down barriers, both within the mind and between minds, or again, do they reconstruct the blockages of the "meat" world? Third, the new technologies can be looked at in terms of how they affect the representation of reality. Do nonlinear tools simply increase the freedom of information or do they provide new methods for controlling information? Finally, the new technologies can be looked at in terms of how they affect human perception of time and space. Do they fundamentally change our perception of and interaction with our own bodies and the "body" of others by breaking down barriers or do they create new blockages?

The Extension of Human Consciousness

Marshall McLuhan is often cited as the first to conceive of technologies in terms of their extension and transformation of human consciousness and thinking processes. McLuhan stated:

> All media work us over completely. They are so pervasive in their personal, political, economic, aesthetic, psychological, moral, ethical and social consequences that they leave no part of us untouched, unaffected or unaltered. The medium is the massage. Any understanding of social and cultural change is impossible without a knowledge of the way media work as environments.[18]

For McLuhan, each technological medium is an extension of some psychical or physical faculty and thus, each medium reorganizes the way we use our senses and the way we perceive the world. The computer or the Internet, for example, are not revolutionary because of the content they carry, but rather because they create a new environment—a technostructure—in which we must live. McLuhan saw humankind as now fully embedded in its technological objects, and accordingly, the space of human interaction is now fully technological.

In general terms, McLuhan's thought has been taken up in analyzing how the computer and the Internet change human consciousness. In order to understand this change we must make a comparison to the supposed past dominant medium—print. Whereas print fosters linear, hierarchical thinking, an inward looking consciousness, visual dominance, and spatial isolation, the computer and Internet foster nonlinear linkages, multileveled thinking, an outward and inclusive consciousness, multisensual perspective, and spatial and temporal interconnection. Ultimately, for followers of McLuhan, the Internet is about abolishing space and time through a reversal of our relationship to technology. Whereas industrial technologies—the printing press—are extensions of our body in space, the new technologies extend the body through space and finally abolish it, for they "extend our central nervous system itself in a global embrace."[19] Followers of McLuhan claim that new media create a situation in which we are inside the machine, that our consciousness is now constructed in the space enabled by the Internet and the computer. This technologically driven space is interpreted as being one that increases our freedom to think and to act.

But as Stamps points out, McLuhan often linked historical and cultural changes too closely with the advent of specific media and thus failed to treat the specific structure of media dialectically.[20] As a result, there are tendencies in McLuhan's thought to equate the specific institutionalized form of a medium, such as the television or the Internet, with the medium per se. He all too easily drops out the social context of the media and instead focuses exclusively on the abstract formal properties of the currently operating institutionally developed form of media.

This social context reveals a set of contradictory principles operating at the core of the computer's architecture. The computer's internal structure, its logical trees and binary processing, resemble the principles of mechanistic rationalization. That is, it realizes a plan installed at its core and methodically carries out the plan. It does not function through the external direction of a conscious agent, instead it replicates the initial plan. This makes it ideal for control purposes. The question is whether this control element conflicts with the communicative capabilities of digital technology.[21]

Due to this underlying structure of control, the microprocessor and the Internet do not fit neatly into the McLuhanite dichotomy of print versus new visual media. The microprocessor organizes and controls, but when inserted into some contexts, it also fragments and isolates. Likewise, the network can serve as an extensive means of control and hierarchical organization when used in the operation of financial markets, but as the basis of an open communication space, it can allow for more equal exchanges and even wild distributions of cultural objects. In actuality, the Internet is a diffused and potentially open architecture, and this in fact may be the way that a large number of Internet users experience it. But underlying the Internet is another architecture—one of hardware and software—that is owned and operated by centralized corporations and which is designed according to the principles of mechanistic rationalization that Feenberg points out.

There is then a fundamental ambivalence surrounding the computer and the Internet. As Feenberg points out, "the computer was not destined by some inner techno-logic to serve as a communications medium."[22] The Internet itself was conceived as a means for engineers and scientists to distribute data. It was only later that the Internet was appropriated for the unintended purpose of communication between diverse users.

The current rhetoric of the "information revolution" would have it otherwise: The internal design of technologies leads to certain results—that is, there is a logic internal to the technology that directly leads to the formation of the Internet in just the way it actually exists. Feenberg, on the other hand, has shown that "technical design is not determined by a general criterion such as efficiency, but concerns the cultural definition of needs and therefore of the problems to which technology is addressed."[23] Only when the technology is settled and accepted does it dictate a certain form of perception or consciousness, and even then this shaping of human experience is contested and struggled over. The personal computer is a perfect example of this. It was launched on the market with no real applications or functions, and only later were its functions discovered and developed. But now we are at a crossroads. The series of technological developments that have resulted in the personal computer, the Internet, and the palm pilot have crystallized into what Foucault called a "regime of truth."[24] The cultural and political struggles that set in place the functions of these new media have been to a large extent settled, and these cultural and political formations are now embedded in the technologies; they form the "unconscious" of the new technology which tends to become invisible. As a result, the new media have taken up the appearance of nature; they are now part of what Feenberg calls a "technical code."[25] The particular technical code of new media technology embodies a set of social values such as speed, transparency, visuality, control, efficiency, and exchangeability. It is through these embodied social values that computerization and communication through the Internet affect our everyday experience and our consciousness of that experience.

Transparency is a concept that is particularly significant in describing how, as an interface tool, the new media affect this everyday consciousness. The new technology has shifted the meaning of transparency. In modernist culture, the technology of the machine is "transparent" in the sense that the user is supposed to be able to rationally construct the "workings" of the machine. For example, even the most technically inept person is aware that the automobile requires fuel that propels an engine that drives wheels, thus moving the vehicle forward. In operating early industrial technology, the worker even directs the mechanisms of gears and pulleys that drive the mechanism. Accordingly, these technologies "transparently" laid out their "rational workings." The invisible magic of the automobile is contained in its cylinders, but no one would imagine the "horseless carriage" contained miniature horses under the hood.

The new postmodern technology defines "transparency" in an exactly opposite manner: Here, the interface screen of the computer "is supposed to conceal the workings of the machine, and to simulate our everyday experience as faithfully as possible" (the Macintosh style of interface, in which iconic signs emulate everyday objects such as trash cans). As a result, the actual digital machinery is more and more inpenetrable and invisible; it is opaque to everyday understanding. The average "user" denounces the endeavor to grasp the functioning of the computer.[26] The new technologies are everywhere, yet we can't see them, their internal workings are invisible, all the more becoming socially and culturally taken for granted. Thus, the new digital technology is totally inpenetrable. In fact, in many cases of microprocessor use, we don't even know it is there—the alarm clock, the coffee maker, the telephone. It is this invisibility that creates a mythic power for the new technology, its magic power. As Zizek puts it:

> If the modernist universe is the universe, hidden behind the screen, of bytes, wires and chips, of electric current, the postmodernist universe is the universe of naive trust in the screen which makes the very quest for "what lies behind it" irrelevant.[27]

The postmodernist cyber-utopians would like to see this as the progressive overcoming of the modernist imposition of the norms of rationality, control, and order. In the transparency of cyberspace we enter an immediate world of sense-events, one that "cannot be reduced to the effect of bodily causes."[28] The cyber-traveler puts aside the rules and becomes submerged in the play of appearances. But such a theory depends on the very actual workings of digital technologies that are, in fact, rigidly ordered and rule driven.

The Self and Others

One claim advanced by postmodernists and cyber-utopians is that human interaction in cyberspace undermines the notion of the self as a centered, autonomous identity. Instead, the experience of cyberspace is one in which individuals play with various identities and thus experience a plastic sense of self. The experience of participating in a variety of MUDs (Multi-User Domains) is one where the "true" identity of the actors is hidden, where one can take on new gender roles and try out a variety of personalities. Further, one can leave the body behind, leaving one's "'subjectivity'" floating around the ether on various listservs, chat rooms, and bulletin boards.

The technical elements that allow for this potential involve the architecture of the network. It is, as we have seen, a network of networks. As such it has no walls, but also, it allows for no point of physical contact. All interaction is through the screen, a screen that does not show the user how her actions reach the other, but instead is based on visual feedback that emulates everyday physical objects. However, at the same time, it can be said that the Web still relies a great deal on the older print culture—it is after all a textual machine.

The experience of print culture is one in which the reader cannot speak back to the author. This is also true of the broadcast world, where the encoders of the news or entertainment media disseminate their messages to a mass of viewers, who can speak back at the tube but cannot be heard. Yet, there is something virtual about all of this communication, for the reader and the viewer don't simply sit there as objects of manipulation, accepting the representations of the media as "reality." It seems evident that communication has always been virtual. Even our day-to-day bodily interactions are not simply a hard reality—we, after all, put on performances for those we meet. Perhaps cyberspace highlights the constructedness of the self and the slipperiness of reality, but it is not as such a total break from our other forms of communication as postmodernists sometimes claim.

A second claim of the cyber-utopians is that the decentered networks of the Internet create new kinds of communities that will create a revolutionary participatory democracy. The desire here is for a transparent world, one in which the "the mystery of the impenetrable bureaucratic state is dispelled."[29] Again, this is a new kind of consciousness, a political consciousness that is dispersed throughout the social landscape, rather than embedded in the opaque institutions of centralized governments. Further, we see here, an undercutting of the notion of representation—individuals have unmediated access to expression and decision-making. But, as Zizek points out, the irony of cyberspace is that it creates these communities inside the machine— "reducing individuals to isolated monads, each of them alone, facing a computer, ultimately unsure if the person she or he communicates with on the screen is a 'real' person."[30] In the cyber-utopian dream the distance between individuals is broken down, we reach across space and time to each other, exploding the limitations of geography and body. But such a dream is not of necessity politically liberating. As Robins and Webster see it, "cyberspace, with its myriad of little consensual communities, is a place where you will go in order to find confirmation and endorsement of your identity, and social and political life can never be about confirmation and endorsement—it needs distances."[31] Democratic life is based in otherness, in the distances that separate individuals and lead to divisions that foster adversarial dialogue. It is "a coming together which can only occur through conflict."

This is not to say that the Internet does not have the potential to assist in the construction of such an agonistic political democracy, for it does provide spaces in which individuals and groups can communicate outside of the centralized space of the government. But we cannot rely on the abstract technology of the Internet to do this for us. As Barglow describes it, "When automobiles first were mass produced, they too were advertised as a technology that would bring us together by making everyone accessible to everyone else. But automobile travel turned out to have quite different implications, including the formations of suburbs insulated from the ghettos of the inner city. Similarly, the 'information superhighway' is as likely to atomize as to integrate."[32]

The Nonlinear Search for Reality

Another claim for the revolutionary nature of new media is that its concrete form is nonlinear in nature (digital) and the resulting representational form is hypertextual. Digitization makes possible the encoding of all possible informational content into an equivalent binary form. Thus, all words, images, and sounds can be stored in a single place, accessed at random, and manipulated into mutated forms. Once put into this form, these different types of texts can be made into one streaming hypertextual multimedia display. In addition, information becomes instantaneously searchable and thus, imminently retrievable. Searching is in many ways the key to new media. But what is searching and why is it not necessarily a desirable mode?

The digitization of information establishes the Internet and particularly the World Wide Web as an information explosion, not the implosion talked about by McLuhan and Baudrillard. This is certainly one of the revolutionary consequences of the new media—the fact that they enable a constant and multileveled searching function. But this availability of information is also potentially responsible for a condition of excess. As Zizek puts it, "general availability will induce unbearable claustrophobia; excess of choice will be experienced as the impossibility to choose."[33] Once again, we see that the effects of the new media are not closed and singularly progressive, but rather are dialectical and conflicted.

Time and Space

Still another claim for the new media is that the network of networks eradicates time and space as human constraints. Distance is no longer an impediment to connection and duration is now instantaneous. If we conceive of the network on a nonbroadcast model, we can see how it decenters space, for it is nothing more than a web of interconnections with no central station. As a result, communication breaks from the sender/receiver model of the mass media. But despite this decentralization, the network still has fixed centers. Around the globe, large centers of finance and technology become key nodes in the network, and it is around and through these centralized sites that people and money flow. In fact, even the network itself is not immune to the broadcast model, as evidenced in the argument over the Internet versus the information highway model of technological infrastructure.[34]

At the personal level, cyberspace offers the false promise of leaving our bodies behind and traveling virtually from any space to any other space, thus eradicating all limitations, all contingencies of our limited actual bodies.[35] Such a promise presupposes something askew in the actual world; fundamental problems in the allocation of social power in the actual world. It is after all, the continual blockage of our ordinary attempts to connect which generates the desire to connect virtually. The fantasy of achieving communion in cyberspace would lose its hold if the fundamental antagonisms of social relations were erased. Yet, cyber-utopians claim just such a future, one in which the virtual overcomes the actual. If this were so, the illusion would be shattered. What, in fact, cyberspace relies upon is an acceptance of the universal necessity of the continued antagonisms of actual social relations. What cyberspace risks substantiating is a willful forgetting of the social power relations within which virtual communities operate.

Information, Economy, Labor

Zizek gives an account of Bill Gates's social fantasy of "friction free capitalism." By "friction free," Gates means an entirely transparent means of exchange in which we can leave aside both the dirty and "friction filled" material world and also the abrasion of class antagonisms. Crucial to this ideology is the notion of cyberspace as a natural organism. Under this notion, "both the earth and global market appear as gigantic self-regulated living systems whose basic structure is defined in terms of the process of coding and decoding, of passing on information."[36] Thus, "information" becomes the key ideological word in the development of the global economy. Information processed through the new technologies takes on at least three functions in contemporary economic processes: (1) it is a resource that provides input into the production process of other commodities, (2) it enables the control of the market itself, and (3) it is an output that is materialized and sold as a commodity.

Information and the Production of Commodities

All of the possibilities of the new technologies depend on one primary element—the microprocessor. Ultimately, what makes the microprocessor different from previous technologies is that it enters into the control of all other technologies. It becomes "the" means of control of all other processes.

As Spencer points out, in traditional organizations, people are given detailed instructions for carrying out assigned tasks that have no direct relation to their own purposes. In doing this labor, the worker primarily follows the prescribed plan and in addition monitors the task "against quality standards."[37] We see this kind of labor in manufacturing plants, in service industries, telemarketing offices, and so on. The microprocessor mirrors these types of human functions. It is used to control and monitor all manner of processes. But the microprocessor cannot think and therefore its directives must be programmed into it.

"This is not merely the truism that computers lack consciousness. It also means that the elements which the device manipulates (0s and 1s, or presences and absences of a state in a given location) do not need to have any meaning in themselves. It must be recognized that any particular string of 1s and 0s existing in a particular area of a microprocessor's memory can 'represent' (be translated from/to) virtually anything."[38]

This capability is what separates the microprocessor from previous technologies—it is what Spencer calls "a meta-technology"—a device that controls all other technologies.[39] What has changed in contemporary technology is that the processing power of these devices is now great enough to allow for immense strings of instructions to be programmed in, to the point where devices appear to mimic human volition and judgment.

The primary use for the microprocessor is not Web surfing or playing video games but the use of control chips in manufacturing processes. As such, the microprocessor displaces human control more and more. It eliminates more and more steering jobs, because it efficiently controls machinery, processes, tabulations, data gathering, even rudimentary communications. The result—human mental activity is reduced, the need for creative labor is reduced. This seems a capitalist dream, for replacing human mental effort exponentially reduces the need for expensive labor. At the same time, this reduction of human labor creates a problem, for capitalism relies upon the productivity of human labor to create profit. It seems then that the continued expansion of the use of the microprocessor as a replacement for human labor will result in fewer and fewer people being economically viable—they will not be producing value and thus will not be consuming value either. As Spencer puts it,

> the continuing adoption of microcybernetic methods results in more and more people who cannot be significant economic consumers, exerting a downward pressure on the demand for goods and services. Unlike earlier revolutionary technologies, this one will not create a demand for new forms of human labour, for it will perform an increasing proportion of all activities itself.[40]

The positive side of this is that, since so much mundane labor is performed by machines and since production is efficient and could be carefully planned, the need for capitalist exchange relations could and should disappear. In other words, in a digital economy the social distribution of wealth according to need is both more feasible and necessary. Of course, the optimal social use of the new technology would not occur simply as a result of that technology but would require a reorganization of society and of social values.

However, it must be recognized that today the economy has not any-where reached this proposed utopia. In fact, new technologies not only replace human labor, but they also tend to make much "knowledge" work mundane and factory-like. A whole array of "information" jobs such as telemarketing, clerical work, manufacturing control, and even sales have become unrewarding rote tasks. Further, the new technologies also serve a primary function of increasing the time of work for those still involved in exercising human judgment. Today, the cutting edge of new media technology is the development of handheld and other portable devices that can be connected to networks through wireless technology. As con-sumer items, they may provide a certain level of convenience, but more importantly they provide for the extension of the workplace into nearly all spaces and all hours of the day. With wireless technology, labor can be in-duced everywhere—imagine the salesman looking up sales charts while driving to the next site, the financial consultant monitoring the stock mar-ket during lunch, the teacher answering student questions while walking the dog. This extension of labor in time and space brings to light a further meaning of Gates's "friction free capitalism."

Information and the Reduction of Uncertainty

One of the preeminent "information society" proponents, Daniel Bell, de-clares that "By information I mean data processing in the broadest sense; the storage, retrieval, and processing of data becomes the essential resource for all economic and social exchanges. These include: data processing of records . . . data processing for scheduling . . . data bases."[41] Bell is pointing to the function of information in providing the basis for knowledge of the market, one of the key components of cybernetic capitalism. Up until the 1970s this was the key focus of information economics—determining infor-mation's place in market performance. As Lamberton notes, "It [information] reduced uncertainty for the firm and for the consumer, both of whom could therefore make decisions. This was basically the information-as-oil view-point."[42] Here, information is the lubricant in the market. This notion of reducing uncertainty fit well with the information sciences, a viewpoint that information is defined by its existence as a bit—in Shannon's formulation, a single decision between two equally plausible alternatives.

The uncertainty referred to in these formulations is the uncertainty of price. Prices, then, are information. Here, information is reduced to the sphere of problem solving and decisionistics, a sphere that obviously points to the computer as the processing device that promises to impose order and hierarchy onto quantities of atomized items. For the information economists this means that information is only information when it reduces the complexity of the decision-making process. Thus, business depends upon the preprocessing of information, controlling the amount of information by eliminating the unnecessary. As Gandy notes, this serves as a definition of rationalization within economic bureaucracy, "that is, rationalization, as preprocessing might be defined as the destruction or ignoring of information in order to facilitate its processing."[43] Once again, information is linked to control, but this time through a process of standardization that closes off certain paths through which the information might flow. If information still has a semantic content, which it does appear to in this case, then the preprocessing of information shuts off certain paths of meaning, it territorializes and closes off certain possible forces and practices. In economic practices, this facilitates routinization, the reduction of skills, stereotyped reactions, the preformation of demand, and the channeling of information resources into methods for structuring production, distribution, and consumption. In offices "information work" is reduced to the routine tabulating and processing of data, where the worker has no actual knowledge of the purposes of the information. Skills that were once markers of workers' accomplishment are now programmed into automatic machinery. Data on consumers is used to sort them into neat stereotypical categories and to generate products and entertainment programs aimed at producing predetermined reactions. Production is structured through "intelligent agents" that constantly monitor the keystrokes of "info workers" such as airline ticketers.

Information as Commodity

The economic rationality behind the information society/economy discourse would like to conceive of all forms of information as homologous "in the monetary sense of easy conversion from one form into another."[44] The impetus is for information commodities to escape any particular form, that is, for the informational message to float free of any specific medium and, thus, to become transferable into as many contexts as possible. Thus, the information society/economy promises a convergence of technologies where print, audio, video, film, and graphic representation appear and reappear in various forms and formats. The first form of economic information, the reduction of uncertainty, creates the conditions for the production of such commodities. This is what Boyle calls "perfect information"—free, complete, instantaneous, and universally available—an uninhibited flow of information that serves as the lubricant for market activity. But information also needs to be treated "as a good within the perfect market, something that will not be produced without incentives. This requires a restriction on the form of information—it must be conceived as a finite good, one whose exchange value can be determined and "deliberately restricted in its availability."[45]

As Morris-Suzuki explains, "the special properties of knowledge (its lack of material substance; the ease with which it can be copied and transmitted) mean that it can only acquire exchange value where institutional arrangements confer a degree of monopoly power on its owner." She goes on to lay out the problems for information economics: information can be copied and reproduced at low cost, it is never consumed, determining its price is nearly impossible to calculate because the buyer cannot know the content until they have bought it, the monopoly of particular information is extremely difficult to maintain (it tends to "flow back into the public domain").[46] These properties are clearly illustrated by the example of software, where the lines between the public stock of social knowledge, the originary "intelligence" behind the design, and the encoding of this onto a "hard" object are nearly completely blurred.

For the producer of the commodity, the meaning of the product is inessential within the exchange process itself; its existence as information consists of the fact that it can be encoded, reproduced, and exchanged as a commodity. Producers would sell each bit of information at the same price if they could and, in fact, they attempt to do just this in certain sectors of the information economy. However, from the consumer's perspective, it is the meaning of the information that is being purchased (at least this is a major factor in the demand for consumer entertainment/information products), and so the distinction of products in terms of the knowledge they contain is always pertinent to the producer. But ultimately, the use value of commodities in terms of their meaning complicates the measurement of value in terms of price. Thus, the producer must come up with strategies to control the exchange of these information commodities and thus must secure the rights to accumulated social knowledge and privately appropriate it for profit. As Morris-Suzuki explains,

> out of informal and formal social knowledge (publicly paid for), corporations produce private knowledge, from which they extract monopoly profits. Eventually, the monopoly is eroded as patents and copyright expire, or as new products and techniques become widely known and imitatable. Information seeps back into the expanding pool of social knowledge, but, in the meanwhile, the corporation has accumulated increased resources that enable it to move forward into a new cycle of private knowledge creation.[47]

The key to this whole process is an emphasis on digitization. The actual meaning of information is sidelined, while the process of encoding it is emphasized, to the point where just the abstract digital quality of the commodity is what sells it. One can see this in the incessant advertisements for digital products of all kinds. In the ads, abstract patterns of digits stream through neon wired patterns that imprint the world with their design—the digital becomes spectacle in its own right.

CONCLUSION: DISORGANIZING INFORMATION TECHNOLOGY

Ultimately, the complex processes and problems of the information economy are clouded in a veil of fetishism. Digital information is conceived of as an inexorable force that will finally enable a faithful representation of reality—both the reality of the external world and the reality of the processes of the market. Information, as the digital rendering of the skills and social knowledge of laborers, is programmed into automatic machinery. Information, as consumer data, is input into "the difference machine that sorts individuals into categories and classifications on the basis of routine measurements."[48] Information, as measurement of the rise and fall of market fluctuations, is encoded and processed as feedback crucial for the control of market chaos.

A critical theory of information technology would emphasize the destruction of meaning that it engenders: the reduction of human thought to binary switching, when it should instead be thought of as an intersubjective activity—a social accomplishment. Further, the critique should be extended to the sphere of mobility and fluidity, particularly in relation to the processes of labor. As Negri put it, informatics becomes accentuated as capital develops a need for "innovation in the instruments and processes controlling the circulation and reproduction of the factors of capital and to the diffuse mechanization involved in the technological control of socialised work."[49] Thus, information becomes the control mechanism within the "workerless factory," it enables operations to disperse in search of cheap sources of labor, it enables surveillance of the workplace and automation of formally skilled tasks through the implementation of "intelligent agents." In short, "the stark goals of control and reduction in the costs of labor" are central to the "information society."[50]

But the information economy is not simply an extension of capital in a smooth transition from its industrial mode of production; it is just as much a response to loss of control, to disorganization and noise endemic to the process of accumulation. As Dyer-Witheford states:

> To coordinate its diffused operations and activate its huge technological apparatus, capital must interlink computers, telecommunications and media in evermore convergent systems, automating labor, monitoring production cycles, streamlining turnover times, tracking financial exchanges, scanning and stimulating consumption in the attempt to synchronize and smooth the flow of value through its expanded circuits.[51]

It appears after all that the new media can fit quite well with the social values of capitalism—the commodification of all knowledge and control of markets. As e-business and e-trading become ubiquitously promoted, they promise not an expansion of new forms of knowledge but a contraction of the potentially chaotic and subversive potential of the Net. Behind the Net is a central memory system that functions through command trees, centered systems, and hierarchical structures that attempt to fix possible pathways of the network and thus to limit the possible variations immanent in the network. Within the new economy of information, technology information becomes defined as nonsemantic discrete bits flowing across space and then directed and stored. Thus, the enemy of the information scientists and economists is heterogeneity, disorganization, noise, chaos. They want an uninterrupted flow, but at the same time, a destruction of the unnecessary—after all, the goal of a market-centered net is control. This encloses or territorializes information; it becomes a part of capitalism's mapping of space and time. But what we may find on the other side of the network is that information's function is precisely to disorganize, interrupt, to remain itself and at the same time to disperse. Information may, in fact, be a keyword connecting the phenomenon we have examined, not as an element, nor as a content, but as a heterogeneous remapping of space and time. If the information society is to be our society, let it be disorganized.

NOTES

1. Louis Rosseto, Editorial, *Wired* 1, no. 1 (1993): 10.
2. Jacques Ellul, "The Technological Order," *Technology and Culture* 3 (1962): 10–28.
3. Marshall McLuhan, *Understanding Media: The Extensions of Man* (New York: Mentor, 1964), 106.
4. McLuhan, *Understanding Media*, 106.
5. Louis Rosseto, Editorial, *Wired* 1, 10.
6. Techno-utopianism is best expressed in the editorial statements of *Wired* magazine, where the new media are heralded as *the* solution to all social, political, and economic problems. Neo-Luddism refers to those (like Kirkpatrick Sale) who reject the new technology in whole or in part. In the nineteenth century, the original Luddites protested the widespread changes brought about by the Enclosures movement and the imposition of new industrial technologies. The Luddites smashed the new machines as a response to political decisions that imposed new forms of labor discipline on them.
7. Kevin Robins and Frank Webster, *Times of the Technoculture* (London: Routledge, 1999), 68.
8. Andrew Feenberg, *Critical Theory of Technology* (New York: Oxford, 1991), 14.
9. I want to distinguish Feenberg's approach to the social construction of technology from what typically goes by the name of social constructivism. I agree that technologies should not be treated as black boxes and think that instead we should examine the inside of technologies to describe their structures, workings, and social origins. (See L. Winner, "Upon Opening the Black Box and Finding it Empty: Social Constructivism and the Philosophy of Technology," *Science, Technology, and Hu-*

man Values 18, no. 3 (1993): 362–78, 365.) However, I do not follow Latour in eradicating the differences between technology and society. This results in a rejection of
any and all views that broach the question of technological determinism. As a result,
social constructivists tend to avoid any evaluation of technological consequences.
This, in turn, results in ignoring the ways in which technologies might be reconstructed.

10. Andrew Feenberg, *Questioning Technology* (London: Routledge, 1999), 79.

11. Feenberg, *Questioning Technology*, 88.

12. Nick Dyer-Witherford, *Cyber-Marx: Cycles and Circuits of Struggle in High-
Technology Capitalism* (Urbana: University of Illinois, 1999), 71–72.

13. Langdon Winner, *Autonomous Technology* (Cambridge, Mass.: MIT, 1977),
226.

14. Gordon Graham, *The Internet:// A Philosophical Inquiry* (London: Routledge,
1999), 21.

15. Graham, *The Internet*, 26.

16. Jerome R. Ravetz, "The Microcybernetic Revolution and the Dialectics of Ignorance," in *Cyberfutures*, ed. Ziauddin Sardar and Jerome R. Ravetz (New York: New
York University Press, 1996), 42–60.

17. Raymond Barglow, *The Crisis of the Self in the Age of Information* (New York:
Routledge, 1994), 14.

18. Marshall McLuhan, *The Medium Is the Message: An Inventory of Effects* (London: Allen Lane, 1967), 26.

19. McLuhan, *Understanding Media*, 19.

20. Judith Stamps, *Unthinking Modernity: Innis, Mcluhan and the Frankfurt
School* (Montreal: McGill-Queen's University Press, 1995), 142.

21. Feenberg, *Critical Theory*, 91.

22. Feenberg, *Critical Theory*, 191.

23. Feenberg, *Questioning Technology*, 83.

24. Michel Foucault, *Power/Knowledge: Selected Interviews and Other Writings,
1972–1977* (New York: Pantheon, 1980), 131.

25. Feenberg, *Questioning Technology*, 88.

26. Slavoj Zizek, *The Plague of Fantasies* (London: Verso, 1997), 131.

27. Zizek, *Fantasies*, 132.

28. Zizek, *Fantasies*, 132.

29. Zizek, *Fantasies*, 139.

30. Zizek, *Fantasies*, 139.

31. Robins and Webster, *Times of Technoculture*, 249.

32. Barglow, *Crisis of the Self*, 202.

33. Zizek, *Fantasies*, 154.

34. Why call the network a highway? It is obvious that to some in the business
community the Internet has similarities to the interstate highway system: It began
with military purposes in mind, it serves as a means of corporate transport, it fosters
individualized automobile travel that is ideal for consumption. It should also be noted
that the highway system also minimizes the development of public transport and its
spread has occurred with little concern for the environment. A model for the network
based in the idea of the superhighway tends to emphasize: a pay-per-use model,
reliance on experts, the use of metering and gathering of data on subscribers, an

asymmetrical flow of information with a heavy flow into the home, functions of entertainment, shopping and e-trade, and mass audiences for centralized sites. The Internet model on the other hand tends to foster: free or low flat fee structures, discovery by chance encounters, information as a public good, an even flow of info with many producers, functions of information and contact, and small diverse audiences.

35. Zizek, *Fantasies*, 154 ff.

36. Zizek, *Fantasies*, 156–57.

37. George Spencer, "Microcybernetics as the Meta-Technology of Pure Control," in *Cyberfutures,* ed. Ziauddin Sardar and Jerome R. Ravetz (New York: New York University Press, 1996), 61–76.

38. Spencer, "Meta-Technology," 64.

39. Spencer, "Meta-Technology," 69.

40. Spencer, "Meta-Technology," 75.

41. Quoted in Dan Schiller, *Theorizing Communication* (New York: Oxford University, 1996), 168.

42. Donald McL. Lamberton, "The Information Economy Revisited," in *Information and Communication in Economics*, ed. Robert E. Babe (Boston: Kluwer, 1994), 12.

43. Oscar Gandy, *The Panoptic Sort* (Boulder, Colo.: Westview, 1993), 42.

44. J. Boyle, *Shamans, Software, and Spleens: Law and the Construction of the Information Society* (Cambridge, Mass.: Harvard, 1996), 7.

45. Boyle, *Shamans*, 29.

46. Tessa Morris-Suzuki, "Robots and Capitalism," in *Cutting Edge: Technology, Information Capitalism, and Social Revolution*, ed. James Davis et al. (London: Verso, 1997), 13–28.

47. Tessa Morris-Suzuki, "Capitalism in the Computer Age and Afterword," in *Cutting Edge: Technology, Information Capitalism, and Social Revolution*, ed. James Davis et al. (London: Verso, 1997), 66.

48. Gandy, *Panoptic Sort*, 15.

49. Antonio Negri, *La Classe Ouvrière Contre L'état* (Paris: Edition Galilee, 1978), 235, 254.

50. Negri, *Contre L'état*, 254.

51. Nick Dyer-Witheford, "Autonomist Marxism and the Information Society," *Capital & Class* 52 (1994): 101.

2

A Critical History of the Internet

Brian Martin Murphy

For most North Americans the Internet arrived sometime between 1993 and 1995. The commercial media popularized the "new" phenomenon.[1] The main theme of these lustrous tales from the electronic interior involved immense economic opportunities for corporations and entrepreneurs.

Wired magazine assembled a group of Web "surfers" and appeared on newsstands to yell that being online was not nerdy but cool. *NetGuide* magazine set the stage for a rash of "how-to" publications like *Yahoo! Internet Life,* and *Internet WORLD.* They advertised things to do and find in much the same way that *TV Guide* listed and featured television network programs. The Net was the new and ever-expanding space of info/entertainment mediated by the commercial imperative. By the end of 1995 the Internet had been featured on the front covers of *Time* and *Newsweek* twice. Most daily newspapers had a "cyber" beat, usually for the business pages.

In the years that followed, a stream of books and Internet-based documents reinforced a dominant narrative for the medium's origin and development. The descriptive genre included time lines and anecdotal testimonies. Typical were titles like *Where Wizards Stay Up Late: The Origins of the Internet* (1996), *The Soul of the Internet: Net Gods, Netizens, and the Wiring of the World* (1997), and *Netizens: The History and Impact of USENET and the Internet* (1998). Emblematic of the online potpourri were "Hobbes Internet Time Line (version 2.4a, 1996), the "Community Memory Discussion List on the History of Cyberspace," and "Bruce Sterling's Short History of the Internet."

All of these efforts shared a common hypothesis: One integrated social formation of United States based hero-scientists and visionary bureaucrats performed an alchemy of technological and institutional innovation transforming

27

electronic networks from prototypes designed to facilitate and safeguard military research into a worldwide digital environment of ever-expanding potential for the commercial exchange of information. The underlying logic of network use reflected the ethos of the techno-corporate social formation. Aside from marginal but highly publicized phenomena like hackers, online crime, and some apparent social-psychological deviance, the network was used by people and institutions operating as consumers within the bounds of an "information-as-commodity" philosophy.

The hypothesis, quietly questioned by a few scholars since 1995, was shattered in November 1999. Well-organized demonstrators occupied the city center of Seattle. Although not the first demonstration against globalization imposed through the corporate controlled World Trade Organization, this event ignited a new level of struggle. The Seattle events and others to follow were paralleled by a broad and sophisticated use of the Internet at many levels, facilitating on-the-ground political organization not seen before by authorities.

Whole institutions with a large and skilled workforce seemed to appear from nowhere to provide network technical support for activist organizations. These institutions, with slogans like "Internet for People not for Profit,"[2] used a different model in their network applications. The techno-corporate hegemony defined use in terms of the transmission of information between people for a fee. These new "others" appeared to use a model of community in which information was freely shared around strategies of action. No matter what network philosophies were juxtaposed, there was a more immediate question resounding through techno-corporate circles after Seattle: How did these institutions spring forth out of nowhere with the technical sophistication and depth to be able to support a worldwide insurgency? Elites searched for answers. Canada's Security Intelligence Service published a report that spoke of the dangers posed by political network warriors. The Rand Corporation expanded its research into threats against the state and military to an analysis of the network support organizations backing the antiglobalization struggle.[3]

What emerged was grudging admission that the Internet may not be the result of a unitary techno-corporate history. The juggernaut of corporate commercialism may have overshadowed other histories during the rush to privatize U.S. government-owned technologies that had been called the Internet during the 1980s. The resulting flurry of commodification and consumer rapture could have created the impression that all aspects of networking were ruled by the commercial transmission approach to the new communication medium. Thus the question became: What are those other histories and how do we find them so as to make sense of the "new" Internet?

One hypothesis proposed that competing social forces could have appropriated available technologies to create a range of networks defined by separate and exclusive ideologies and rules for inclusion and use. Later, in the

face of the corporate juggernaut, these other institutions integrated their independently developed networks into the emerging corporate dominated
convergence. They confirmed that the new "network of networks" would resemble the "old" Internet in name only. Instead, as these alternative social
formations and their institutional structures survived and reproduced they insured that the twenty-first-century Internet would be a space of both dominant and resistant use values—a place where virtual insurgencies could support and parallel material struggles.

There are a number of theoretical perspectives that may be used to focus
a search for the diverse and contested Internet history. Raymond Williams,
for one, understood that a technical invention may emerge from one social
formation but does not become a technology of significance until it is applied for precise social uses under conditions in which power is contested.[4]

Carolyn Marvin's research into the development of electricity in the late
nineteenth century resulted in a model in which new media technologies
evolve in three phases. In the first phase inventions are constructed by a
techno-science establishment wedded to prevailing power elites bent on in-
stitutionalizing the innovation in their own interest. In a second phase new
media technologies become both the subjects and the platforms used by existing social groups that are negotiating power relations. In a third phase one
form of a new media technology is institutionalized, bound by these power
relations.[5]

Brian Winston has expanded the model into a series of steps. He saw in
the emergence of each "new" media technology a period of scientific
ideation and prototype experimentation dependent upon elite resources.
There follows a period of "invention" driven by a range of "social necessi-
ties." Next comes a process of diffusion in which many social formations define their own uses for the media form. In that time dominant forces seek to
repress any radical potential.[6] From a broader perspective Stuart Hall and
Michel de Certeau have postulated the existence of negotiation and resistance existing within any media/culture form.[7]

The focus of all these critical theories is on the radical break occurring in
the historical moments when an "invention" diverges from its controlled path
of development. Different social formations appropriate the technologies to
use in their own ways. The narrative of action shifts from the technology itself with its defining protocols to the socially constructed rules of selection
and access and use arranged by each appropriating social formation.

In the case of precursors to the Internet, Winston's period of ideation and
prototype development corresponds to the years between 1957 and 1973. At
that time the concept of a publicly distributed computer network was a
closely held secret of the U.S. military establishment. Through a revolving
door between the Massachusetts Institute of Technology and the U.S. Defense Department, budding computer scientists built a "safe" network of

university and military contractor mainframes. It was modeled on a system developed to manage the distant early warning system of radar stations erected during the 1950s and 1960s in the Canadian arctic as a shield against possible Soviet attack.[8]

The turning point in this process, and the moment at which diffusion occurred, was when the results of a military-sponsored research program into the development of protocols for computer communication between systems with different operating programs was published widely in scholarly journals in 1973 and 1974. It was named TCP/IP: Telecommunications Control Protocol/Internet Protocol and it defined the basis for networking.[9] From this time forward the model and resource for network organization was open to anyone capable of appropriating a range of technologies to do the job.

With the technology available, the more interesting aspect of the history of networks is the way that people organized themselves to use the technology. Networks work when they are structured according to rules. The history of computer networks since 1973 is not so much about the technologies as about the rules that people adopted in order to use the technologies.

Different groups will make different rules that will structure the uses of a technology. These rules become policies governing the networks. People with an opportunity to gain access to a network must accept the rules by which the system is structured. In the case of evolving computer networks the rules revolved around practices that were "acceptable" to the people and institutions that formed and managed the systems. To use a network people must agree to the "acceptable use policy" (AUP) governing that system.

During the second half of the 1970s four social formations appropriated available networking technologies and protocols. The acceptable use policies established by each formation represented an institutional structure with technological and bureaucratic expertise and established procedures capable of enforcing boundaries on an individual's interaction with a computer network. They can be broadly categorized as (1) State/Public, (2) Corporate, (3) Civil Society, and (4) Social Movements. It is possible to say that the history of today's Internet was forged in the differing rules of acceptable use evolved by the four social formations.

In the Public/State domain the U.S. government transferred responsibility for national computer networking from the military to the National Science Foundation (NSF) at the end of the 1970s. By 1984 more than 1,000 systems or "hosts" were interconnected. This mega-computing capacity became the de facto "hub" of the Internet and was known as the NSFNet.

The most important aspect of this new backbone network was that NSFNet required all users, no matter which sector they may be entering from, to agree with an acceptable use policy (AUP). Since the AUP related to the use of the backbone itself, it meant that all AUPs administered within all interconnecting networks were superseded. In the AUP network, use for any private business or profit-making activity was specifically prohibited. In effect the public computer networking domain was bounded as an electronic research, education, and communication park.

The dismantling of the park came through a series of bureaucratic and legislative operations. In the late 1980s NSFNet made a range of contracts with corporations that effectively ceded management to the private sector. Legislation got under way with the High Performance Computer Act (HPCA) of 1991.

The HPCA was guided through Congress by then-senator Al Gore. As vice president, Gore created the governmental structures that would ease public networking into the hands of large-scale corporations. He worked through the White House-based Information Infrastructure Task Force (IITF) to craft a wide-ranging policy for a National Information Infrastructure (NII). Gore's vision saw private corporations taking the "lead role" as managers and operators.

Gore's privatization strategy was executed through a flurry of congressional acts: The Information and Infrastructure Technology Act of 1993, and the National Information Infrastructure Act of 1993 were at the core of enabling legislation. Gore also used portions of the Telecommunications Authorization Act of 1992.

The command posts for the privatization of public networking was, appropriately, positioned within the Department of Commerce. In that bureaucracy grew the National Telecommunications and Information Administration, which was mandated by the Telecommunications Authorization Act with an annual budget of $32 million, as a research and development program aimed specifically at helping businesses connect to commercialized networks. Other programs inside the Department of Commerce included creation of "technology extension" centers around the country to help small businesses using computer networks and databases; an Advanced Technology Program (ATP) matching money dollar for dollar spent by corporations in networking research and development; and a range of new contract and service tendering procedures prioritizing delivery via electronic networks.[10]

The final link in the chain of enabling legislation came with the Communications Act of 1996. The new law governing the operations of all media in the United States affirmed that "the market will drive both the Internet and the information highway."[11] But the key period enabling privatization came between 1990 and 1993. At that time the NSF amended the network's AUP to allow commercial for-profit information transmission.

However, commercial enterprises did not come by public networking by accident in the early 1990s. The corporate prehistory of the Internet may be sketched along three trajectories: (1) Huge corporate enrichment via government research and manufacturing contracts; (2) Internal knowledge network development fostering transnationalization; and (3) Consumer product development creating a platform for the commercialization of the Internet.

The documentation of public assistance for the development of American corporate monopolies in culture and communication is well established.[12] The commitment of public resources created a vortex of financial capital. It sparked growth of a huge academic/corporate science and technology juggernaut. The government in Washington, D.C., operated a de facto subsidy to private science and technology based companies equalling up to 90 percent of their revenues.

One report from the Organization for Economic Co-operation and Development at the end of the 1950s noted that computer manufacturers were getting more than a billion dollars a year in research subsidies, equalling total income from actual sales and dwarfing any subsidies provided to the engineering industries in other nations. Corporate networking emerged from an effective state-sponsored initiative.[13] During each stage in the development of the "Internet," whenever a publicly funded resource had been created it was sold or contracted out to private corporations.[14]

A principal spin-off benefit for American transnational corporations was the internal development of digital knowledge. When technological capital was transferred through research and manufacturing contracts, aerospace corporations were left with the ability to maintain and develop computer communications. In most cases, for example in the motor manufacturing industry, the capability was put towards developing dispersed computer-based systems of product development and management. In a few cases corporations made their internal expertise into a product and consulting capability sold to other corporations. An example is the McDonnell Douglas Corporation, which was a major defense aeronautics contractor.[15]

One of the best examples of internal and intercorporate knowledge networks was the development in the 1970s of the global financial trading system.[16] By the end of the 1980s digital knowledge networks embodied as information technology had become both a tool in the reproduction of global capitalism and a justification for the integration of local/national territories into transnational corporate telecommunications regimes of surveillance and negotiation.[17]

Computer networked consumer product development evolved along two parallel tracks. First, a mass consumer computing product: the microcomputer. The first generation of microcomputers, in development during the early 1970s, were brought to the consumer marketplace in 1978 and 1979.[18] By 1984, 10 percent of U.S. homes had microcomputers, and a fifth of them were equipped with modems. Six years later in 1990, 22 percent of U.S. households had computers, more than half of which were capable of telecommunications.[19]

On a parallel track, large-scale corporations developing internal digital knowledge networks conceived the idea of selling space and time on these networks as consumer entertainment products. The first of these "videotext" public commercial services arrived at the same time as the first microcomputers—1979. Typically, the H & R Block companies of Columbus, Ohio, created CompuServe. In the early 1990s the largest of these online entertainment operations, Prodigy (2 million subscribers), was competing with CompuServe (1.9 million) and a clutch of other players including America Online.[20]

The ideological impact of the three trajectories in corporate development of computer-communications was to create a "commonsense attitude" among policymakers that networking "progress" is best left to the large-scale transnational commercial sector. The impetus is summed up in recent global discussions about the approved route towards national and international information policies.

The formula offers that governments should not be tempted to practice protectionism that would undermine multilateral trade, investment, and finance structures. International organizations are seen as key players, facilitating trade in services, international investment, technology, standards, transborder data flow, and intellectual property rights. The guiding notion is that of free trade between transnational corporations in line with intergovernmental treaties administered by international agreements and organizations like the Organization for Economic Co-operation and Development (OECD).[21]

The policy guideline established by the OECD effectively delineated the de facto acceptable use policy of the corporate domain. But two other social formations contested the public/corporate appropriations and their AUPs: civil society and social movements.

In civil society computer-communication fascinations grew with public availability of microcomputers and cheap telecommunication devices (modems).[22] A century earlier the same popular fascination with electricity was embodied in bands of home-based experimenters, dismissed by engineers as "public library" electricians."[23] In the early 1980s a similar wave of experimentation and appropriation focused on personal computers connected to the telephone.

In 1983 Boston computer programmer Tom Jennings moved to San Francisco, and in a moment of unemployment designed a communication protocol to send files between microcomputers over the phone line. It was called Fidonet. By the end of the year Jennings was operating a microcomputer-based bulletin board system (BBS) that was capable of exchanging files with other microcomputers automatically.

"The name 'Fido' came out of an incident at a small company where Jennings previously worked. The company computer belonged to Jennings; it was a mongrel collection of different parts. One night, drinking beer after work, somebody wrote 'Fido' on a business card and taped it to the machine. The name migrated to the BBS."[24]

In its early incarnation the software directed computers to come alive at the cheapest public telephone time, phone a computer with the same installed communication protocol, and exchange updated files. Jennings, a political anarchist, gave the software away on the condition it would never be used for profit. Hundreds of boffins upgraded its capabilities, sometimes daily.

By 1990 more than 10,000 amateur computer network operators in thirty nations were linked into the "store and forward" system that could exchange electronic mail and files.

Each one of the 10,000 local "nodes" was a bulletin board that, in turn, had many subscribers. As Bob Barad and Wendy White explained in 1992, "because Fidonet technology emerged in an environment where individuals operated each system independently and covered their own costs for phone calls and equipment, it had to be very flexible, decentralised, and designed to operate inexpensively with standard modems and microcomputers connected over ordinary phone lines.

"Fidonet-compatible systems, relative to other electronic mail and computer conferencing systems are cheap and easy to install. They do not require powerful computer hardware and do not use packet switching [whereas TCP/IP does—author's note] and thus are attractive in countries that do not have highly developed computer and communications facilities."[25]

Dissemination of the amateur protocol was so dramatic that users had to devise an encyclopedic naming index to differentiate each computer system. It was called "The Node List" and was updated and circulated to all Fidonet computers around the world, sometimes every twenty-four hours. "Today 'Nodes' are broken down primarily by zones, which are generally delineated by continental boundaries (i.e., Zone 1—North America, Zone 2—Europe, Zone 3—Oceania, Zone 4—Latin America, Zone 5—Africa, Zone 6—Asia)."[26]

Fidonet maintained its inventor's principles by enforcing a noncommercial acceptable use policy. The AUP was contained in guidelines that Node computer system operators were required to apply to their users. Sysops were responsible for restricting two activities: Excessively Annoying Behavior and Commercial Use.[27]

The existence of Fidonet as early as 1984 made the system the first popular or citizen-run alternative to public and corporate computer networking. The fact that it was free (after purchase of computer and interconnection equipment) and had a robust communication software capable of traversing very low grade phone lines anywhere on earth meant it was the network of choice for those who could not afford or did not have access to the public/corporate precursors of the Internet. It would become the platform for communication amongst activists, development workers, and nongovernmental organizations in Latin America, Africa, and the former Soviet Union providing a source of institutional support and technological access evolving over fifteen years before the explosion of global Internet action supporting the antiglobalization struggle.[28]

Paralleling the worldwide Fidonet explosion, civil society groups in North America developed the concept of Free Nets. In 1986 American computer scientist Tom Grundner needed to link the far-flung clinics of Cleveland's Chase Western Reserve University. The result was The Cleveland FreeNet, the first self-described community network mirroring a local civic society on a computer system. In the months and years following the 1986 Cleveland initiative, community networks emerged throughout the United States, Canada, and around the world.

The first wave of networks, constructed between 1986 and 1990, were the result of initial steps taken by universities (usually after prodding from a few activist professors). The idea was to construct university outreach to local communities, providing "Internet" access "free" based upon the logic that the U.S. public had already paid for the service through taxes. The scheme for democratic network practice had two objectives: (1) break the enclosure of expert knowledge and (2) challenge a government/corporate monopoly over the development of the Internet.

Jay Weston, a communication professor, was a key figure in the creation of the National Capital FreeNet in Ottawa, Canada, when he brought the Internet resources of his Carleton University to the wider community. He later explained:

> It was understood from the first, for instance, that the relatively narrow and concrete act of having electronic mail and Usenet newsgroups available, and at their real cost to the community, would ensure widespread acceptance, and that the acceptance rate would be stunning. It was also understood that once these were made freely available, it would be difficult to take global electronic mail away or to introduce it at the leisurely rate and higher tariffs that are customary with market driven services.[29]

By the early 1990s there were fifty FreeNets with a second wave of one hundred being developed throughout the United States. A purpose-written communication software, called Freeport, was in circulation. The software offered users a text-based electronic environment where they could move around as if visiting the buildings of the resources available in a town. In the United States, FreeNet advocates formed the National Public Telecomputing Network (NPTN). Headed by Grundner, the organization lobbied federal regulators to make FreeNets the basis for a universal access service model for the development of the Internet.

The universal service access model was ignored as the U.S. government privatized its public online park using a commercial model for the Internet. But some small support was forthcoming through the National Information Infrastructure program developed under Vice President Al Gore. The NPTN received a $900,000 federal grant to help create twenty rural community networks. However, no further funding was received. NPTN went bankrupt and was wound up in 1999.[30]

Nevertheless, community networking grew in the United States and abroad. There was a range of start-up models. The most common saw one or more locally based institution provide encouragement and meeting space for volunteers using computer-communications equipment donated by local commercial entities. As FreeNets prepared to celebrate the thirteenth anniversary of the concept in 1999 there were 114 in the United States, sixty-seven in Canada, five in the United Kingdom, and up to four each in Australia, Finland, Germany, Hungary, Israel, Italy, Netherlands, New Zealand, Russia, Singapore, Spain, Sweden, and Ukraine.

In Canada, which contained the largest number of FreeNets in proportion to its population, the facilities were seen as data networks operated by nonprofit organizations providing affordable access to information of local relevance.[31] These ideals were reflected in most acceptable use policies constructed for community FreeNets. The model taken up by most of Canada's FreeNets was designed by the National Capital FreeNet (www.ncf.ca).

Free accounts were to be for personal use only. This meant one account per person. Accounts could not have multiple users in institutions, companies, or families. The accounts could not even be shared among friends. In FreeNets one person equaled one account, equaled one vote. Commercial use could exist but could not be intrusive. Personal users could exchange commercial information, note their business in their address at the end of all their e-mails, or place "properly identified advertisements when invited by discussions groups." Further provisos limited mass mailings, abusive language, and personal attacks. This policy accepted the commercial sector as a community fact but did not allow the commercial imperative to drive the nature of the network. Rather, people from the commercial sector might participate as individuals.

Both Fidonet and FreeNets can be categorized as "civil society" initiatives. Their acceptable use policies place them within at least two philosophical conceptualizations of the social formation. Fidonet can be characterized by the autonomous tradition while FreeNets may be defined by the materialist tradition.

In the autonomous tradition, civil society is not a contractually dependent component of authority power relations. It is an opening or freeing of public space reconstituting relations of power in autonomous self-regulating associations creating a web of affinities and structures over and against "state" or "hegemonic authority."[32]

Fidonet might correspond to this form of civil society. The emergence of the system was spontaneous and predicated upon an antiauthoritarian circulation of communication software. The structure of the network was organized around the principle of the right of ordinary people to self-regulate their computer-communications relationships without any reference to state or commercial entities. The constitution of a computer network outside any authority of censorship, community restriction, or national boundaries also qualifies Fidonet for designation as a kind of autonomous civil society computer network.

The Hegelian/Materialist tradition sees the category of civil society as a space of negotiation or opposition which encompasses three activities: (1) economic relations, the formation of classes, and the machinery of the judiciary; (2) public administration; (3) social cooperation.[33] Karl Marx took the Hegelian tripartite civil society and gave it only the meaning of economic relations which, he wrote, was the decisive base on which political superstructures were erected. Antonio Gramsci asserted that civil society was not a representation of economic forces at the base of society but a component of the superstructure, an arm of the state or arrangement of power relations operating through the state as a network of ruling elites constructing hegemony. Thus oppositional politics remain debates within hegemonic elites.[34]

FreeNets can be placed within this framework. With AUPs that include economic elites as well as "ordinary people" FreeNets appear to be dependent for their existence on the ability of individuals with positions within state and commercial apparatuses. They operate in the Gramscian sense as places where the local social/political elites establish their extra-institutional networks as individuals. FreeNets are a space of negotiation/opposition within existing social elites.

But no matter how they "fit" in a civil society nomenclature their virtually "hidden" history added a significant nonstate and noncorporate institutional component to the "new" Internet. Compared to Fidonet's global infrastructure offering a direct alternative to the Internet FreeNets are small, scattered, and dependent upon the existence of the Internet to make community linkages. But where they have grown they have diffused knowledge and expertise from the enclosed public/corporate world of computer-communications to ordinary civilians. Between 1984 and 1999 these institutions provided another source of expertise in networking that might be drawn on for community mobilization.

The history of online institutions capable of giving in-depth technical and institutional support to resistance activities evolved as a convergence between progressive social movement activism and international alternative journalism.[35] The beginning of that convergence can be traced to the "New Left" temperament that emerged during the 1950s and 1960s in many national spaces with differing antecedents. At its core was opposition to "ideological dogmatism, bureaucratic authority, and cultural conformity" operating in both "capitalist" and "communist" worlds.[36]

The legacies of this rupture marked the latter decades of the twentieth century and the start of the twenty-first century in many ways.[37] One important change was the reconceptualization of "politics" as both coalitions of opposition to oppressive authority (rather than parties jousting for office) and cultural practice.

Activism worked through "movements" (feminist, environmental, peace, human rights, communitarian, international solidarity, etc.). Movements saw party politics as just one tactical option for struggle. Other possibilities included the enunciation of "multiple realities" (identities) and the "prefiguring" of more democratic forms of life in the organization of community-based structures.[38] Further, as social movements unfolded they were quickly aware of being "framed" by the dominant ideologies coursing through commercial mass media. Spaces of public discourse were recognized as terrains where the struggle was over application of pejorative "frames." At the same time efforts were initiated to erect a network of alternative media voices supporting the aims of social movements.[39] In effect, preeminence was given to culture: a practical focus on exposing the strategies of "hegemonic" ideologies,[40] the creation of "counter-cultures,"[41] and the production of critical/analytical alternative journalism inside oppositionally organized media.[42]

The multifaceted thrust of these activities created a symbiotic relationship between people who made media and people who acted out the social politics of movements, in many cases through the activities of international nonprofit or nongovernmental institutions (NGOs).

Alternative media producers expanded the reach and efficiency of their cultural constructions by appropriating "new" media technologies.[43] Social movement organizations like NGOs working on international political action and development employed media techniques for educational outreach and documentation assisting in the continuous process of fund-raising.[44] The technique insured financial stability and made the NGOs more like communication-based institutions.[45]

Over the years a cadre of media producers moved back and forth between the sectors uniting a flair for technology appropriation with the financial capacity for innovation in communication. The NGOs provided a kind of infrastructure and access to capital through grants and donations which was seldom available to journalists working inside hand-to-mouth alternative media.

Between 1980 and 1982 workers from both sides of this revolving door viewed the recently available results of public/corporate computer networking and speculated on the possibilities of appropriating the technology to be used for social movements and NGOs on an international level. Things started to move during 1982. In Canada the Canadian International Development Agency (CIDA) commissioned a two-year study into the possibilities of using computer networking for education and documentation between activist groups in Canada and the so-called "Third World."[46] The Canadian research led to formation of the first Fidonet bulletin board service dedicated to social movement action and NGOs.

Meanwhile similar initiatives were being considered in other nations. Starting in 1982 the United Nations-funded, Italian-based International Documentation Centre (IDOC) had been supporting a series of meetings that brought together NGO administrators, documentalists, and alternative media practioners from around the world. The aim was to plan workshops and prototypes on computer networking using any and all available technologies.

In 1984, at the end of the workshops, NGOs and their media colleagues from nine nations signed an international agreement to develop computer networks for education and documentation in relation to activist work. The document, named for the town in Italy where the final meeting took place, was called "the Valletri Agreement" and it created a new institution that would guide NGOs in the operation of international computer networking. The new coalition body was named Interdoc.

Signers of the Valletri Agreement included IDOC alongside Instituto Brasileiro de Analises Sociais e Economicas (IBASE, Brazil), the International Coalition for Development Action (ICDA, Belgium), CODESRIA (Senegal), Asia Monitor Research Centre (AMRC, Hong Kong), Antenna (the Netherlands), SATIS (Netherlands-based NGO database development organization servicing 100 grassroots technology groups), Human Rights Information and Documentation Systems (HURIDOCS, Norway), Instituto Latinamericano de Estudios Transnationales (ILET, Chile), DESCO (Peru), and the International Development Education Research Agency (IDERA, Canada).

Passages of the Valletri Agreement serve as the boundary marking Acceptable Use Policy for the first social movement computer network. The agreement's preamble registers the commitment to make a network as open as possible:

> The well-being of an individual and a community depends on their access to and ability to apply information. Information is thus central in the development process in all societies. . . . Recent rapid developments in new information technology have opened up new possibilities for NGOs to communicate and share information. . . . such a global network only has a valid role to play in development if it is created by, linked to and at the service of local activities. . . . It must be stressed that the management of information is not a goal in itself, but is simply an essential element in action for concrete and sustainable results and improvements in people's lives. Information management and related practices of networking must be geared to the mobilisation of information, not its immobilisation.[47]

By 1989 Interdoc had a technical advisory committee and a secretariat. The organization saw itself not so much as "one big network" but as an "informal network of NGOs established to facilitate the adoption of appropriate information handling techniques in order to permit the better delivery of services to their constituents."[48]

The online centerpiece of Interdoc was an e-mail and bulletin board conferencing facility. For example, the Dutch member (Antenna) made arrangements with GeoNet, a commercial electronic mail service based in Germany, to act as a server for conferencing and document exchange. The network started with seventy-five institutional members using the system. By 1985 the "for-profit" GeoNet system had expanded, providing access points in most Western European countries and the United States.

GeoNet was "sympathetic to the idea of providing a service to non-commercial users."[49] A group of NGO volunteers formed Poptel in London under the aegis of GeoNet to serve not-for-profit entities. By the end of the decade Poptel/GeoNet was handling 600 NGO institutional users from forty-five countries.

Interdoc did more than provide a networking facility. Members travelled the world attending meetings with NGOs and conducting training sessions for the use of the new medium.

While Interdoc was developing at an international level, an initiative from the United States was expanding to Europe. Three computer networks for U.S. activists grew together as the Institute for Global Communications (IGC) based in San Francisco. In 1987 they started an experiment in connecting with a like-minded group in England called GreeNet. A concept of building one world network exclusively for NGO/activist use got people from the IGC, GreeNet, and Interdoc talking.

During May of 1990 Interdoc organized a meeting held in Amsterdam as a forum where NGOs, campaigning organizations, resource workers, and researchers could meet and exchange views with technical consultants and e-mail systems operators.[50] Over the following months NGOs dedicated to operating a computer network focused on communicative action with the aim of creating a world alternative computer network: The Association for Progressive Communications (APC).

The APC expanded Interdoc's AUP with a mission statement declaring the need for a unique world computer network institution dedicated to activism:

> The APC arose in response to the need for a more efficient and effective tool to promote international communications among non-profit organizations, non-governmental organizations (NGOs) and individuals working in the peace, environmental, conflict resolution, health, and public interest communities. The APC networks are used primarily by citizens and NGOs working in related issue areas. APC networks serve to educate and meet the organizational and advocacy needs of international users, providing users with the tools and services for communication, collaboration and information sharing.[51]

As the privatization of the American online park called the Internet approached in 1993, the APC had already developed the technical and administrative skills to use computer networking as part of global resistance struggles.[52]

By 2000 the APC had affiliates in more than fifty nations. It had evolved since Interdoc with more than eighteen years of technical and administrative experience in facilitating online communication for activism. It had become one of the core structures of the "new" Internet contesting corporate hegemony.

CONCLUSION

The Internet has diverse institutional histories. One narrative of its history has come to dominate the public discourse. But the story that relates a triumph of American public sector innovation transformed into private corporate implementation and control obscures the multiplicity of use values.

A different perspective is generated when research starts from a theory that all technologies arise out of social contexts and are reformulated according to how they are used by divergent groups struggling for power. Then it is possible to track the hidden history of the Internet. The perspective allows for a move away from focusing upon technologies and techniques and towards the trace of rules and boundaries marking off each distinct social use of the media form.

In this case, a history of the Internet drawn from an examination of technology appropriations around unique Acceptable Use Policies demarcates four distinct precursors. All four jostle together in the "new" Internet. Each brings its own culture to the online spaces. The public/corporate forces attempt to dominate with the commercial imperative. But the structures of civil society and social movement computer networking exist and can operate support for a resistant form of online communitarian communication.

It is early days in the excavation of these precursors. The monuments to public/corporate computer networking rise high in the fields of digital dogma. But the footprints of civil society and social movement networking remain intact. The path marked out may explain in more depth the roots of a future Internet where insurgencies can burst into the shuffling and murmuring consumer mall of cyberspace apparently from nowhere.

NOTES

1. A survey of American popular magazines conducted for this chapter by using the Info-trac database shows a dramatic increase in reports about "the information superhighway" after February 1993.

2. www.igc.org.

3. "Anti-Globalization—A Spreading Phenomenon," in *Perspectives: A Canadian CSIS Publication Report # 2000/08*. Ottawa: Canadian Security Intelligence Service, online at www.csis-scrs.gc.ca/eng/miscdocs/200008e.html. See also, Roger C. Molander, *Strategic Information Warfare Rising* (Washington, D.C./Santa Monica, Calif.: U.S. Department of Defense/Rand Corporation), 1999.

4. Raymond Williams, *Towards 2000* (Hammondsworth, U.K.: Penguin, 1985), 129–30.

5. Carolyn Marvin, *When Old Technologies Were New* (New York: Oxford University Press), 1988.

6. Brian Winston, *Media Technology and Society, a History: From the Telegraph to the Internet* (London: Routledge), 1998.

7. See, for example, Michel de Certeau, *The Writing of History* (New York: Columbia University Press, 1988); Michel de Certeau, *The Practice of Everyday Life* (Berkeley: University of California Press, 1984); and Stuart Hall, "Notes on Deconstructing the Popular," in *People's History and Socialist History*, ed. Raphael Samuel (London: Routledge, 1981), 227–40.

8. For a typical techno-history of the Internet see Daniel P. Dern, *The Internet Guide for New Users* (New York: McGraw-Hill, 1994). See also Neil Randall, *The Soul of the Internet: Net Gods, Netizens and the Wiring of the World* (London: International Thomsom Computer Press, 1997).

9. Ed Krol, *The Whole Internet: User's Guide and Catalog* (Sebastopol, Calif.: O'Reilly and Associates Inc., 1992), 23.

10. Steven E. Miller, *Civilizing Cyberspace: Policy, Power, and the Information Superhighway* (New York Association for Computing Machinery/Addison-Wesley Publishing Co./Reading, Mass.: 1996), 107–10.

11. Robert W. McChesney, "The Internet and U.S. Communication Policy-Making in Historical and Critical Perspective," *Journal of Communication* 46, no. 1 (Winter 1996): 104.

12. Herbert Schiller, *Who Knows: Information in the Age of the Fortune 500* (Norwood, N.J.: Ablex Publishing Corporation, 1981); Armand Mattelart, *Multinational Corporations and the Control of Culture* (Brighton: Harvester Press, 1979).

13. Brian Martin Murphy, *The World Wired Up: Unscrambling the New Communications Puzzle* (London: Comedia/Routledge, 1983), 21.

14. Zakon, Internet Time Line, online at www.zakon.com.

15. Zakon, Internet Time Line, online at www.zakon.com. Tom McGovern, *Data Communications: Concepts and Applications* (Scarborough, Canada: Prentice-Hall, 1988), 129–31.

16. Cees Hamelink, *Finance and Information: A Study of Converging Interests* (Norwood, N.J.: Ablex Publishing Corporation, 1983).

17. Martin Hewson, "Surveillance and the Global Political Economy," in *The Global Political Economy of Communication*, ed. Edward A. Comor (New York: St. Martin's Press, 1994), 61–80; and D. Harvey, *The Condition of Postmodernity* (Cambridge: Blackwell, 1991).

18. Ken Polsson <ken.polsson@bbc.org>, Chronology of Events in the History of Microcomputers (1995).

19. Jay Black and Jennings Bryant, *Introduction to Media Communication* (Madison, Wis.: Brown and Benchmark, 1995), 387.

20. Jay Black and Jennings Bryant, *Introduction to Media Communication* (Madison, Wis.: Brown and Benchmark, 1995), 387.

21. Meheroo Jussawalla, Tadayuki Okuma, and Tosihiro Araki, eds., *Information Technology and Global Interdependence* (Westport, Conn.: Greenwood Press, 1989).

22. "Computer information signals are usually digital in nature, but to be transmitted over telephone lines they must be converted to analog signals. The process of conversion is called modulation. The device that performs the conversion is called the Modem (MOdulator-DEModulator) or data communication equipment (DCE)" McGovern, *Data Communications*, 10.

23. Marvin, *When Old Technologies Were New*, chapter 2.

24. Howard Rheingold, *The Virtual Community: Homesteading on the Electronic Frontier* (Reading, Mass.: Addison-Wesley, 1993), 136.

25. Bob Barad and Wendy D. White, "Einstein at NAS/BOSTID: Exploring Fidonet Technology Applications for Scientific Communication and Networking," in *Electronic Networking in Africa*, ed. African Academy of Sciences/American Association for the Advancement of Science (Washington, D.C.: Sub-Saharan Program, American Association for the Advancement of Science, 1992), 41–44.

26. Carol Anne Dodd, "What Is a FidoNet? Discussion of the Growth and Development of an Amateur Computer Network." Mass Communication, Carleton University, Working Papers in Communications Technology and Society, March 1992, 4, online at jweston@ccs.carleton.ca.

27. Fidonet Policy—Introduction, online at www.fidonet.org, p. 3.

28. Graham Lane, *Communications for Progress* (London: CIIR, 1990); Jack Rikard and Gary Funk, "The International Fidonet—22067 Bulletin Boards with an Attitude," *Boardwatch Magazine* (August 1993), 66–68; Gannady Kudrayshoff, Fidonet Systems Listed in Nodelist, *FIDONEWS* 15, no. 26, July 6, 1998, online at www.fidonet.org.

29. Jay Weston, "Old Freedoms and New Technologies: The Evolution of Community Networking." Paper delivered to Free Speech and Privacy in the Information Age Symposium, University of Waterloo, Canada, November 26, 1994, 5.

30. Victoria Telecommunity Network, Community Computer Networks, Free-Nets and City Regional Guides, online at www//victoria.tc.ca/Resources/freenets.html, p. 7.

31. Telecommunities Canada, Response to Phase I Submissions, CRTC PN 1994–130, 5.

32. John Ely, "Libertarian Ecology and Civil Society," *Society and Nature* 2, no. 3 (1994): 98–151.

33. G. W. F. Hegel, *Hegel's Philosophy of Right*, trans. Knox (Oxford: Oxford University Press, 1965).

34. Antonio Gramsci, *Passato e Presente*. Page 164, as quoted by Norberto Bobbio, "Gramsci and the Concept of Civil Society," in *Civil Society and the State*.

35. Social movements are defined here as those consistently representing antihegemonic positions. Following Sara Diamond, they are differentiated from right wing social movements that support the "state" as enforcer of authoritarian infringements of civil liberties and a religiously derived code of behavior while using the rhetoric of "antigovernment" to restrict the "state" as a redistributor of wealth and

power. See Sara Diamond, *Roads to Dominion: Right Wing Movements and Political Power in the United States* (New York: Guilford Press, 1995), 7–9.

36. George Katsiaficas, *The Imagination of the New Left: A Global Analysis of 1968* (Boston: South End Press, 1987), 19.

37. See, for example, Andrea Levy, "Progeny and Progress? Reflections on the Legacy of the New Left," *Our Generation* 24, no. 2 (1994): 1–39; Linda Hutcheon, *The Politics of Postmodernism* (London: Routledge, 1989), 10; David Pepper, *The Roots of Modern Environmentalism* (London: Routledge, 1989); Hester Eisenstein, *Contemporary Feminist Thought* (Boston: Hall, 1983); Arthur Hirsch, "Part III: Beyond May 1968, the Legacy of the French New Left," in *The French Left: A History and Overview* (Montreal: Black Rose Books, 1982); and Katsiaficas, *The Imagination of the New Left: A Global Analysis of 1968*, 19.

38. Chantal Mouffe, "Radical Democracy: Modern or Postmodern," in *Universal Abandon? The Politics of Postmodernism*, ed. Andrew Ross (Minneapolis: University of Minnesota Press, 1988), 35–36; George McRobie, *Small Is Possible* (New York: Harper and Row, 1981).

39. See, for example, Bernadette Barker-Plummer, "News as a Political Resource: Media Strategies and Political Identity in the U.S. Women's Movement, 1966–1975," *Critical Studies in Mass Communication* 12 (1995): 306–24; Linda Steiner, "Oppositional Decoding as an Act of Resistance," *Critical Studies in Mass Communication* 5 (1988): 1–15; and Todd Gitlin, *The Whole World Is Watching: Mass Media in the Making and Unmaking of the New Left* (Berkeley: University of California Press, 1980), 16–17.

40. See, for example, John Fiske, "Commodities and Culture," in *Understanding Popular Culture* (Boston: Unwin Hyman, 1989), 37–52; de Certeau, *The Practice of Everyday Life*; Foucault and Bourdieu; and Stuart Hall, "Notes on Deconstructing the Popular,'" in *People's History and Socialist Theory*, ed. Raphael Samuel (London: Routledge and Kegan Paul, 1981), 227–40.

41. Neil Nehring, *Flowers in the Dustbin: Culture, Anarchy, and Postwar England* (Ann Arbor: University of Michigan Press), 1993; Griel Marcus, *Lipstick Traces: A Secret History of the Twentieth Century* (Cambridge, Mass.: Harvard University Press, 1990); Cynthia M. Lont, "Women's Music: No Longer a Small Private Party," in *Rockin' the Boat: Mass Music and Mass Movements*, ed. Reebee Garofalo (Boston: South End Press, 1992), 241–53; Robin Denslow, "Born under a Bad Sign," in *When the Music's Over: The Story of Political Pop* (London: Faber and Faber, 1989), 1–30; Simon Frith, *Sound Effects: Youth, Leisure, and the Politics of Rock 'n' Roll* (London: Constable, 1987), 48–52; Dave Morley and Ken Worpole, eds., *The Republic of Letters: Working Class Writing and Local Publishing* (London: Comedia Publishing Group, 1982); Hans Magnus Enzensbeger, *Raids and Reconstructions* (London: Pluto Press, 1977); and Guy Debord, *Society of the Spectacle* (Boston: Red and Black, 1970).

42. See Nigel Fountain, *Underground: The London Alternative Press, 1966–74* (London: Routledge/Comedia, 1988); Charles Landry, David Morley, Russell Southwood, and Patrick Wright, *What a Way to Run a Railroad: An Analysis of Radical Failure* (London: Comedia Publishing Group, 1985); David Armstrong, "Rise of the Underground Press; Sexual Politics; and The New Muckrakers," in *A Trumpet to Arms: Alternative Media in America* (Boston: South End Press, 1984); Eileen Cadman, Gail Chester, and Agnes Pivot, *Rolling Our Own: Women as Printers, Publish-*

ers, and Distributors (London: Comedia Publishing Group, 1981); and Brian Martin Murphy, Scottish Community Newspapers (Edinburgh: Scottish International Institute, 1977).

43. See John Downing, Radical Media: The Political Experience of Alternative Communication (Boston: South End Press, 1984); Alan Marshall, Changing the Word: The Printing Industry in Transition (London: Comedia Publishing Group, 1983); and Robert J. Glessing, The Underground Press in America (Bloomington: Indiana University Press, 1970).

44. Stephen Dale, McLuhan's Children: The Greenpeace Message and the Media (Toronto: Between the Lines, 1996).

45. See Tim Broadhead and Brent Herbert-Copley, Bridges of Hope: Canadian Voluntary Agencies and the Third World (Ottawa: North South Institute, 1988); and Tim Broadhead, "NGOs: In One Year, Out the Other?" World Development 15, Supplement (Autumn 1987).

46. Chris Pinney, Brian Martin Murphy, and Richard Kerr, "A Study into the Feasibility of Establishing a Development Communications Centre." International Development Education Research Centre, Vancouver, 1984.

47. Preamble to the Valletri Agreement. Interdoc, Nijmegen, the Netherlands, 1984.

48. Lane, Communications, 47.

49. Lane, Communications, 39.

50. Lane, Communications, 48.

51. Susanne Sallin, "The Association for Progressive Communications: A Cooperative Effort to Meet the Information Needs of Non-Governmental Organizations, A Case Study Prepared for the Harvard-CIESIN Project on Global Environmental Change Information Policy," Internet resource available from the CIESIN Human Dimensions Kiosk anonymous FTP, online at ftp://esin.org (version current at February 1994).

52. Howard Frederick, "Computer Networks and the Emergence of Global Civil Society," in Global Networks: Computers and International Communication, ed. Linda M. Harasim (Cambridge, Mass.: MIT Press, 1993), 112–31.

II

NET ARCHITECTURE

3

The Case of Web Browser Cookies: Enabling/Disabling Convenience and Relevance on the Web

Greg Elmer

Few would argue, especially now that the so-called dot-com investment bubble has burst, that the Web has been charged with unrealistic democratic and economic duties. As an amalgamation of many previous forms of communication technology—as multimedia—the Web and the Net in general has seemingly taken on the monumental task of rationalizing a myriad of social, political, and economic spheres. As such, the Web continues to be a lightning rod for often heated debate over such contemporary social issues as free speech, pornography, globalization, and information "poverty." And while the Web continues to focus attention on broad social issues, we must also remember that—as with the computer in general—the Web's interface offers a decidedly individualized medium. As opposed to the socially accommodating screens of television and film, or even video game consoles that offer at least two joysticks, Web browsers are enabled by a single mouse or touch pad, increasingly form fitted for an individual palm. The Web-PC is, in short, enabled by an individual interface.

As a medium marketed to—and bought for—individuals, the Web-PC offers users perhaps the most revolutionary promise of the new information age: simply, the possibility of an easier life. The Web, in other words, hyperaccentuates the universal solution to the complexities and demands of modern life in Western industrialized nations: convenience. This is not to suggest, however, that the PC-Web experience is unproblematically user-friendly or "friction free," as Bill Gates has suggested. The Web and other personal computer technologies have clearly posed significant barriers to the easing of life's trials and tribulations. Any personal computer user will, no doubt, have a long list of gripes about software crashes, installation problems, compatibility issues, lost data, and printer malfunctions—never mind keeping up with the latest software version learning and expense curve. And of course from both the user and media industries' perspective, the Web's decentered and hypertextual architecture has fundamentally challenged the topography of media production and consumption. Without linear formatting of media content, via numbered TV channels or similarly ordered radio station frequencies, major new media firms such as Microsoft, Yahoo!, America Online (AOL), and others have increasingly deployed a range of corporate strategies to attract or divert otherwise nomadic Internet users to their respective all-in-one portals. Microsoft, for instance, has partnered with the U.S. technology retailer Best Buy to offer $300 retail coupons in exchange for a three-year commitment to Microsoft's Internet service provider. The practice of hyperlinking common Web pages together in "Web rings," bypassing the dominant Webguide/index/portal model of Web searches, was recently bought out by portal giant Yahoo! (Elmer 1999). And as Korinna Patelis (2000) documents, America Online offers perhaps the most centralized—and customized—all-in-one Internet platform where the "Web" per se is but one of a number of possible options that AOL members may choose to investigate. Thus, according to AOL's promotional literature, now "It's *easier* than ever to stay connected with friends and your information on AOL"[1] (emphasis added).

RELEVANCE, CONVENIENCE, AND COOKIES

The Web's promise of an easier, more convenient life is inherently tied to its ability to deliver relevant (AOL's "your") information to Web users. The entire search engine, Internet service provider, and Web portal industry has sought to cut through the seemingly limitless and decentralized clutter of the Web by offering more precise, personalized, and customized services, searches, and Web interfaces. While the search engine industry—with its nonstop traffic flow of users requesting specific sites of relevance—has recently taken up the task of filtering out "irrelevant" information,[2] the Web as a whole was made decidedly more convenient and relevant through the widespread adoption and use of Web browser cookies.

As one of the primary means of identifying individuals on the Web (particularly for e-tailers), cookies have become the source of much concern for privacy advocates worldwide. As but one element of the online privacy debate, this chapter will question the relationship between the development of Internet software (specifically Web browsers and their accompanying cookies) and the implications of online users exerting their privacy rights (defined as their desire to maintain control over the dissemination of their personal demographic and psychographic information). Specifically the chapter discusses a study of Netscape's Navigator and Communicator Web browsers (specifically, versions 1.12, 2.02, 3.0,

4.01, and 6.01), in which the following research questions are posed: (1) Where are the preferences for cookies located? (2) What options are offered to control the use of cookies? (3) Where are the cookie files located? 4) Where can users find information on cookies (via their respective browser)? As a whole, the study is predicated upon the question of user knowledge and control over cookie operations via their Web browser and on their respective PC hard drives. As such, the research questions attempt to ascertain the degree to which Netscape encodes knowledge and control preferences for Web browser cookies. Findings from a brief follow-up study also question the implications of users actually changing the default settings[3] of their cookie operations (when available). In short, both studies suggest that exerting one's privacy rights in cyberspace significantly disables the Web's ability to offer convenient services and relevant information (in particular those offered by industry leaders such as Yahoo! and Excite). Before we move on to a more detailed analysis of the studies and its findings, let us first investigate the technology of Web cookies.

COOKIES: CULTIVATING THE ONLINE CONSUMER-STATE

Upon visiting a Web site a small identifying piece of information, or "cookie," is sent to a personal computer within an HTTP header. In other words, when a user browses the Web, stopping to view certain Web sites and pages, the user not only receives the text, graphics, streaming media, etc., on their screen, but they also receive a small packet of information that is first stored in the browser's memory, then later upon closing the browser is stored on the user's own hard drive (Whalen 2001). Privacy expert Roger Clarke offers a clear step-by-step explanation:

1. a Web-browser requests a page from a web server;
2. the Web-server sends back to the Web-browser not just the requested page but also an instruction to the browser to write a cookie (a record) into the client-computer's storage;
3. unless something prevents it, the Web-browser does so;
4. each time a user requests a Web-page, the Web-browser checks whether a cookie exists that the Web-server expects to be sent with the request;
5. if there is such a cookie, the browser transmits the record to the Web-server, along with the request for the page;
6. when a Web-server receives a request that has a cookie associated with it, the server is able to use the data in the cookie in order to "remember" something about the user.[4]

The purpose of employing cookies, according to the technical language of the Net, is to overcome a "stateless protocol" (Whalen 2001). Cookies provide a relatively stable platform for interactions between users (clients) and Web site owners (or servers). Cookies essentially provide servers (and their owners) a means of identifying repeat visitors to their Web sites, in so doing fundamentally challenging the ability of users to remain anonymous on the Web.[5] Thus, in addition to the possibility of online user surveillance, early use of cookie technology also clearly offered the aforementioned ease of use and relevant/personalized information sources. Approximately eighteen months after the technology was first introduced (December 1994) cookies were being used for three main purposes: retaining information at e-tailing sites such as items placed in online "shopping baskets," personalizing content on Web sites, and lastly, providing Web owners (or "masters") information on how users are navigating their respective Web sites (Randall 1997).

With seemingly obvious benefits to online consumers, one must wonder why Netscape, and later Microsoft (Internet Explorer), neglected to publicly promote its use of cookie technology in 1995 and early 1996.[6] In hindsight such a declaration might have diffused some early criticism and ongoing distrust of cookie technology. Without doubt, the first published reports of cookie technology were a public relations challenge for Netscape. Not surprisingly the specter of an Orwellian World Wide Web was repeatedly raised by reporters and other critics of Netscape. One of the earliest newspaper articles on cookies, published in the *Financial Times*, for example, exclaimed that "Technology is already in place—and ready to be put to use on the World Wide Web of the Internet—that will allow Web site owners to gather an alarming range of information on the people who look at their Web pages from PCs at home" (Jackson 1996). Defenders of such technology might argue that cookies transmit but a few pieces of information on to Web page owners and e-tailers: namely, the user's IP address,[7] the type of Web browser, and the operating system of the personal computer (U.S. Department of Energy). However, as the upcoming discussion of cookie control preferences will demonstrate, the relatively small amounts of information transmitted by cookies have been greatly increased by linking their use with a host of server side data collection and diagnosis techniques (most prominently user profiling, collaborative filtering, and recommender systems).

Consequently, as cookie use became widespread, both from the client (user), and most importantly server side (largely by e-tailers, but also government),[8] Netscape began, with the release of every new version of its popular browser, to provide some additional information and options for controlling the use of cookies. As we shall see, though, Netscape's changes highlight not only the growing importance of PC-Web "literacy," but also, more importantly, the effects of choosing Netscape's own cookie control preferences (namely, the disruption and disabling of web convenience and relevance).

THE EVOLUTION AND DEVOLUTION OF COOKIE
PREFERENCES: A VERSION-BY-VERSION ANALYSIS

As noted in the introduction, five versions of Netscape's browser were studied (see chart 1.0). While the author chose to investigate Netscape's browser on a Macintosh platform, or operating system, there were few significant variations and options offered by Netscape for Windows or even Microsoft's competing Internet Explorer browser,[9] though its bundling and use with MS Windows 98 operating system would require a full chapter unto itself. While there have been forty-one browser versions (not including beta or testing versions) released by Netscape, the study chose to focus on only those versions that made substantive changes to cookie preferences, defined as either information or control/alert options. Continuing from left to right on the headings of chart 1.0, then, *preferences location* relates to the place in the respective version of Netscape's browser, typically pulldown menus, where users can find and change the preferences for cookies. "Preferences" is the term widely used by the computer software industry to refer to the options users are given to change various software functions. Many software programs, including Netscape for Macintosh, use the label "preferences" for their pulldown menus. The preferences pulldown menu for Netscape offers a daunting list of potential options, including appearance options (including fonts), network proxies, cache, and of course cookies. More to the point, such software preferences or control options serve as a key indicator of a software's flexibility and usability. There is no one established list of options or preferences for all software. Some software programs are fairly rigid providing few options for customization and adaptation to a range of computing requirements. Other programs, conversely, offer a lengthy and exceedingly complex number of options, some of which pose potential system-wide hazards in the hands of all but the most learned and time oblivious computer user.

"Preferences" and similar control options thus shed light upon the limits of software, as they bring into focus the choices made in the process of producing software. And while such programming decisions are clearly made consciously and decisively (e.g., so that they will be compatible and complementary to their other products or allied corporation's software), other "preference" decisions are often made for reasons of cost, time, and efficiency, or simply because of ignorance of other possible options. Regardless of reason, such decisions often result in the shelving of more dynamic plans.[10] Consequently such production decisions—on the part of computer programmers and software industry executives—have clear social, political, ethical, and of course economic implications.[11] Seen in this light, default settings of various preferences, the factory set, "generic," or assumed lowest common denominator software user, therein suggests a "recommended" or

Chart 1.0

Netscape Version (for Mac)	Preferences Location	Privacy Control Options	Cookie Files Located	Information on Cookies
1.12 8/95	None	None	System Folder/ preferences folder/ Netscape Folder/ Magic Cookie File	None
2.02 5/96	None	None	System Folder/ preferences folder/ Netacape Folder/ Magic Cookie File	None
3.0 8/96	Options, Network Preferences, Protocols	"Show an Alert before Accepting a Cookie" *Default setting:* Off	System Folder/ preferences folder/ Netscape Folder/ Magic Cookie File	Preference Panels Guide, Netscape Navigator Handbook
4.01 6/97	Edit, preferences Category: Advanced	"Accept all cookes" "Accept only cookies that get sent back to the originating server" "Do not accept cookies" "Warn me before accepting a cookie" *Default setting:* "Accept all cookies"	Netscape Communicator older/ communication/ "user name" folder/Magic Cookie File	Help, advanced panel
6.01 2/01	Tasks, privacy and security, cookie manager *Other option:* edit menu, preferences, advanced	"Enable all cookies" "Enable cookies for the originating web site only" "Disable cookies" "Warn me before storing a cookie" "View Stored Cookies" "Allow Cookies from this Site" "Block Cookies from this Site" "Remove Cookie" "Remove all Cookies" "Don't allow removed cookies to be accepted later" *Default setting:* "Enable all cookies"	Mozilla folder/ Users50/default folder/ mgb93svy.slt folder/cookies file	Help, understanding privacy Also, "more information" tab in the cookie preference section leads to the understanding privacy document

to varying degrees preferable mode of use (not only for the benefit of users but also for the software developer and its corporate allies). More on these points as we move through each browser version.

Continuing along the chart, *Privacy Control Options* are the actual preferences themselves. For the individual user, they are the boxes, circles, and other interactive buttons that let users change the function of cookies. In addition to their location and default setting the terminology used for such options also provides some insight into Netscape's attempts to respond to social criticism of cookie technology. Next, the question of where cookie files are located, meaning where they are stored after a user has visited a Web site, calls into question not only the accessibility of cookie files, but also their appearance (are they presented in plain language, expert PC vernacular, or computer code), and the very preferences for the files themselves (can they be edited, deleted, renamed, or color coded like text, graphics, or html files).

Lastly, the *Information on Cookies* column attempts to show the extent to which each version provided documentation on the workings of cookie technology. Typically almost all computer software and programs today are accompanied by either a "read me" txt or text file, or for more advanced products an online "help" index or FAQ. While the chart focuses primarily on the location of the information, the text itself obviously suggests Netscape's preferred reading, interpretation, and use of cookies.

Versions 1.12 and 2.02

First released in 1995, Netscape's earliest browser versions are completely devoid of any preferences, control options, or information on cookies. That is to suggest that while cookies were operational in all version 1 and 2 browsers, there was no ability to manipulate their workings, or in fact even to be aware of their existence. Obviously since there are no preferences or options to control the use of cookies, the first version of Netscape, by default, accepted all cookie files that were sent back by Web sites. Subsequently, the new cookie-enabled Internet (as a networking of computers) meant that personal computers, and their accompanying hard drives, were no longer personal.

The only evidence of cookies in versions 1 and 2 is the generated "Magic Cookie File" (see under Cookie Files Located). There is no clear path to this file, nor any pointers or information anywhere that would suggest its existence, never mind its greater significance for the individual user. The file itself is a simple generated text file that cannot be edited in any manner. Even a lengthy reading of the accompanying *Netscape Handbook* (version 1), with its tutorial, reference guide, and index, renders no mention of cookies or client-server states at all. In fact, the "filling in [on-line] forms" section of the

"Learn Netscape" portion of the handbook would seem to be the most obvious and applicable place to mention cookie technology, given that such online forms employ cookies to "remember" repeat visitors. The section, however, merely offers the following passage, parenthetically, reiterating the convenience of the Web browser:

> Typically, forms are used to give you a fast and easy way to make a request or send back a response regarding the page you are reading. Forms can supply an interface to databases with fields that let you query for information and perform Internet searches. (Netscape 1995)

Version 3.0

As noted in the introduction, the very earliest discussions of cookie technology were published in newspapers and popular technology periodicals just prior to the release of the 2.02 browser. As a consequence there is no evidence of substantive change from version 1.12. However, as concern over cookies mounted in the spring of 1996, news reports indicated that Netscape would offer options for cookie use in its upcoming 3.0 version (Rigdon 1996). From chart 1.0 one can see that the preferences for cookies, the aforementioned control options, were obscurely labeled (Options/Preferences/Protocols), giving no indication or hint of "cookies" or other common language such as "privacy or identity controls." In other words, in the first instance, without substantial knowledge of cookies or computer language, the cookie preference was not easily found or recognizable. While the "magic cookie" file remained in the same place as previous versions, information on cookies was added to an expanded *Netscape Handbook 3.0*. Surprisingly, particularly given the amount of criticisms lodged at Netscape's treatment of the cookie issue, the handbook offered very little in the way of explanation of cookie technology. Indeed as with earlier *Handbooks*, discussions of client-server interactions—the raison d'être of cookie technology—lack any reference to cookies:

> The server transmits page information to your screen. The Netscape application displays the information and leaves the connection to the server open. With an open connection, the server can continue to push updated pages for your screen to display on an ongoing basis. (Netscape 1996)

Indeed, of all the information provided by Netscape, including a cookieless eighteen-page document that lists "What's New Since 2.0?" the new Cookie preference receives a scant three-sentence description:

> The Alert check Boxes determine whether you receive a notification dialog box (popup alert) when accepting a cookie (unchecked, by default) or submitting a

form by mail. (A cookie is a piece of limited, internal information transmitted between server software and the Netscape application.) The dialogs notify you before information is transmitted. (Netscape 1996)

The most significant and relevant change to version 3.0 of course was the option "Show an Alert Before Accepting a Cookie." If a user changes the preference from the default "no" position (do not alert) and visits a cookie enabled Web site, a notification appears in a box asking the user: "Do you wish to allow the cookie to be set?" Buttons with the options "No" or "Yes" are provided. The Yes option is set as a default, meaning that if a user were to simply hit return, the Yes option (allow cookies) would be chosen.

Moreover, such seemingly minor changes to the Netscape browser, while hinting at the political debate over privacy and anonymity online, also point to the broadening use of cookie technology throughout the burgeoning Internet industry. To unearth the expansion of cookie technology a small but somewhat representative sample of Web sites, encompassing the search engine (Excite.com, MyYahoo), content provider (NY Times), and e-commerce (Yahoo shopping) industries, were visited using the new cookie "Alert" option for the 3.0 browser (see chart V 3.0 below). Upon receiving the alert both options—(1) do not accept cookie and (2) accept cookie—were tested. The results below show that while the Netscape browser seemingly offered users the ability to control the storage of cookies on their respective hard drives, the choice to decline cookies blocked access to the aforementioned sites. In other words, if a user wanted the convenience of reading the *Times*, shopping online at Yahoo, or personalizing content at the Yahoo or Excite Web sites, they in effect had no ability to control cookie files.

Version 4.01

With concerns still mounting over its use of cookies, in the summer of 1997 Netscape released the 4.0 versions of its browser. Additional cookie

Chart V 3.0

Options	NYTimes.com	MyYahoo	Yahoo Shopping	MyExcite.com
A.) "Show an Alert Before Accepting a Cookie." (i. "No"—the cookie is not set, ii. "Yes"—the cookie is accepted).	i. "In order to access NYTimes.com your Web browser must accept cookies." ii. Access allowed	ii. "An Error Occurred Setting Your User Cookie." ii. Access Allowed	i. "Sorry! You must configure your browser to accept cookies in order to shop at this merchant." ii. Access Allowed	i. "Please enable your browser to accept cookies." ii. Access Allowed

control functions were no easier to find, nor did they particularly encourage novice users to experiment with the cookie control functions. The preferences panel now simply offered cookie controls under the daunting title "advanced." In addition to accepting and declining cookies, the browser offered the option of being warned before accepting a cookie and accepting only cookies being sent back to the "originating server." The latter choice was a response to the news that third parties, originally hackers, were able to "read" cookies left behind by a host of Web sites, potentially offering the raw materials for a personal profile of the user (based upon the history of sites visited by the user). Initially, of course, cookies were meant to bridge an individual user's computer to a single server only (e.g., from the user to a respective e-tailer such as Amazon.com or CDNOW.com). Individual hackers were, however, not the only ones trying to bypass this initial one-to-one cookie setting. The online advertising giant Doubleclick, for instance, partnered with a number of online Web sites to set their individual server addressed cookies from multiple "remote" sites. Visiting a page from a Doubleclick partner, regardless of its URL (Web address), would thus result in the storage of a Doubleclick cookie. Doubleclick used the information collected at these partnered sites to target specific and "relevant" commercial messages to individual users. Responding to criticism of such online profiling, Doubleclick would later offer an "opt-out" option through its Web site. Ironically, the ability to opt-out was contingent upon having to accept a cookie from Doubleclick.

Version 6.01

After having been taken over by Internet service provider giant America Online (AOL), Netscape's most recent browsers have taken a decidedly different approach to cookies, especially in their accompanying help material. Netscape 6 and all following updates provide by far the most comprehensive documentation on cookies. The "Privacy" document contains over five pages specifically on cookies, and yet more on online privacy issues in general. Perhaps tired of receiving the overwhelming bulk of criticism over cookie use, Netscape now provides documentation that points its finger at rogue Web sites and other interests less concerned about privacy. In the section that asks "Why Reject Cookies?" Netscape's "Privacy" documentation now reads:

> If a site can store a cookie it can keep track of everything you've done while visiting the site by writing these things into a cookie that it keeps updating. In this way it can build a profile on you. This may be a good or a bad thing depending on what the site does with the information. It might be bad if the bookseller then sold that information to the local dog pound so they could

cross-check for potential dog owners who do not have valid dog licenses. (Netscape 2000)

Netscape's attempts to pass some blame around has, however, not resulted in any radical modifications in the way cookies are encoded into its browser preferences. Why not, for instance, make "do not accept cookies" the default setting, so that new and intermediate users do not have to dig deep into the program to find out about privacy and cookie controls? Clearly part of the answer to this question is that the Web would become a much less convenient and relevant place with generic "lowest common denominator" portals, leaky online shopping bags, and advertisements for products and services never previously bought or browsed. Moreover, such inconvenience would most surely and disproportionately fall upon Netscape and its Web browser—especially when Web sites such as Yahoo remark (if one visits with cookies turned off) that "The browser you're using refuses to sign in. (Cookies rejected)."

Having a cookie warning set as the default choice would be even more maddening, though potentially it's the most instructive way to demonstrate the extent to which cookie technology is used on the Web. A browse through Amazon.com, for instance, with the "warn me before accepting a cookie" option chosen, will inevitably result in multiple interruptions with the question "The site amazon.com wants to set a cookie. Do you want to allow it?" posed.

Chart V 4.0

Options	NYTimes.com	MyYahoo	Yahoo Shopping	MyExcite.com
A.) "Accept only cookies that get sent back to the originating server."	Access Allowed	Access Allowed	Access Allowed	Access Allowed
B.) "Do not accept cookies."	"In order to access NY Times.com your Web browser must accept cookies."	"An Error Occurred Setting Your User Cookie."	"Sorry! You must configure your browser to accept cookies in order to shop at this merchant."	"Please enable your browser to accept cookies."
C.) "Warn me before accepting a cookie." (i. "Cancel"— Cookie is not set, ii. "Ok"—Cookie is accepted.)	i. In order to access NYTimes.com your Web browser must accept cookies." ii. Access Allowed	i. "An Error Occurred Setting Your User Cookie." ii. Access Allowed	i. "Sorry! You must configure your browser to accept cookies in order to shop at this merchant." ii. Access Allowed	i. "Please enable your browser to accept cookies." ii. Access Allowed

What could be more inconvenient than being asked to make such a choice on multiple pages within a site? One must also wonder on what basis a user would knowledgeably discriminate between one Web site cookie and another, particularly when bombarded with requests from page to page. The cookies manager in version 6.0 follows a similar logic by offering the option of deleting individual cookies, with little to no help in attempting to distinguish one cookie file from another (save perhaps a warning about the aforementioned "foreign cookies" employed by advertising brokers such as Doubleclick).

CONCLUSION

Today it seems as though every popular discussion of technology must begin with an expert analysis offered in simplified language intended for the lay user. The case of browser cookies is no different. A quick survey of initial, one sentence, technical descriptions of cookies shows quite startling uniformity in definitions of cookies. From technological periodicals, academics, and newspaper articles, cookies are routinely defined as "a few lines of text," "short pieces of information," "a record," or simply "a number." Ironically, Netscape is one of the very few sources that more accurately define cookies as "a mechanism." In the broader socially circulated "data" definition

Chart V 6.0

Options	NYTimes.com	MyYahoo	Yahoo Shopping	MyExcite.com
A.) "Enable cookies for the originating Web site only."	Access Allowed	Access Allowed	Access Allowed	Access Allowed
B.) "Disable cookies."	"In order to access NYTimes.com your Web browser must accept cookies."	"An Error Occurred Setting Your User Cookie."	"Sorry! You must configure your browser to accept cookies in order to shop at this merchant."	"Please enable your browser to accept cookies."
C.) "Warn me before storing a cookie." (i. "No"—cookie is not set, ii. "Yes"—cookie is accepted.)	i. "In order to access NYTimes.com your Web browser must accept cookies." ii. Access Allowed	i. "An Error Occurred Setting Your User Cookie." ii. Access Allowed	i. "Sorry! You must configure your browser to accept cookies in order to shop at this merchant." ii. Access Allowed	i. "Please enable your browser to accept cookies." ii. Access Allowed

though, we find a consistent client (user) side definition after the fact, that is to say absent the process by which such pieces of "data" come to be stored on—or accessed via—a user's hard drive. And while Netscape's definition correctly focuses on the technology and not the product of the technology, their actual deployment of cookies since 1994 has a much closer affinity with the "data" definition. In other words, the Netscape browser's privacy solutions or controls for cookies largely focus on the cookie files on users' own hard drives. However, as this chapter has shown, the act of disabling cookies clearly highlights their link to the server side of the Web where once convenient and relevant sites such as MyYahoo now inform users that their decision to refuse cookies has produced an "error."

Thus, with the help of default set "accept cookie" preferences, and cookie options that significantly limit, disable, or disrupt the convenient flow of relevant online information and services, the release of personal online information, previously automated in early versions of Netscape browsers, has now become an automatic "choice" for PC-Web users.[12]

NOTES

1. Online at www.aol.com, accessed March 2001.

2. The portal and search engine Dogpile.com, for instance, distinguishes itself by providing "All results, no mess."

3. Computer software, including Web browsers, come "prepackaged" or "bundled" on PCs with certain settings "factory" set.

4. Online at www.anu.edu.au/people/Roger.Clarke/II/Cookies.htm, accessed March 2001.

5. The problematic of anonymous online identities was of course a central question of many early studies of "computer-mediated communication."

6. Interestingly some three years later (February 1999) Intel's heavily promoted (online and off) ID function for their Pentium III chip was heavily criticized by privacy advocates, spawning the relatively successful "Big Brother Inside" campaign (a spoof of the corporation's "Intel Inside" logo). Intel's Web site today, specifically pages dedicated to their Pentium III chip, is now devoid of any information about the controversial ID chip and its accompanying "Web outfitter" service.

7. This address is unique and fixed if the user is on an internal internet system (ethernet) or DSL connection. Any Internet connection that uses a dial-up (telephone) connection has a random IP address assigned to the user for the duration of the connection.

8. According to the Associated Press (2000), thirteen U.S. government agencies use cookies to track Internet visitors.

9. In contrast to Netscape, Internet Explorer 4.0 offers its privacy options under the title "cookie."

10. Cf. Elmer for a discussion of Tim Berners Lee and the development of hypertext for the Web.

11. Indeed the preferences of Microsoft's products, namely, its Windows operating system and accompanying Explorer Web browser, have served as key points of contention in the ongoing dispute between the corporation and the U.S. Department of Justice.

12. More advanced users, however, hardly receive preferential treatment. A recent study of Internet users (close to 80 percent of which self identified as being "Very Comfortable" with the Internet) found that while 47 percent of users were concerned enough to change their default cookie preferences, less than 7 percent chose to "Never Accept Cookies." GVU WWW 10th User Survey, www.cc.gatech.edu/gvu/user/survey-1998-10/graphs/use/q81.htm.

BIBLIOGRAPHY

Associated Press. 2000. "Agencies Record Web Users' Habits." *Boston Globe*, October 22, A25.

Elmer, Greg. 2001. "Hypertext on the Web: The Beginning and End of Web Pathology." *Space and Culture* 10.

———. 1999. "Web Rings as Computer-Mediated Communication." *CMC Magazine*, online at www.december.com/cmc/mag/1999/jan/elmer.html.

Jackson, Tim. 1996. "This Bug in Your PC Is a Smart Cookie." *Financial Times,* February 12, 15.

Netscape Communications Corporation. 2000. *6.01 Handbook.*

———. 1996. *3.0 Handbook.*

———. 1995. *1.12 Handbook.*

Patelis, Korinna. 2000. "E-Mediation by America Online." Pp. 49–63 in *Preferred Placement: Knowledge Politics on the Web*, ed. Richard Rogers. Maastricht: Jan Van Eyck Akademie Editions.

Randall, Neil. 1997. "The New Cookie Monster: Everyone Is Afraid of Cookies Lately, but They Can Be Good for You!" *PC Magazine Online*. Online at www.zdnet.com/pcmag/issues/1608/pcmg0035htm, accessed April 22.

Rigdon, Joan E. 1996. "Internet Users Say They'd Rather Not Share Their Cookies." *Wall Street Journal,* February 14, B6.

U.S. Department of Energy. 1998. I-034: Internet Cookies. Computer Incident Advisory Center (March 12), online at www.ciac.org/bulletins/i-034.shtml, accessed May 2001.

Whalen, David. 2001. The Unofficial Cookie FAQ, Version 2.54. Online at www.cookiecentral.com/faq, accessed March 2001.

4

Surfing for Knowledge in the Information Society

Richard Rogers and Andrés Zelman

INTRODUCTION

Quite distinct from its other popular manifestations as library, marketplace, darkroom, rumor mill, parliament, or pasteboard for the creative and the homely, the World Wide Web also may be conceived as a public "debate space," made up of a series of "issue networks."[1] Indeed organizations, especially those practicing an "org-style'" mode of communication, openly make their positions known on their Web sites. Either in preparation for a major summit, or as a matter of course, active .org-style nongovernmental organizations (NGOs), governments, corporations, and less frequently scientific groups (organizations in the .org, .gov, .com, and .edu domains, or the national subdomain equivalents) all put their viewpoints online per issue. In doing so, they publicly position themselves vis-à-vis other parties debating particular issues from a researcher-surfer's point of view. Such organizational positionings put debate on public display, or what we call public debate on the Web, with significant participatory implications.

Note that this definition of public debate on the Web and the prospect of participation by other active groups are to be distinguished from more popular, cyber-democratic notions of debate and participation, resident in the notions of a speaker's corner, a debate cafe, or other single comment spaces, like bulletin boards and forums. There, surfers are invited to leave comments for other passersby, and for more specific surfing audiences that soliciting organizations have in mind. In these cases, participation in public debate is mainly for its own sake, largely because the channels of dissemination beyond the forum itself are rare, unclear, or absent.[2] In such a case, a surfer may feel as if she is participating, publicly, in a debate, but the stakes may be no greater than those of phoning in to a radio talk show. This is not participation in public debate on the Web to which this chapter refers.

In other words, we do not put our hopes on a single forum site and analyze participating surfers' inputs as if they were the makings of meaningful debate with high stakes for current or future information societies. Rather, we view a spectrum of major and minor organizations' sites (and the "deeper" pages on their sites dealing with specific issues) as the makings of an issue network, and possibly public debate. The key is to determine which organizations belong to the network of organizations dealing with the issue, and to analyze the characteristics of the networked debate. (Later we come to a strict definition of who's in the "issue network," and who's out, thereby defining the notion of an issue network by a demarcation technique.[3] We subsequently look for certain network properties to ascertain whether the parties in the issue network are engaging in debate.) The determination of the relevant players in an issue network is made by analyzing hyperlinking patterns.

It has been shown that organizations display their interorganizational affinities, or make known their strategic affiliations, through hyperlinking.[4] For some time now, the question to whom to link has been a serious matter of organizational policy.[5] While the rationale behind making a hyperlink may be viewed in many ways, the very act of linking and the selectivity it implies are emphasized here. Through selectively hyperlinking, parties are made relevant by the Webmaster of an organization. In this way, the act of not linking, nonreciprocal linking, or unlinking similarly reveals a politics of association.

The extent to which networks of Web sites debate an issue has to do with common recognition of positions (the use of similar language), common routing directions (shared link recipients), and cross-domain participation (transdiscursivity among .org, .com, .gov, .edu, etc.). The last criterion is of crucial significance, for it may be stated plainly that narrower groupings through selective hyperlinking (interlinking and network formation between only .coms, or between only .coms and .govs) loosely map onto forms of laissez-faire or expert decision-making, respectively. As opposed to .com-centric or .gov-.com-centric networks, issue networks exhibiting transdiscursivity are chosen as the exemplary Web debate spaces, to be navigated by surfers and the debating parties themselves.[6]

In all, the Web, when methodically charted, furnishes the surfer with a kind of debate geography, composed of different topographies of social interaction and decision-making. We see these topographies as implying different kinds of information societies, made up of different kinds of knowledgeable participants. That is to say, if that topography is well charted and well navigated, it may be read and understood as a knowledge map for debate rapporteurs and participants. The topography also may lead to novel forms of participation in public debate. Webby participation is achieved not by leaving a comment on a site (as in the cyberdemocractic school),[7] but rather by mounting a site, by positioning one's own viewpoints on the site vis-à-vis others in the issue network, and by becoming a "stop" (or network node), preferably along the more heated (heavily hyperlinked) routes through the debate. In order to become a node in the issue network, relevant organizations must link to you. Such is the achievement of certain actors in the Genetically Modified (GM) food debate.[8] The achievement of relevance in an issue network (making it onto the map) should not be underestimated at a time when agenda-setting authorities (not to mention security agencies) are beginning to look to the Internet and to vocal, well-organized, and highly mobile Web networks for discussion partners, online and offline.[9] Locating new groupings of debating parties, in online and offline spaces, at any given time and for any given issue, has implications for putting forward as well as organizing preferred information societies.

To understand (by navigating) any charted issue, however, a surfer-researcher must choose the starting points (or initial entry points to the Web) with care. That is to say, an understanding of an issue may follow from initial surfer preferences, and these understandings may differ greatly. Beginning with .orgs, for example, the surfer may be given to understand an issue through the particular discursive framings and hyperlinking behaviors characteristic of NGOs. Alternatively, .com or .gov starting points may open up different networks, routes, and storylines.[10] Indeed, in a recent study of the climate change debate on the Web, it was found that .coms did not participate in the story of climate change and developing countries, and that .orgs did not participate in the story of climate change and uncertainty.[11] The converses held. So understandings of the climate change issue may differ substantially depending on the surfer-researcher's preferred entry points to the Web, as .orgs and .coms are (typically) organizing different climate change debates to be explored. These .org-centric or .com-centric issue networks, explored by surfers, are very much unlike the multicultural and pluralistic space the Web is often held up to be.[12] By charting and then analyzing "transdiscursive issue networks," we attempt to rescue a neopluralistic potential of the Web.

For the purposes of finding debates and recommending preferred information societies, this chapter outlines five entry points for creating an issue network, with varying combinations of .orgs, .govs, .coms, .edus, depending on various surfer-researchers' preferences and judgment. We consider the extent to which the issue networks, created by different preferences, may be thought of as "transdiscursive debates," the preferred information society. Counter-intuitively, we have found that controversial sites sometimes lead to an absence of debate, while more mainstream sites—such as the Monsanto.com and Greenpeace.org sites—introduce a world of highly contested positions and hot routes where the most Web traffic may flow.[13] Here, the Web assumes the guise of a "space of contestation" (in Saskia Sassen's phrase), where the "great conversations" are taking place, not so unlike the ideal "great good place" that idealistic Net rhetorics seek and sometimes find.[14]

MAPPING DEBATE SPACES ON THE WEB

Prior to mapping issue networks, debates, hot routes, and storylines, parties must be sought. Here it is instructive to point to methods of locating relevant parties and mapping debates on the Web. In a series of papers, we have outlined various schools in the Web navigation and source recommendation debate.[15] At the outset, a crucial distinction is made between two approaches that pinpoint sites relevant to finding and studying Web materials, and ultimately Web debate. The first uses surfer recommendations (surfer tracing or collaborative filtering) to find relevant materials on the Web. The second (network rubbing or debate landscaping) sees the Webmaster, not the surfer, as the recommending party. Whereas the tracing approach views hits by collaborating surfers (assumed to be like-minded and symmetrically relevant) as the means to measure the relevance of Web materials, the rubbing approach uses links by divided Webmasters as a means of measuring the relevance of parties to a debate. The key is to determine the authority of such sites, i.e., which issue sites should be recommended (and landscaped in a knowledge map) for a debate navigator to explore.[16]

To determine the value of the landscaping technique, we carried out an initial case study. In the study—on the emerging climate change debate—we found that hyperlinks are meaningful. Individual organizations link selectively, not capriciously. We also discovered distinctive hyperlinking styles for .org, .com, and .gov, with .orgs highly networked; .govs only highly intranetworked; and .coms lowly networked—with the exception of Shell, which uses the Web like a .org to mobilize support. We also found that organizations take discursive positions on climate change on their sites, which can be mapped and read, as discussed above. Here, the key players are similarly located and mapped. In contrast to the climate change study, however, we have not mapped discursive positions; rather, the findings are made (and stories told) from mapping hyperlinks alone. In this chapter, we employ largely the same approach and sampling method for mapping online debates as in the climate change case, but with a series of different starting points and a number of methodological permutations different from those used in previous research. We are interested in finding the extent to which different starting points (URLs) yield similar or different issue networks, and similar or different debates.

In keeping with the much propagated Web finding that, on average, all sites are nineteen clicks (or nineteen degrees of separation) away from each other,[17] we ask: Is it possible to locate similar issue networks on the Web using different entry points? By which entry points to the Web are similar qualities of networks found? Certain findings derive from overlaying the networks, as if on transparencies; the analogy is with archaeological guidebooks. Thus, atop pictures of the ruins of Pompeii one may place transparencies showing how the city looked before the eruption of Mt. Vesuvius.[18] Layering information in an archaeological approach to Web debates may not only bring debate to life (or make the Web speak in new ways) but also provide a knowledgeable tour. This chapter asks whether and on what conditions there are preferred paths for debate navigators, and ultimately preferred constitutions of information societies.

There is an overarching reason for exploring issue networks and mapping debates on the Web. It may be argued that there are two basic epistemological problems with respect to the Web and its use.[19] That is to say, the Web designers (of .com, .org., .gov, and .edu sites) as well as Web designer-engineers (of search engines, portals, etc.) face issues of maintaining a reliable and authoritative status for online versions of their institutions and viewpoints (as well as for their recommendation devices and spaces). Moreover, those who use the Web confront indexing issues, uncertainty, and a diversity of entry points to any given topic. We believe it is important to become better equipped to evaluate different Web entry points, and to grapple with the basic epistemological problems of coming to an understanding (via the Web) of an issue—one type of key word that search engines handle. In addition, we also consider what a Webmaster (and by extension, an organization) may do to organize, knowledgeably, an issue for a surfer-researcher. How, too, can a Webmaster aid an organization in becoming a relevant party (gain significant presence) in an issue network?

WEB ANTHROPOLOGY: SURFER-RESEARCHER PREFERENCES AND THE LOCATION OF ISSUE NETWORKS

The preliminary step of the research involved a brainstorming session in which a number of methods (loosely defined) to evaluate one's choice of entry points to the Web was enumerated. They include hits, links, search engines (key words), conventional media stories, public trust logics, associative reasoning, directories, experts, (Dutch-style) science shops and science help lines, and discussion lists. Significantly, each kind of starting point stakes some claim to recommending authoritative sources, and leading the surfer-researcher to potentially relevant networks of sources. The relevance of information yielded by hits, for example, rests on site popularity among surfers, by links on

Webmaster recommendations, by media stories on journalistic method, by public trust logics on publicly trusted actors, by associative reasoning on Web literacy and playing hunches, by directories on taxonomy and encyclopedic completeness, by experts on recognized acumen, by (Dutch-style) science shops and science help lines on institutionalized public services, and by discussion lists on informed discussants. While each has its merit, the ten were collapsed and narrowed to five distinct means for determining entry points. Each method was then assigned to someone familiar with it: search engines (to a frequent searcher of AltaVista and its fancy features), associative reasoning (to a literate Web-user), public trust (to a researcher versed in the public understanding of science), media stories (to a media researcher and designer of tools for digital journalism), and discussion lists (to a discussion list analyst).[20] Each trusted his or her own method; the methods were the surfer-researchers' own preferences (or personal net-archaeological methods to unearth potentially relevant and reliable material). Most of the surfer-researchers also depicted the networks of sources in their preferred manners in order to understand them (and navigate them, if need be).

The starting points yielded by the researchers' preferences set into motion a more formally defined method to demarcate an issue network. The method was followed through to varying stages of "completion" depending on the surfer-researcher's ideas about the relevance of the network of parties found through the initial entry points and demarcation method. Thus at various stages of demarcation, certain networks of sources were abandoned, as is the surfing norm. Other surfer-researchers, however, remained "on message," so to speak, locating and understanding issue networks.

The sampling method begins by locating central players for the issue at hand, deemed to be the most relevant. (Details are provided below on the different means by which the researchers located central players, according to their net-archaeological expertise and preferences.) Common outward links from the central players are then found, and a pool of organizations (the central players as well as the common recipients of links) become candidates for relevant parties in the issue network. In this group of candidates those organizations receiving common links (often three, depending on the preferred authority threshold) were deemed to be elected as relevant by the issue network. Thus beyond individual preferences (and the expertise of the methodologists, broadly defined) is a commonly held viewpoint. Once the starting points are chosen, the Web (or networks on the Web) decide upon relevance. Such a move is largely in keeping with the core assumption built into all (automated) search engine logics promising relevant rankings, that is, that the Web, one way or the other, is the judge. Thus, our epistemology is "non-voluntaristic."[21]

As for the entry points, briefly, the search engine technique follows from key word inputs, and involves interlinking the results of a search on GM food using AltaVista. Associative reasoning involves educated guesses of relevant URLs, for example, by typing intuitively significant URLs, as milk.org, into the browser and then mapping the interlinking relationships between the outward links located. Public trust involves a familiarity logic whereby the surfer-researcher seeks sites that are expected to be involved in the debate; in this case Monsanto.com and Greenpeace.org are the starting points. The media story technique follows all parties listed in an authoritative media source (in this case, a BBC online news story) to determine the degree of interlinking between these sites. Finally, the discussion list technique interlinks all URLs listed during a select time period on an active discussion list on the issue (GenTech).

Each final network map reveals relationships between sites found with respect to their degree of interlinking, and their neighborhoods.[22] The research then explores what the networks share and how they differ (mainly with respect to the presence of nodes and routes; density is not included here). Do the networks provide diverse assemblages of sites involved in, for example, different contexts or subcultures of the GM food debate? Are the networks found contingent upon the different ways the Web is accessed and the respective preferences of the surfer-researchers, or is there ultimately one authoritative "mother network" or type of network to be sought for the issue in question? Furthermore, is it worthwhile to locate and recommend one type of network by a triangulation of techniques, or through an analytical as well as normative argument for the network yielded by only one technique? (A similar debate concerns the value of using Metacrawler.com or other engines that amalgamate the results of leading engines for one query, or just Google.com, often considered to house the finest relevance logics of all leading search engines to date.)

As indicated, the debate on GM food has been selected as a salient example of an emerging science and technology debate. In part, this topic was chosen to provide a contrast to the climate change project, and more specifically to enquire into whether the GM food debate was globalizing in the same manner as climate change. The research on climate change revealed that the debate was well formed and key players were well established; it was found to be a global debate, centering on a principle knowledge claim made by the Intergovernmental Panel on Climate Change (IPCC)—its statement on "the balance of evidence suggests a discernible human influence on global climate." The discursive positionings of the relevant players in the climate change debate could be mapped. In separate discursive analysis (mentioned above), broader climate change storylines and those participating in, for example, "climate change and developing counties" and "climate change and uncertainty" also were found. By contrast, the GM food debate is much fresher, and seems much less defined; in this way it can be perceived as a prospective structure awaiting surfer-researcher routing instructions. Perhaps the primary reason that the GM food debate appears so fresh is that there seems to be no statement around which a debate is formed. (Hence the absence of discursive analysis in this chapter.) Thus, as we touch on below, the terminology of the issue itself is only beginning to settle around genetically modified food from earlier terms such as "genetically engineered food" or "genetically altered food" (from the North American context). The terminological differences also point to only a gradual emergence of a global or globalizing debate. Here it should be noted that the research does recognize the value of providing time series analysis, that is, a series of snapshots of the different stages or states of the issue networks (and the discursive and organizational positionings) over time in order to chart the globalization of issues in the making, among other interests.

ENTERING ISSUE NETWORKS
BY SURFER-RESEARCHER PREFERENCES

Search Engine (AltaVista)

Search engines crawl and index information in significantly different ways.[23] It is beyond the scope of this chapter to recount the logics of search engines, leading or otherwise. Suffice it to say that of all key word entries, issue searches, unlike those for single institutions or individuals, yield considerably different sets of returns across engines, as was found in the climate change research and anecdotally noted in the GM food work. (Hence both the value, in terms of diversity, and the dubiousness, in terms of authority, of metacrawlers.) For the search engine entry point, we used AltaVista because of is relevance logics, the above-average size of its database, and its capacity for advanced search specifications (fancy features). Boolean syntax permits (among other things) an assessment based on the number of inward links to each located site.

The search engine sampling technique involved the following.

1. AltaVista was queried for "genetically modified food" and "genetically engineered food." GM food was selected for further analysis because international organizations (UN and NGOs), European bodies (EU as well as national governments and NGOs), and transnational corporations (Monsanto and Novartis) were found to be using the terminology.
2. In the top ten returns, only four organizations appeared, which became obvious when the amount of links into the individual pages and the amount of links into the sites as a whole were examined.
3. Next, the surfer-researcher followed a preference to assemble the DNS information for the four core sites.[24] (Viewing the actual names and ad-

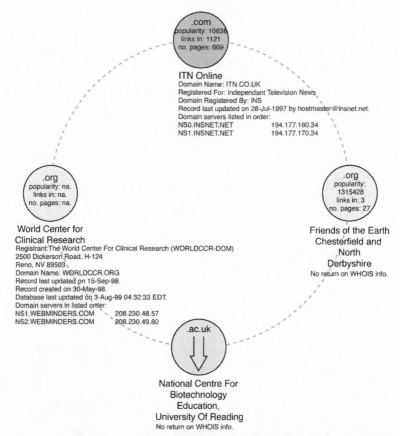

Figure 4.1.   Search Engine Technique. Depiction of the Four Organizational Pages (with no interlinking between them) returned in AltaVista's first ten results from the query "GM Food," 26 July 1999. Image by Alexander Bruce Wilkie.

dresses of organizations, as one may do using Alexa, presumably informs the surfer-researchers about their relative authority.) Figure 4.1 displays the four core sites, the lack of interlinking between them, and their DNS information (for the sake of completeness).

4. The researcher concluded the exercise because of the apparent absence of a network yielded by AltaVista. (None of the four core sites was interlinked.) The surfer-researcher lost interest.

Associative Reasoning

The Associative Reasoning technique addresses the issue of personal interpretative processes (educated guesses) in Web navigation. Here the GM food debate is entered from URLs selected on the basis of a hunch about the relationship between a domain name and the issue. Such thinking is in keeping with general Web-literate expectations; that is, one could expect the most basic terms for a product or an issue would be turned into a domain name by a relevant source, perhaps after that source has purchased the domain from a poacher—an individual or company that reserves a name only to sell it. In the technique, a series of generically relevant domain names was chosen, and plotted in the following steps.

1. The researcher's initial hunch about a potential relationship between milk and genetic modification led to the selection of a URL to begin the analysis: www.milk.org. From milk.org the links out were followed in the hopes of finding a set of intuitively relevant parties (on the basis of domain name alone). Of the relevant parties found—a Dutch Ministry, two UN bodies, and two main EU sites—there were no common link recipients; indeed there appeared to be distinctly separate networks around the EU and the UN, with GM food being one of many subjects. (A similar problem was encountered in the initial stage of the public trust logics method, below.) The organizations found were not deemed central for their lack of network. They were abandoned.

2. Keeping to the idea that relevant domain names are owned by relevant parties and that a series of .orgs is more likely to lead the surfer-researcher to a network, to milk.org was added corn.org and grains.org as potentially relevant parties. (The domains gmfood.org as well as gmfood.com had been reserved by a poacher and a hit- and banner ad-seeker, respectively; the former is not online and the latter site contains only banner ads and a borrowed engine.) Between these newly selected candidates for central players, four common link recipients were located: fao.org, wto.org, usda.gov, and econ.ag.gov (a branch of the USDA). In previous work, of the candidates in the pool—the starting points and common link recipients—central players were chosen owing to the scope of their presentation of the issue, in terms of coverage and the transdiscursivity of the links in their link lists. Here the surfer-researcher now had seven sites (milk.org, corn.org, grains.org, fao.org, wto.org, usda.gov, and econ.ag.gov) in the pool of actors to create a GM food issue network from associative reasoning and common link following. It was assumed that a .org/.gov mix of starting points would produce an issue network of sufficient scope and transdiscursivity.

3. All the outward links from the pool were captured, and, applying an authority threshold, only those organizations (sites) receiving three or more links from the central players were elected as relevant. The following sites were captured (but not depicted).

www.epa.gov
www.econ.ag.gov
www.wto.org
www.fao.org
www.usda.gov
www.fas.usda.gov
www.ars.usda.gov

The researcher decided to abandon the mapping of the network dominated by U.S. governmental agencies, the UN, and the WTO owing to the lack of transdiscursivity. It had become an intergovernmental issue network.

Public Trust Logics

Public trust involves a familiarity logic of a different kind from associative reasoning. Here the individual seeks organizations they trust and/or expect to be involved in the GM food debate. Here, the researcher trusted Monsanto.com and Greenpeace.org to be in the GM food debate.

1. The method began with comparing the outward links from Greenpeace.org and Monsanto.com. The first sweep revealed that these two URLs had no links in common, and it was unclear which organizations discuss GM food. This phase resulted in an amorphous set of only generally related bodies. A preliminary assessment suggested that on the global level the GM food debate has not been articulated, institutionalized, and internetworked in the manner of the climate change debate. The phase was abandoned.
2. While the debate is not well formed on an international level, a national focus might reveal more telling interlinking patterns. Thus the new experimentation began with the U.K. sites of Monsanto and Greenpeace. Here it was found that several organizations appear on both link lists. Then the link lists of the linkees (link recipients) were consulted, and from these lists the interlinkings between all the organizations in the pool (the central players plus the common link recipients) were plotted.
3. In keeping with the general network sampling method, it was decided to increase the authority threshold of the organizations within the network. For this sample of organizations only those organizations with more than three links in from the pool were selected.
4. An interlink map outlining the network relationships between the key players in the (U.K.) GM food debate was crafted (see figure 4.2); among other things it reveals (only) a gradual globalization of the (scope of the actors in the) debate beyond the national context.

Govs
English Nature
Ministry of Agriculture, Fisheries and Food (MAFF)
Department of the Environment, Transport and the Regions (DETR)
Department of Trade and Industry's Bioguide (DTI)
UN: Food and Agriculture Organization (FAO)
Department of the Environment,
Advisory Committee on Releases in the Environment (ACRE)
Biosafety Information Network and Advisory Service, UNIDO (BINAS)
Organisation for Economic Co-operation and Development (OECD)
International Centre for Genetic Engineering and Biotechnology (ICGEB)
The United States Animal and Plant Health Inspection Service (APHIS)
European Federation of Biotechnology (Euro Fed of Bio)

Orgs
Union of Concerned Scientists (UCS)
Greenpeace International
Friends of the Earth (uk) (FOE)
Soil Association
Genetics Forum
Oneworld Online
Rural Advancement Foundation International (RAFI)
Third World Network (TWN)
Institute of Food Science & Technology (IFST)
Genetic Engineering Network (GEN)

Coms
Monsanto International
Novartis
Biotechnology Industry Organisation Online (BIO Online)
BioSpace
Food for Our Future Food and Drink Federation
European Association for Bio Industries (EABI)

Edus
Biotechnology and Biological Sciences, Research Council (BBSRC)
National Centre for Biotechnology Education, University of Reading

Figure 4.2. Public Trust Technique. Depiction of the Organizations (and their inter-linkings) in the GM food issue network, October 1999. Image by Noortje Marres and Stephanie Hankey. *(continued on p. 75)*

Media Stories

Instead of employing a search engine, guessing URLs (in the associative reasoning method) or following the usual suspects (in the public trust method), surfer-researchers may prefer to read and follow links from a story by an authoritative online (or offline) news source to understand the issue. The attempt here is to ascertain whether, at least in this particular case, the story leads to an issue network (and, perhaps, reveals whether the journalist followed conventional snowballing or newer link-following techniques in an emerging form of digital journalism). The media story demarcation procedure began with a piece from BBC Online News entitled "GM Experiment

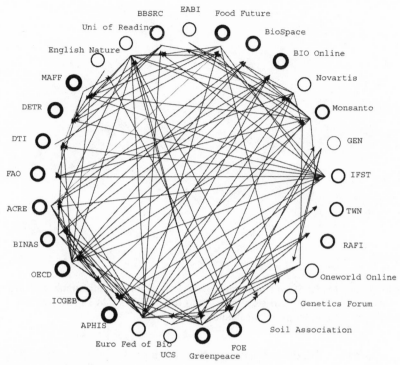

Figure 4.2.   *Continued*

Will Continue," July 26, 1999. The links within the story as well as those listed as related links were collected.

1. Six URLs were listed on the story page. The surfer-researcher also was able to locate the URL for the other leading actor in the story, a lone scientist, whose homepage or institutional Web site was not listed on the BBC story page. The interlinkings of the seven sources were depicted (for the actors in the story and their interlinkings, see figure 4.2). Given the authority of the news source, all sources were retained as central players.
2. All the links out of the seven URLs were captured, and given the large quantity of candidates for the pool only those organizations receiving two or more links from the central players in the BBC news story were captured. Thus the surfer-researcher employed an authority threshold at an earlier stage.
3. The interlinkings between all twenty-one actors were then sketched (see figure 4.3a).
4. All the links out of all twenty-one actors were collected (some 720 in all). Applying the authority threshold only those organizations receiving three or more links from the network were mapped as relevant

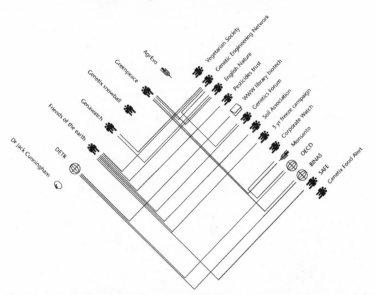

Figure 4.3a.   Media Stories Technique. Depiction of the Organizations (and their interlinkings) in the GM food story pool, from BBC online's GM Experiment Will Continue, 26 July 1999. Image by Stephanie Hankey.

parties to the debate. Twenty-one actors made the map (including the original seven). Seventeen actors, receiving two links from the network, were stricken from the map. A lower authority threshold, which we could dub "high" inclusiveness in the debate, would have allowed these actors onto the map. Here, however, they were deemed less relevant for a debate with "medium" inclusiveness. ("Low" inclusiveness would mean that the authority threshold is raised to four links in from the sample.) The technique seeks the highest authority threshold that still exhibits transdiscursivity. Such strictness also is in keeping with a perceived need to avoid "democratic overload" in meaningful online and offline public debating.

5. The surfer-researcher made an alternative depiction of the network through "actor profiles" (see figure 4.3b). In depicting the quantity of links each actor has received from the sample, these actor profiles demonstrate the relative authority of the actors according to the network.

Discussion Lists

Some of the more Net-literate and interested users subscribe to discussion lists to gain insight on an issue, often from other subscribers of similar mind, politics, and/or profession. (The outcomes of such like-mindedness with regards to the content of the discussions as well as the link recommendations

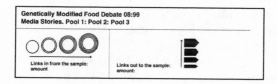

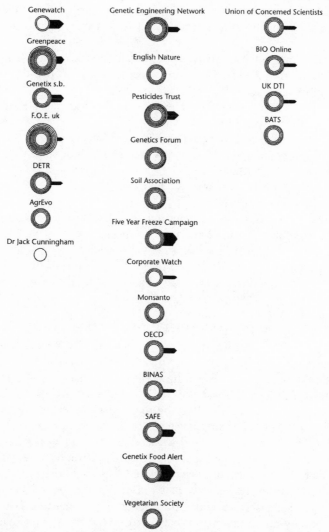

Figure 4.3b. Media Stories Technique, Actor Profiles. Depictions of the Relative Authorities (by quantities of links received from the network) of actors in the GM food story network, from BBC online's "GM Experiment Will Continue," 26 July 1999. Image by Stephanie Hankey.

made could be dubbed the list effect.) The discussion list technique described here interlinks all URLs listed during a five-day window (July 28–August 1, 1999) on an e-mail discussion list debating GM food. The discussion list, GenTech, was located by following links from the BBC story, discussed above. Though the lists could be reached by the surfer-researcher inclined to follow media stories together with discussion lists, we decided not to combine the URLs recommended by the discussion list with those recommended by the BBC story. We decided to keep the methods separate in this analysis for the sake of clarity. Network demarcation ensued.

1. The mailing list archives for e-mail discussion list GenTech (www. gene.ch/archives.html) were accessed for a five-day period (July 28–August 1, 1999).
2. The URLs mentioned or referenced in the discussion list were collected, yielding seven individual URLs.
   www.econ.ag.gov/whatsnew/issues/biotech/
   www.econ.ag.gov/whatsnew/issues/gmo/index.htm
   www.ul.ie/~biotech
   www.biotech-info.net/RR_yield_drag_98.pdf
   www.greenpeace.org
   www.monsanto.com/monsanto/investor/summary/default.htm
   www.hfxnews.southam.ca/story6.html
3. Owing to the absence of a network around Greenpeace.org and Monsanto.com (found with the public trust method), the search for a network around these sites was abandoned by the surfer-researcher.

PRELIMINARY FINDINGS: HOT ROUTES
AND STORYLINES THROUGH ISSUE NETWORKS

It should be emphasized, without remorse, that surfer-researcher preferences, which lie at the heart of "finding and knowing" on the Web, were behind the decisions to abandon the makings of potential, incipient issue networks on GM food at various stages of the formal method, especially in the case of the search engine and less so for associative reasoning and the discussion lists. Apart from the surfer-researchers' preferences, however, there are more formal (or intuitively obvious) reasons to discount the prospect of locating authoritative issues networks from the search engine. Since AltaVista indexes sites in its database according to self-described metatags and the location and frequency of key words in the site, the database, queried by the surfer, contains any number of sites with mention of GM food. The ones rising towards the top of the rankings are those receiving links from the entire Web (and not necessary from GM food sites). (Other engines, as Direct

Hit, further boost sites on the basis of what surfers, querying the same term, have in turn clicked from the engine returns.) The top ten returns may not lead directly to an issue network, not only because "issue network authority logics" are not built into AltaVista, but also because relevant organizations may not be heeding AltaVista's and other search engine watchers' tips to rise in the rankings.[25] In order to gain a quick idea of a network surrounding an issue, using AltaVista, one or more intuitively authoritative entities may be chosen, and their links in checked through fancy features. The sites occurring frequently may hint at candidate central players. The surfer-researcher decided to abandon such a method owing to the lack of candidate central players in the first set of ten returns.

While further empirical research has yet to be carried out on its efficacy, associative reasoning is rather hit and miss. While the domain name wars (a summary term for battles between poachers and legal entities wishing to secure online equivalents of their names, with any number of grey cases) are beginning to result in a loose correlation between well-known institutions and domain names, "issue names" may hardly correspond to authoritative issue associations, lobbies, researchers, institutions, what have you. This much is obvious. In our case, specifically, gmfood.com and gmfood.org are reserved by individuals or companies, and await purchase. Moreover, it is a stretch to expect even the most Web-literate to guess truefood.org (the name of the URL for Greenpeace's GM food campaign), though the network yielded by milk.org, corn.org, and grains.org should cause more formal surfer-researchers to take notice.

The discussion list results are a different matter, for the URLs collected are based on informed discussant recommendations. Though a larger scale analysis would be necessary, it could be expected that the level of the list would produce different outcomes. Net-discussants generally assuming a high level of understanding of the issue may suggest more specific and obscure links ("interesting to the discussion"), while lists exhibiting a tolerance for neophytes to the issue may suggest more basic starting points. In comparison with the outcomes from the other starting points in this research, the discussants recommended any number of palpably relevant parties (e.g., Greenpeace.org and Monsanto.org), but these did not yield an issue network, as was found in the opening stages of the public trust logics method. Only behind the U.K. domains was an authoritative network later discovered.

Where the media stories method is concerned, there is merit in assuming that the links recommended in online news stories by traditionally authoritative sources could lead to an understanding of the issue (or, intuitively, the story behind the story), however much the journalist's method may not (yet) be that of a "digital journalist." Indeed, it is an empirical question whether stories by individual journalists or individual news companies generally come (in the "related links" sections following the story) with an understanding of "networked sources." Such research, again with larger data sets, would have to be undertaken.

Here, however, we can put the issue differently (and more radically), in order to pursue an understanding (by navigating) of a relationship between digital journalism and online news stories. Could the journalist have written the story by following (her "related" and subsequently recommended) sources in a single surf? In other words, is there a route through which the media surfer-researcher could find the journalist's storyline, on the basis of the recommendations made on the story page? Can one surf the story? With the caveat of the unlinked, lone scientist being absent from the Web, here the answer is in the affirmative, at least with the use of the map.[26] Below, the single-surf story is highlighted within the original media stories GM food network map. Since the surfer-researcher could not navigate this debate by following links from the sites alone (the directionality is missing), the map would have to be inserted into the surfing process for a "line" through the journalist's "story" to be located. For the original seven story nodes to be surfed properly (so to speak), DETR would have to solicit a link from Genewatch.

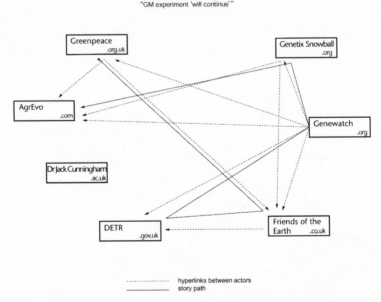

BBC news online 26th July 1999
"GM experiment 'will continue'"

Greenpeace .org.uk

Genetix Snowball .org

AgrEvo .com

Genewatch .org

Dr Jack Cunningham .ac.uk

DETR .gov.uk

Friends of the Earth .co.uk

--------------- hyperlinks between actors
———————— story path

Figure 4.4.   Digital Journalism abstracted from BBC story. Depiction of a potential "story path" between interlinked organizations mentioned in BBC online's GM Experiment Will Continue, 26 July 1999. Image by Stephanie Hankey and Auke Touwslager.

One may compare node and route findings by overlaying the maps. To begin, it is noted that of the BBC journalist's recommendations, only four of the seven made the public trust logics map. Comparing the final outcomes of the media stories and the public trust network maps, each, however, with a somewhat different network location technique, one notes the overlap of nine nodes. The meta-map with interlinkings, figure 4.5, could serve as a GM food navigator for surfers inclined towards a personal net archaeology of trusted actors and authoritative media stories.

Note that next to highly recognizable NGOs, two U.K. networks on genetics have achieved great presence on the map—a notable attainment of social relevance for groups presumably without great offline notoriety. Other parties desiring relevance would have to solicit links from the mapped organizations. In keeping with the organizational policy of strategic hyperlinking, the soliciting parties (practicing hyperlink diplomacy) would presumably be vetted by the relevant organizations in their consideration of the (potential) value of granting them a link. In other words, any solicitation on the part of the aspirants would be an attempted demonstration of relevance, in not so much a beauty contest, but rather a show of the value of their content, affinity, and reputation. After all, a hyperlink is an invitation issued to leave one's own site for another.

Note, too, that the organizations link-listed presumably would not accept payment for granting a link. Thus the much criticized practice of "preferred

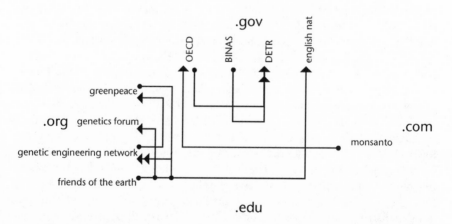

Figure 4.5. Digital Journalism abstracted by overlay of two maps. Depiction of the overlay of the GM story map (figure 4.3a) and the GM public trust map (figure 4.2), showing relevant interlinked organizations and new, potential story paths. Image by Marieke van Dijk and Richard Rogers.

placement"—buying a top slot (i.e., a link and the subsequent hits that go with it) in certain search engine returns—would not apply here. Having located the relevant players in particular issue networks, one could also challenge other seating allotments and "preferred placements" offline, as at Davos, where one buys a place in that network in order to participate.

CONCLUSION: ISSUE NETWORKS AS DEBATE SPACES—ONLINE AND OFFLINE IMPLICATIONS FOR THE INFORMATION SOCIETY

The means by which a debate navigator may surf routes (and potentially stories) through the GM food debate online has been treated in the case of the BBC online news story as well as in the outcome of the comparison of the media stories and public trust methods. Maps were overlaid and routes between hot nodes were depicted. These are the new surfer-researcher recommendations, quite distinct in method and spirit from those served up by certain search engines, using metatags and link counts from the entire Web, and by collaborative filtering, using previous surfer paths to point another potentially lost surfer to more Web sites, to phrase it somewhat bluntly. Whereas the collaborative filtering method assumes that surfers on the whole know how to find the authoritative and relevant sources (and makes recommendations from the surfers' "findings and keepings"), here it is assumed that aid may not be forthcoming from the collective surfer, often exploring issues through search engines or by other means. Indeed, the somewhat anthropological side of the research described above points to any number of abandoned routes made by allegedly expert surfers using not only the search engine, but also associative reasoning, public trust logics, conventional media stories, and discussion lists techniques. These abandoned, expert surfer routes, traced and collectively filtered, probably should not be recommended to other surfers. Instead the recommendations made by Webmasters aids in the demarcation of the issue networks in which they operate, and aids in providing sources the network recommends. These are the authoritative recommendations of choice, it is argued.

More importantly, however, the Web is beginning to reveal distributions of relevant debating parties that have ramifications far beyond surfing for knowledge. In the piece arguing for the public trust logics method, the case is made for the location of an authoritative network displaying the greatest amount of transdiscursivity, or cross-domain acknowledgment.[27] It was pointed out that such a network exhibited one state of the debate from one particular authority threshold (three links in from the sample). Higher authority thresholds revealed only .govs and .coms, and lower thresholds resulted in the inclusion of supermarkets, alternative lifestyle societies, as well as rogue Web sites, which impersonate other sites to parody and critique.[28]

A compromise between democratic overload and expert governance was made, in order to put forward a state of the debate with the highest authority measure, still exhibiting transdiscursivity (threshold three).

The public trust network depiction, borrowed from astronomical charts, may be understood as a roundtable. (Where the overlay map is concerned, the comparative researchers—the authors—decided to depict the parties as on distinct sides of a rectangular boardroom table, owing to the lack of interlinkings between the .govs, .coms, and .orgs. Kinship linkers, each keeps largely to its own domain.) The roundtable network, contrariwise, exhibits the prospect of neopluralist participation, as well as potentially reflexive understandings of each other's viewpoints.

Though an issue network may be found through different entry points and by different Net archaeological skills and preferences, the larger issue concerns the preferred "information society" implied by the network. Here, normative recommendation has been made for the authoritative, transdiscursive network (the roundtable), with sets of relevant parties on the Web awaiting invitation to at least the virtual GM food summit, with potential storylines already in place for the agenda. As discussed above, the parties off the map are left to devise a new Web presence strategy. (They may use the maps.) If the network still does not acknowledge their authority in the debate, they would have to endeavor to buy their way in.

NOTES

The work described here has been conducted under the auspices of the Design & Media Research Fellowship, Jan van Eyck Akademie, Maastricht, funded by the Dutch Ministry of Foreign Affairs, and the Ministry of Education, Culture, and Science. The authors wish to acknowledge close collaboration with Noortje Marres as well as the valuable input of the other members of the Research Fellowship, Stephanie Hankey, Ian Morris, and Alexander Wilkie. Finally, we wish to thank those assisting with the image-making, Marieke van Dijk and Auke Touwslager of the Govcom.org Foundation, Amsterdam. This chapter is © Govcom.org Foundation, 2000–2001.

1. On the Web as library, cf. Christine L. Borgman, *From Gutenberg to the Global Information Infrastructure: Access to Information in the Networked World* (Cambridge, Mass.: MIT Press, 2000); on the Web as marketplace, cf. Dan Schiller, *Digital Capitalism: Networking the Global Market System* (Cambridge, Mass.: MIT Press, 1999); on the Web as dark room, cf. Allucquere Rosanne Stone, *The War of Desire and Technology at the Close of the Mechanical Age* (Cambridge, Mass.: MIT Press, 1995); on the Web as rumor mill, cf. Richard Rogers, "Introduction: Towards the Practice of Web Epistemology," in *Preferred Placement—Knowledge Politics on the Web*, ed. Richard Rogers (Maastricht: Jan van Eyck Akademie Editions, 2000), 11–23; on the Web as parliament, cf. Roza Tsagarousianou, Damian Tambini, and Cathy Brian, eds.,

Cyberdemocracy (London: Routledge, 1998); on the Web as creative space, cf. George Landow, *Hypertext 2.0* (Baltimore: Johns Hopkins University Press, 1997); and on the Web as homely space, cf. Christine Hine, *Virtual Ethnography* (London: Sage, 2000).

2. See Richard Rogers and Noortje Marres, "Landscaping Climate Change: A Mapping Technique for Understanding Science and Technology Debates on the World Wide Web," *Public Understanding of Science* 9, no. 2 (2000): 141–63. The more standard case for meaningful public participation on the Web, with major consequences for government, may be found in numerous government documents in northern European and Scandinavian countries, e.g., Netherlands Scientific Council for Government Policy, *Governments Losing Ground: An Exploration of Administrative Consequences of Information and Communication Technology* 54 (The Hague: Netherlands Scientific Council for Government Policy, 1999).

3. Our use of the term "issue network" contrasts sharply to that of previous authors, who conceive of "networks" much like "communities." Cf. Heclo's and McFarland's notions in David Ronfeldt and John Arquilla, *The Zapatista Social Netwar in Mexico* (Santa Monica: Rand, 1998).

4. For hyperlinking as an act of organizational strategy, see Graphic, Visualization and Usability Center, *10th Internet User Survey* (Georgia Tech, 1998), online at www.gvu.gatech.edu/user_surveys/survey-199810/graphs/Webmaster/q51.htm.

5. Cf. Loet Leydesdorff and Michael Curran, "Mapping University-Industry-Government Relations on the Internet: The Construction of Indicators for a Knowledge-Based Economy," *Cybermetrics* 4, no. 1 (2000), online at www.cindoc.csic.es/cybermetrics/vol4iss1.html; and Moses Boudourides, Beatrice Sigrist, and Philippos D. Alevizos, "Webometrics and the Self-Organisation of the European Information Society," paper for the SOEIS project (Brussels: European Commission, 1999), online at http://hyperion.math.upatras.gr/webometrics.

6. See Noortje Marres and Richard Rogers, "Depluralising the Web, Repluralising Public Debate: The Case of the GM Food Debate on the Web," in Richard Rogers, ed., *Preferred Placement—Knowledge Politics on the Web*, 113–36.

7. For example, Shell, a highly relevant actor in the climate change debate, sets up a forum (or surfer "vent space") on its site where surfers may and do leave highly critical comments, which are sometimes answered by Shell employees, in one kind of participatory debate space. See www.shell.com.

8. For the notion of "becoming a relevant social group" and "achieving relevance," in reaction to W. Bijker's notion in his Social Construction of Technology (SCOT) approach, where groups are defined as relevant a priori, see Stuart Blume, "The Rhetoric and Counter Rhetoric of a 'Bionic' Technology," *Science Technology and Human Values* 22 (1997): 31–56; and Wiebe Bijker, *Of Bicycles, Bakelites and Bulbs: Toward a Theory of Sociotechnical Change* (Cambridge, Mass.: MIT Press, 1999). See also Richard Rogers and Noortje Marres, "French Scandals on the Web and on the Streets: Stretching the Limits of Reported Reality," *Asian Journal of Science* 30, no. 3 (2002), forthcoming.

9. Cf. David Ronfeldt and John Arquilla, *The Zapatista Social Netwar in Mexico* (Santa Monica: Rand, 1998); and Robin Mansell and Uta Wehn, eds., *Knowledge Societies: Information Technology for Sustainable Development* (Oxford: Oxford University Press, 1998).

10. For a basic overview of the study of (nonlinear) storylines through hypertext, from a literary studies perspective, see Paul Levinson, *The Soft Edge* (London: Routledge, 1997).

11. See Noortje Marres, "The Debate on Climate Change on the World Wide Web: A Network Analysis," unpublished ms., 1998; and Richard Rogers and Ian Morris, "In the Bubble: Operating Issue Networks on the Web," *Science as Culture* 11, no. 2 (2002), forthcoming.

12. Saskia Sassen, *Globalization and Its Discontents: Essays on the New Mobility of People and Money* (New York: New Press, 1998).

13. "Freshness" is gauged by the modification dates of Web pages, and is a feature of the Alexa toolbar. Among other things, the toolbar retrieves "files not found" from the Internet archive. See www.alexa.com; and www.archive.org.

14. While not concerned with the Web, Ray Oldenberg's book is often referred to by Web enthusiasts in this context: Ray Oldenberg, *The Great Good Place* (New York: Paragon, 1989).

15. Noortje Marres and Richard Rogers, "To Trace or to Rub: Screening the Web Navigation Debate," *Mediamatic* 9/10, no. 4/1 (1999): 117–20.

16. On the manners by which electronic journals appear authoritative (and survive or not), see Rob Kling, "What Is Social Informatics and Why Does It Matter?" *D-Lib Magazine* 5, no. 1 (1999), online at www.dlib.org:80/dlib/january99/kling/01kling.html. We also have explored automating the process of locating issue networks. The "De-Pluralising Engine" (aka the "Net Locator") crawls selected sites and returns co-linked sites; it has been crafted by the Design & Media Research Fellowship, Jan van Eyck Akademie, Maastricht, 1999–2000. The next generation of the co-link machine is to be used for the creation of an Atlas of Globalization Issues, at www.govcom.org.

17. Reke Albert, Hawoong Jeong, and Albert-Laszlo Barabasi, "The Diameter of the World-Wide Web," *Nature* 401 (6749), (1999), 130–31.

18. See, for example, *Pompeii-Herculaneum* (Roma: Vision, 1996).

19. These problems with the Web are summarized in Richard Rogers, "The Future of Science and Technology Studies on the Web," *EASST Review* 15, no. 2 (1996), 25–27; and Richard Rogers, "Playing with Search Engines and Turning Lowly Information into Knowledge," *Mediamatic* 9, nos. 2/3 (1998): 122–30.

20. The search engine explorative exercise was performed by Alex Bruce Wilke, associative reasoning by Ian Morris, public trust by Noortje Marres, media stories by Stephanie Hankey, and the discussion list by Andrés Zelman and Richard Rogers. The overlay work was done by Richard Rogers.

21. By contrast, Yahoo has human evaluators for every page submitted to the "directory"; Yahoo thus should not be confused with a search engine.

22. Neighborhoods have degrees of separation, which is to say that a site that is two clicks away is "farther" than a site which is only one click away.

23. For example, AltaVista and Google both boost ranking based on the amount of links into a site; whereas HotBot and DirectHit boost ranking based on the amount of hits a site receives. See www.searchenginewatch.com for a basic overview of search engine logics; for a lengthier discussion of search engine logics, and their implications, see Lucas Introna and Helen Nissenbaum, "The Public Good Vision of the Internet and the Politics of Search Engines," in Richard Rogers, ed., *Preferred Placement: Knowledge Politics on the Web*, 25–47.

24. DNS refers to the basic identification information about an individual site (e.g., to whom it is registered). The reader will note that the information for two of the four core sites was unattainable at the time of search.

25. On the issue of search engine manipulation, and the drama behind seeking the top ranking, see Richard Rogers, "Introduction: Towards the Practice of Web Epistemology," in Richard Rogers, ed., *Preferred Placement—Knowledge Politics on the Web*, 11–23.

26. As many others before us, we refer here to the future envisaged by one pioneer of "paths of meaning" through hypertext, Vannevar Bush: "There is a new profession of trail blazers, those who find delight in the task of establishing useful trails through the enormous mass of the common record." Vannevar Bush, "As We May Think," *Atlantic Monthly* 176, no. 1 (1945), 107. Cf. Greg Elmer, "Hypertext on the Web: The Beginning and End of Web Path-ology," *Space and Culture* 10 (2001), 1–40.

27. The GM Food Debate Map is inserted in Richard Rogers, ed., *Preferred Placement—Knowledge Politics on the Web*.

28. A taxonomy of rogue Web sites (and a "rogue Web site gallery") appear in Richard Rogers, ed., *Preferred Placement—Knowledge Politics on the Web*.

III

RETHINKING NET COMMUNITIES

5

The Myth of the Unmarked Net Speaker

Alice Crawford

Cyberspace consists of transactions, relationships, and thought itself, arrayed like a standing wave in the web of our communications. Ours is a world that is both everywhere and nowhere, but it is not where bodies live.

We are creating a world that all may enter without privilege or prejudice accorded by race, economic power, military force, or station of birth.

We are creating a world where anyone, anywhere may express his or her beliefs, no matter how singular, without fear of being coerced into silence or conformity.

—Declaration of the Independence of Cyberspace[1]

DREAMS OF A TECHNOLOGICALLY ENABLED COMMUNITY

From its beginnings, the Internet has been enthusiastically promoted as a medium that will break down barriers of social and cultural inequality, flatten hierarchies, and thus bring about a world in which radical, participatory democracy is not only possible, but almost inevitable. This "techno-populist" rhetoric has taken a tenacious hold in business, governmental, and, naturally, technological circles, and shows little sign of remitting. In the words of MCI's long-running advertising campaign, "There is no race. There is no age. There are no infirmities . . . is this Utopia? No, it's the Internet." Then President Clinton travels to China and makes the claim that the one thing that will guarantee Chinese children human rights is that they have access to the Internet. In my own town of Pittsburgh, Pennsylvania, meetings of the Technology Council, including developers, researchers, and IT business people are rife with talk of the "level playing field" and "pure meritocracy" that universal access to the Internet will bring about.

While it is unsurprising to hear such sentiments from parties with a vested interest based on billions in research and development dollars, it is perhaps more surprising that numerous academics and cultural critics have continued to make similar claims. It is not unusual to read in "critical" approaches to IT that a technologically determined brighter future is on the way, with claims along the lines that: "These technologies are inherently democratic and transnational. They will help create new and hitherto unimagined forms of democracy, political involvement, obligation, and power."[2] Even a generally skeptical critic such as Mark Poster has suggested that the nature of online communication is, in important respects, inherently democratic:

> [online speech] does connote a "democratization" of subject constitution because the acts of discourse are not limited to one-way address and not constrained by the gender and ethnic traces inscribed in face-to-face communications. The "magic" of the Internet is that it is a technology that puts cultural acts, symbolizations in all forms, in the hands of all participants; it radically decentralizes the positions of speech, publishing, filmmaking, radio and television broadcasting, in short the apparatuses of cultural production.[3]

Together, these various claims form a narrative that is consistently reiterated through multiple channels and that tells a tale about the formation of an unprecedented form of community. Perhaps the boldest claim about this community is that all people, from all backgrounds, will be able to actively participate in political discourse and debate.

COMMUNITY AND THE
DISEMBODIED/DESPATIALIZED INTERFACE

A key assumption that underwrites the techno-populist rhetoric of the "level playing field" and of "pure meritocracy" is the proposition that speech on the Internet is "unmarked," taking place as it does in the absence of a body coded by racial, class, and gender markings. The claim that all disembodied voices are equal goes largely unquestioned. The allegedly "unmarked" character of Internet interlocutors has been the cause for both celebration and anxiety, as any casual observation of the debates will demonstrate. There is clearly a great deal of optimism about the "democratic" character of public discourse, loosened from the moorings of inconveniently embodied subjects. There is also much hand-wringing about the dangers of "unmarked" communication, seen especially in the hysteria over pedophiles posing as children, men posing as women, and other socially unsanctioned moves in the game of self-presentation.

While these two attitudes are clearly opposed in many respects, both are heavily invested in the assumption that "Net-speech" is somehow stripped or "purified" of the markings of social difference, taking place as it does in the disembodied, despatialized place of the Net. As William J. Mitchell, the highly quotable dean of the School of Architecture and Planning at M.I.T. has put it:

> [In the standard sort of spatial city] you may come from the right side of the tracks or the wrong side, from Beverly Hills, Chinatown, East Los [Angeles], or Watts . . . and everybody knows how to read this code. . . . You may find your-self situated in gendered space or ungendered, domains of the powerful or margins of the powerless. . . . But the Net's despatialization of interaction destroys the geocode's key.[4]

Mitchell himself backpedals a bit on this claim, noting that "the incorporeal world of the Net has its own mechanisms for coding and class construction,"[5] however, the manner in which he qualifies his claim is worth noting: coding and class construction in the despatialized, "soft" city of Internet relations is, he maintains, almost entirely a matter of bandwidth, access, and technological prowess.

Mitchell's caveat is characteristic of the vast majority of objections to the techno-populist line. When questions of access to decision-making power are raised, they are almost entirely construed as technological questions; either as a question of access to the technology itself, or of access to specifically technological skill sets. The enormous amount of attention being paid to "wiring" schools and promoting technology education is, in part, a response to the concern that, without universal access to Internet technology and an understanding of how to use it, the promises of a technologically enabled community of equals will most certainly go unfulfilled.

BEYOND THE TECHNOLOGICAL FIX

While questions of access are clearly important I argue that even if universal technological access were to be achieved the level playing field of the techno-populists would still not be realized. Access to technology and technical education is a necessary, but far from sufficient, precondition for equal access to decision-making power within any "wired" community. In fact, the access and education position is founded on a strikingly common though untenable understanding of the way in which language operates in relation to social and political power. This perspective holds that language can function somehow "outside" or "above" embodied, material relations between people and groups of people, a point of view that participates in a long tradition of understanding language in isolation from the contexts in which it operates. Such theories of "linguistic idealism" consider language in an abstracted form neglecting the sociohistorical conditions underlying the formation of language itself, treating language as if it were separable from its development and use in the day-to-day situations of embodied, material existence.

As mentioned above, the assumptions made by techno-populists regarding the way in which language functions are assumptions embedded in a long history of linguistic theory. In short, techno-populists make the same abstractions and buy into many of the same illusions as the most idealist of linguistic theorists. Accordingly, I will argue that the position of the techno-populists can be submitted to many of the same critiques that have been launched against idealist linguistics. In the field of communication theory, a number of more materially grounded perspectives have attempted to address the relationship between language, identity, and society. One of the most effective and influential critiques of linguistic idealism has been offered by the French sociologist and cultural critic Pierre Bourdieu. Bourdieu's critique of idealist linguistics can, I believe, be usefully employed to question a number of key assumptions of techno-populist rhetoric. To elaborate upon both the nature of the abstractions perpetuated by the techno-populists and their most problematic shortcomings, a short detour through the major assumptions of linguistic idealism may be useful at this point.

LINGUISTIC IDEALISM AND THE
HOMOGENEOUS SPEECH COMMUNITY

The classic treatment of language as an abstracted, self-sufficient system of signs is the structuralist linguistic analysis of Ferdinand de Saussure. In one of the foundational works of twentieth-century linguistics, the *Course in General Linguistics*,[6] Saussure suggests that the way in which language functions is largely determined by internal relations within the system of symbols which make up the language. On this account, language forms a self-sufficient system (*langue*) that exists and has meaning independently of particular instances of its use (*parole*). This form of analysis conceives language as having an objective inner logic, rather than as a contextualized process where language is acquired, modified, and articulated. In a famous passage, Saussure bypasses the question of the social framework within which language functions with the rather astonishing claim that:

> Language exists in the form of a sum of impressions deposited in the brain of each member of a community, almost like a dictionary of which identical copies have been distributed to each individual. Language exists in each individual, yet is common to all.[7]

On this perspective, language is a resource that is equally distributed and shared by all. This claim, along with Saussure's proposal that the social nature of language is internal to language itself, rather than being a matter determined at least in part by extralinguistic contexts, underwrites the related notion of a homogeneous language or speech community in which all individuals are fundamentally capable of participating. If each member of the community has identical access to the dictionary that has been mysteriously and almost mystically implanted in everyone's brain alike, why wouldn't each member of the community have equal power to express themselves, be heard, be listened to? August Comte, a prominent linguist of the nineteenth century whose views closely parallel Saussure's in a number of key respects, had the following to say about the distribution of the resources of language:

> Language forms a kind of wealth, which all can make use of at once without causing any diminution of the store, and which thus admits a *complete community of enjoyment*; for all, freely participating in the general treasure, unconsciously aid in its preservation.[8]

While the observations of such early structuralists are interesting in their own right, what is more pertinent to the argument being made in this chapter is the fact that similar abstractions are clearly being made in our own time. By assuming that language in its "pure," disembodied form is shared in equally by all, contemporary techno-populists propose the possibility of a homogeneous speech community in which all voices will have the same amount of power. Stripped of the more obvious markers of social difference, such a disembodied, despatialized Internet community would seemingly offer a pluralist democracy where all voices could be heard equally.

PIERRE BOURDIEU AND THE "ILLUSION OF LINGUISTIC COMMUNISM"

Bourdieu's theory of language provides a markedly different perspective regarding the origin of the real powers of language. As such, his critique of structuralist linguistics, particularly as elaborated in *Language and Symbolic Power*, provides the foundation for a reexamination of the claims of techno-populists. Bourdieu's *Language and Symbolic Power* is a sustained attack on structuralist analyses inspired by Saussure, and, by extension, on all other forms of analysis that treat the actual uses of language as separable from the political and social contexts in which they take place. His critique is a thoroughgoing one: Rather than merely supplementing these abstracted, "idealist" analyses with a consideration of sociohistorical conditions, Bourdieu wants to demonstrate that language is itself a sociohistorical phenomenon. On this account, language use, rather than being a matter of participating in an ideal realm somehow separate from the other activities of life, is itself a "mundane" (in the sense of "worldly" and quotidian), practical activity, an activity thoroughly enmeshed in the other practical activities that constitute the life of an individual or a culture. Apropos of Comte's description of the way in which linguistic power is acquired, Bourdieu asserts that:

> In describing symbolic appropriation as a sort of mystical participation, universally and uniformly accessible and therefore excluding any form of dispossession, Auguste Comte offers an exemplary expression of *the illusion of linguistic communism* which haunts all linguistic theory.[9]

This assertion is directly opposed to the idealistic notion of *langue* as a self-sufficient, homogeneous system of signs, accessible to all, in which the meaning of an expression is determined strictly by the relation between it and other elements in the language system. The resources of language, rather than being freely shared by all, are unevenly distributed, and distributed in patterns, as we will see, that are broadly homologous to the distribution of other social resources within a community. Inequalities in distribution make it highly problematic to assume, as the techno-populists tend to do, that online speech communities are free of social hierarchies, privilege, and oppression, which characterize embodied life, and can function as realms of radically egalitarian debate and conversation.

If language is itself fully embedded in other practical activities and in the material conditions of everyday life, then the homogeneous speech community of structural linguistics does not exist. Rather, it is an *idealization* of a particular set of linguistic practices that have in fact developed historically, and, accordingly, have particular social conditions of existence. The chief example of the social conditions at play here is, of course, access to education. While the idealist perspective holds that everyone in a community has the same access to the "proper" way of expressing herself, Bourdieu takes pains to demonstrate the way in which this seemingly "natural" ability is differently distributed among community members according to their level of access to educational institutions, and the social position of their families (in which a great deal of language acquisition takes place). By overlooking the way in which extralinguistic institutions such as education and family affect the distribution of access to education in "proper" modes of expression, the idealist perspective assumes that everyone has equal access to the power of language. The assertion of a homogeneous, decontextualized community of speakers papers over the social conditions of language acquisition, and also the sociohistorical conditions (including broader power relations within a culture or across cultures) that have established a particular set of practices as legitimate while delegitimating others. As Bourdieu puts it, linguistic theory that abstracts linguistic practice from its context simply takes the victorious language for granted as superior, rather than reflecting upon how its victory was achieved.

To clarify his position, Bourdieu gives the example of the establishment of "French" as the legitimate, national language after the French Revolution. Rather than occurring naturally, as is often assumed, the installation of the dialect we now recognize as "French" was as much a political process as any military campaign. As Bourdieu points out, the members of the upper classes, who already spoke the dialect that was to be installed as the legitimate language, had everything to gain from this policy, as it would provide them with a de facto monopoly on political power.[10] Bourdieu's theory could also be applied to the spread of the English language as the lingua franca of economic and other discourse on the Internet. The international spread of English as the language of "choice" on the Internet is in large part the result of deliberate choices made by institutions such as the World Trade Organization in which de facto economic sanctions are threatened against nations who "stubbornly" insist on using their own languages and dialects for Internet transactions.[11] Near monopolistic control over the world software market by American companies has also contributed a great deal to the "choice" of English as the common language for programming and communicating in high-tech circles, a choice that has trickled down into interpersonal communication on the Internet as well.

On an international level, it is clear that the establishment of English as the "common language" of Internet communication is not a process that has taken place on an entirely linguistic plane, but, rather, that this state of affairs is the product of a particular set of historical and social institutions with extralinguistic powers, such as the power of economic sanctions, market controls, etc. Far from being separable from extralinguistic institutions, the power of language is thoroughly imbricated in these institutions, as they have both *produced* the legitimacy of the common language,[12] and are reproduced by the language. The language of the powerful, installed as legitimate, perpetuates the legitimacy of those who speak it. Those members of the world community who have access to the social conditions of acquisition of "proper" English are empowered by their mastery of an ability that is far from "natural" or equally shared by all. From this vantage point, language is not a neutral medium, and the homogeneous speech community in which the resources of language are as equally distributed as the air we breathe is shown up as a convenient fiction. In Bourdieu's metaphor, the "market" in which language circulates is far from "free":

> This [abstract] market, which knows only pure, perfect competition among agents who are as interchangeable as the products they exchange and the

situations in which they exchange, and who are all identically subject to the principle of the maximization of informative efficiency . . . is as removed from the real linguistic market as the "pure" market of the economists is from the real economic market, with its monopolies and oligopolies.[13]

It follows that, if the language system (*langue*) itself cannot be abstracted from the social conditions of its establishment, then neither can individual instances of its use.

IN/FELICITY AS A PRACTICAL AFFAIR

In the same manner in which "idealist" theories of language tend to decontextualize the speech community as a whole, they also tend to analyze individual occasions of language use[14] in isolation from the social conditions in which they take place. The implications of an act of speaking, Bourdieu argues, cannot be understood merely in terms of "execution," as structuralist linguistics has assumed for over a century: that is, as if what is most important about the act of speaking is the fact that the speaker can successfully organize and reorganize ("execute," in linguistic parlance) the elements of a language system in the form of grammatically correct sentences (such as "I am the boss here," or "On the Internet, nobody knows you're a dog"). While certainly a prerequisite to linguistic power, the ability to form recognizable sentences is clearly not an adequate description of what is required for language use to be effective. The varying linguistic powers that speakers possess are more complex than this, and also more thoroughly grounded in networks of social interaction.

True linguistic competence is not the capacity to generate grammatically correct sentences in a vacuum, but rather it is the capacity to produce expressions that are appropriate for specific social situations. As Bourdieu puts it, linguistic competence is the capacity to produce expressions "a propos." It is in this sense a practical affair, involving much more than an abstract ability to "execute the code," producing grammatical sentences. This more inclusive notion of competence is more chiefly concerned with a speaker's capacity to generate utterances that are effective, versus merely coherent. A truly "competent" speaker has command of the implicit and explicit rules of legitimacy—rules that govern the likelihood of being listened to versus merely heard, to having one's utterances given credibility; of being obeyed, and the like. "Making sense" on a grammatical level lays the foundations for linguistic competence but is not its end goal. Bourdieu is influenced here, as many others have been, by J. L. Austin's "speech-act theory,"[15] which draws attention to the fact that utterances do more than report on or describe the world. In fact, one of the more interesting and salient things about language is that, though it is in a sense immaterial, we can use it to make things happen in the material world. The class of utterances Austin calls "performatives," such as the utterance "I do" spoken in a wedding ceremony, are a type of action through which the speaker participates in social practices with real, material effects. Successful utterances of this sort are "felicitous," those that fail, "in/felicitous."

To be "felicitous," utterances must be given voice by a person who is authorized to do so, and who makes use of a conventional procedure; otherwise, utterances will not "perform." What class of people are "appropriate" for performing certain types of utterances, and what the conventional procedures are, are determined by social and historical conditions. In Bourdieu's words:

> A performative utterance is destined to fail each time that it is not pronounced by a person who has the "power" to pronounce it. But perhaps the most important thing to remember is that the success of these operations of social magic . . . is dependent on the combination of a systematic set of interdependent conditions which constitute social rituals.[16]

These social rituals are authorized by institutions that cannot, in many cases, be circumvented simply by speaking as if one were authorized to do so. For example, if I stand in a 7-11 parking lot and pronounce two passersby to be "man and wife," their status vis-à-vis the law, the IRS, any religious institutions they may be associated with, and Pottery Barn mailing lists does not change in the slightest. Or, more to the point of the question at hand, if I perform a wedding ceremony for two women in a chat room on the Net, very little will come of it. I cannot make myself an "appropriate" person to perform a wedding ceremony that changes two people's legal status, etc., just by uttering the words. I cannot authorize myself by fiat in a way that will make it felicitous in these (and other) cases.

Furthermore, the conventional procedures that determine felicity are not subject to change simply by any random group of people simply stating that "the rules have changed." Quite the contrary: Linguistic conventions are decided by social and historical factors, in this case, extralinguistic factors such as legal, religious, and other institutions place the utterance "I pronounce you wife and wife" outside the realm of felicitous statements. Power or felicity does not stem from the utterance itself, but from institutional recognition of that utterance as legitimate, a recognition that is, in this case, lacking.

A less legalistic example would be a conversation regarding the allocation of resources within a community. Imagine a hypothetical, fully wired community in which choices regarding education were under debate online. Since everyone in this hypothetical community is technically enabled to participate in the debate, does that mean that a Laotian woman with a G.E.D. for whom English is a second language is going to be able to participate in the conversation with the same level of felicity as the Stanford-educated superintendent of schools, or other individuals holding an Ed.D.? Certainly her interlocutors will not be able to see her cultural background, markers of class carried in her clothing or the way she carries herself, her level of education, her gender, but does this mean that her speech will magically be freed of these extralinguistic facts of her everyday life when she goes online? On the contrary: Online speech is marked by a highlyreadable system of differences encoded in grammar and syntax, vocabulary, allusions, regionalisms, dialect, and all the other ways in which we signify our cultural and class positions via language.

To reiterate this key point, the conditions that decide who is likely to succeed in performing felicitous linguistic acts, and when and where they can do so, are primarily social conditions, embedded in particular sociohistorical relations, marked by both hierarchy and struggle over power. The right to speak, the ability to be heard and not silenced, and the authority to be obeyed come not from the utterances themselves, but from their origin in a speaker positioned vis-à-vis social institutions in a particular fashion. This perspective provides a useful tempering of the idealistic thinking that holds that simply speaking without our socially situated bodies on view will have a "democratizing" effect that will carry over into our everyday lives in a fairly uncomplicated fashion, a line of thinking that underwrites claims such as "if a black man can talk to a white woman on the Internet as pure, disembodied voices, they'll be equal." No matter if he can't get a loan to buy a house in her neighborhood due to extralinguistic factors such as long-standing practices in financial institutions and real estate markets that reinforce segregated and unequal access to housing along racial lines.

It has become fairly commonplace to claim, as W. Mitchell has done, that, because of the disembodied, despatialized nature of the Internet interface, in cyberspace. "There is no such thing as a better address, and you cannot attempt to define yourself by being seen in the right places in the right company."[17] However, in light of Bourdieu's analysis, it seems disingenuous to claim that Professor Mitchell—whose e-mail address is "wjm@mit.edu"—would have no more authority in a discussion of, say, new technology protocols, than someone speaking from the position of "joe_shmoe@aol.com." An online debate of this sort would be marked by a wide number of differentiating factors, for example: long-standing familiarity and, hence, ease with the "terms of art" of technological debate; the status and prestige conferred through association with legitimated institutions (such as M.I.T.); mastery of the explicit and implicit rules of debate in engineering and policy circles; as well as basic markers that indicate the speaker's education level. All of these factors serve as powerful markers that determine what speech will tend to be recognized as legitimate and valuable in this context.

DISPOSITIONS AND SUBMISSION

A final aspect of Bourdieu's linguistic theory that calls into question popular assumptions about speaking subjects on the Net is his notion of "*habitus*," which is related to "habit" in that both are a kind of "second nature" that give form and pattern to our behavior without necessarily being available to conscious thought. With "*habitus*," Bourdieu gives a name to the practices and dispositions brought about by our cultural, historical, and social contexts (such as family, education, class background) that, through their familiarity, become "natural" to us. One of the more interesting qualities of *habitus* is that the dispositions described are simultaneously the product of a particular set of sociohistorical conditions while they also generate practices that reproduce that very history. For example, a woman raised in a sociohistorical context in which women are expected to be silent or agreeable will tend to develop over the course of her life a set of dispositions that will generally be productive of utterances (or silences) that are agreeable to others, particularly to individuals invested with more authority than she.

On the other hand, a highly educated person socially positioned from early childhood to consider her statements worthy of being heard and even obeyed will, regardless of any formal investiture with authority, tend to express herself in a fashion that is more likely to be accepted as authoritative. The way in which expressions are coded and decoded is part of a broader, highly recognizable pattern of social differences and differentiation, which affect whose speech is likely to have a high degree of legitimacy (and therefore felicity) and whose speech is not. Mastery of Standard English, of the specific terms of whatever debate is at hand, a predisposition to expect one's words to be respected rather than ignored, an understanding of oneself as a legitimate speaker in any particular situation— all of these factors are shaped by the structures and institutions of our everyday, embodied life, and are reproduced in generally recognizable ways in our habits of speech. With this in mind, it becomes highly problematic to claim, with the techno-populists, that a speech community in a disembodied, despatialized medium will necessarily be a "level playing field" or a "pure meritocracy," or that, in the words of the widely cited cyberbooster Jaron Lanier, computer mediated communications represents "the ultimate lack of race or class distinctions, or any other form of pretense, since all form is variable."[18]

The manner in which offline, embodied inequities shadow us on the Internet has been noted by a number of scholars who have been investigating this issue. For example, in the case of female Internet speakers, it has been noted that the "inequities of face-to-face interaction migrate on-line, where women speak less and are less likely to have their topics pursued."[19] In short, the dispositions of a speaker who is invested with little authority (little "linguistic capital" in Bourdieu's terms) will be generative of the kinds of linguistic practices she will be willing and able to engage in, and also the value her speech will have in different speech communities or "linguistic markets." Since utterances are always produced in particular contexts or markets, and the properties of these markets endow certain types of linguistic products with a certain "value," part of linguistic competence is to be able to produce expressions that are highly valued on the markets concerned, not just the ability to create grammatically comprehensible expressions:

> The competence adequate to produce sentences that are likely to be understood may be quite inadequate to produce sentences that are likely to be listened to, likely to be recognized as acceptable in all the situations where there is occasion to speak.[20]

Furthermore, "Speakers lacking the legitimate competence are de facto excluded from the social domains in which this competence is required or are condemned to silence."[21]

What is crucial to understand at this juncture is that *habitus* is not something that the individual consciously manipulates or controls to any significant degree in the course of daily life. Different speakers possess different quantities of linguistic capital as the result of long and complex training that can't be overcome by a simple act of will[22] and is frequently not even available to conscious thought without careful and deliberate introspection. In the wide array of speech styles and patterns are reflected a set of differences significantly associated with social differences. In Bourdieu's words, in linguistic *habitus* we can discern the "re-translation of a system of social differences" in the form of speech.[23]

The disembodiment of Internet speech may, under the right circumstances, provide an environment in which such speakers may overcome some of the barriers erected by embodied difference. Such results have been found, for example, in studies conducted within educational settings, such as Bellman et al.'s findings that Latin American women participating in class discussion online tended to assert themselves more than they normally did in face-to-face classroom discussion.[24] However, the bulk of empirical studies to date have indicated that offline patterns of speech and silence tend to cross over into online speech, finding that, for example, men and women generally have recognizable, gender-specific styles of communication online, that people in positions of offline authority tend to post more frequently and to garner more responses in the conversations they are involved in online, and that cultural differences inflect online communication in much the same way they shape our communications in everyday, embodied life.[25]

Accordingly, not only our bodies, but our linguistic practices themselves carry the markings of our backgrounds, betraying or trading on the training of a certain social position. Since the distribution of access to legitimated modes of expressing oneself (one's share of "linguistic capital" in Bourdieu's terms) is related in specific, predictable ways to the distribution of other forms of capital, many of the inequalities that determine who gets listened to in life offline will tend to carry over into online speech. A speaker whose grammar, vocabulary, repertoire of allusions, and style of expression is readable as lower class, and marginally educated will not, in many speech communities on the Net, have the same authority, or even ability to be heard, as someone with the linguistic *habitus* that comes with a privileged social position.

It is worth repeating that a subject's relation to authorizing institutions and her *habitus* are generative of the choice to speak at all in certain communicative settings, or to simply remain silent, knowing her utterances will be invested with negligible value. Rather than sharing equally distributed resources in the context of a homogeneous community, speakers take into account what constitutes legitimacy within different contexts, and judge both their own and others' ability to "measure up" according to these criteria. The capacity to reliably produce contributions to the conversation that will be received and valued by others, as well as the tendency toward self-censorship, varies with background. Clearly there are many, many voices that are silent in cyberspace, and not only because they do not have access to equipment, as is so often assumed to be the case.

CONCLUSION

Rather than focusing attention so narrowly on technological approaches to access, it would be more realistic and more effective to understand technological empowerment as a small part of a much larger array of movements that need to take place in order for a truly egalitarian democracy to take hold. The solution is not to disregard the very real impact that online speech communities can have in the world, but to avoid allowing the "technological fix" to function as a substitution for other forms of empowerment that need equal if not greater attention if the roots of structural inequalities are to be addressed. Consider, for example, Clinton's claim that Chinese children could be guaranteed human rights primarily through access to the Internet, a statement that implies a notion of cyberspace as a locale in which social and political relations can be worked out in isolation from the inequalities that structure everyday life. While an online conversation regarding child labor, for example, could well bring attention to the issue and aid dramatically in organizing efforts (as we have recently observed in global organization to protest the policies of the World Trade Organization and World Bank), such a conversation would not naturally and inevitably lead to concrete changes in policy and in the lives of the children in question. It is only after being articulated to actual political movements taking real-world actions such as boycotts, embargoes, educational campaigns, and the like that such conversations will have real traction.

By clarifying the very tangible relationships between the practical affair of speaking and the material conditions of social and political life, Bourdieu's approach to understanding the power of language provides a much needed contextualization of the putatively "pure" and unencumbered speech of Internet communities. Bourdieu's treatment of the social and historical grounding of the in/felicity of all speech acts brings the techno-populist dream of technologically produced free speech down to earth. This is of more than theoretical interest at this point in our collective political life, as the assumption of the "unmarked" nature of the Net speech frequently underwrites the claims of powerful techno-libertarians as they enthuse about a new form of world citizenship ("netizen-ship," in *Wired*-speak) in which identities are cut loose from the classed, gendered, racially marked "meat" in which they have previously inhered, and, so we are encouraged to believe, take on a new mobility that allows for respect, status, and advancement to be rewarded on the basis of something like "pure merit." Ignoring the very real constraints on this idealistic form of "free speech" can only serve to prolong the infelicity and silencing of many voices that need to be heard if substantive change is going to take place.

NOTES

1. John Perry Barlow. A Declaration of the Independence of Cyberspace. Davos, Switzerland, February 8, 1996, online at www.eff.org/pub/Publications/John_Perry_Barlow/barlow_0296.declaration. While Barlow is generally perceived as being a bit daft, his proclamations often merely put common claims regarding Internet Technology into more turgid prose. A quick Internet search will also show that Barlow's "Declaration" is posted on a wide range of Web-pages hosted in a remarkable number of countries.

2. J. Hillis Miller, "Literary Theory, Telecommunications, and the Making of History," in *Scholarship and Technology in the Humanities*, 17–18.

3. Mark Poster, online at www.humanities.uci.edu/mposter/writings/democ.html.

4. W. J. Mitchell, *City of Bits*, 10.

5. W. J. Mitchell, *City of Bits*, 10.

6. A book compiled by his former students from notes taken in a series of courses on general linguistics offered by Saussure during the period 1906–1911.

7. Ferdinand de Saussure, *Course in General Linguistics* (New York: McGraw-Hill, 1959), 19.

8. Auguste Comte, quoted in Bourdieu, *Language and Symbolic Power*, 43 (italics mine).

9. *Language and Symbolic Power*, 43.

10. *Language and Symbolic Power*, 47.

11. The role of international organizations and trade relations in establishing English as a global lingua franca has been widely explored. Some of the more compelling arguments have been made in the context of international conferences concerning the broader topic of globalization. See for example the proceedings of the April 2001 Global English: The European Lessons Conference (www.guardianunlimited.co.uk/GWeekly/Global_English/) and those of the 1997 Human Security and Global Governance Conference, especially Yukio Tsuda's paper, The Hegemony of English and Strategies for Linguistic Pluralism: Proposing the Ecology of Language Paradigm (www.toda.org/conferences/hugg_hon/hugg_hon_6_97.html).

12. In the same manner in which the French-speaking merchant class helped to produce "French" as the common language of France, an explicitly political process that Bourdieu describes in some detail in *Language and Symbolic Power* and elsewhere.

13. *Language and Symbolic Power*, 56.

14. The *parole* of structuralist linguistics.

15. See particularly J. L. Austin, *How to Do Things with Words* (Oxford: Oxford University Press, 1975).

16. *Language and Symbolic Power*, 111.

17. Mitchell, *City of Bits*, 11.

18. Jaron Lanier, cited in Peggy Orenstein, "Get a Cyberlife," *Mother Jones* (May/June 1991), 63.

19. N. Baym, "Agreements and Disagreements in Computer Mediated Discussion," in *Research on Language and Social Interaction* 29, no. 4 (1996): 315–45, 325.

20. *Language and Symbolic Power*, 55.

21. *Language and Symbolic Power*, 55.

22. Although sustained and conscientious effort can bring about changes—"The rain in Spain, falls mainly on the plain, Professor 'Iggins!"

23. *Language and Symbolic Power*, 54.

24. Bellman, Tindimubona, and Arias Jr., 1993.

25. See, for example: Lynn Cherny, "Gender Differences in Text-Based Virtual Reality," *Proceedings of the Berkeley Conference on Women and Language* (April 1994); V. Frissen, "Trapped in Electronic Cages?: Gender and New Information Technologies in the Public and Private Domain: An Overview of Research," *Media, Culture and Society* 14 (1992): 31–49; Susan C. Herring, "Gender and Democracy in Computer Mediated Communication," *Electronic Journal of Communications* 3: 2 (1993).

BIBLIOGRAPHY

Austin, J. L. *How to Do Things with Words*. Oxford: Oxford University Press, 1975.

Bellman, B., A. Tindimubona, and A. Arias Jr. "Technology Transfer in Global Networking: Capacity Building in Africa and Latin America." Pp. 237–54 in *Global Networks: Computers and International Communication*, ed. L. Harasim. Cambridge, Mass.: MIT Press, 1993.

Bourdieu, Pierre. *Language and Symbolic Power*. Cambridge, Mass.: Harvard University Press, 1991.

———. *The Logic of Practice*. Stanford, Calif.: Stanford University Press, 1992.

Cherny, Lynn. "Gender Differences in Text-Based Virtual Reality." *Proceedings of the Berkeley Conference on Women and Language* (April 1994).

Frissen, V. "Trapped in Electronic Cages?: Gender and New Information Technologies in the Public and Private Domain: An Overview of Research." *Media, Culture, and Society* 14 (1992): 31–49.

Gates, Bill. *The Road Ahead*. New York: Viking, 1995.

Herring, Susan C. "Gender and Democracy in Computer Mediated Communication." *Electronic Journal of Communications* 3, no. 2 (1993).

Miller, J. Hillis. "Literary Theory, Telecommunications, and the Making of History." Pp. 11–20 in *Scholarship and Technology in the Humanities*, ed. May Katzen. London: Bowker Saur, 1991.

Mitchell, William J. *City of Bits: Space, Place, and the Infobahn*. Cambridge, Mass.: MIT Press, 1995.

Orenstein, Peggy. "Get a Cyberlife." *Mother Jones* (May/June 1991): 63–68.

Poster, Mark. CyberDemocracy: Internet and the Public Sphere, online at www.humanities.uci.edu/mposter/writings/democ.html, 1995.

Saussure, Ferdinand de. *Course in General Linguistics*. Glasgow: Collins, 1974.

6

Digitizing and Globalizing Indigenous Voices: The Zapatista Movement

Donna M. Kowal

Social movements on behalf of indigenous and disenfranchised peoples are rhetorically constrained by the establishments that seek to suppress them and by their corresponding lack of political representation in the dominant public sphere. However, the rise of the Internet as a democratic communication technology and its increasing accessibility to diverse populations has resulted in the opening of new opportunities for "speaking" as well as being "heard." The ongoing cyber campaign launched by the Zapatistas of Mexico on January 1, 1994, the inauguration day of the North American Free Trade Agreement (NAFTA), is a model example of the potential of the Internet to function as a forum for the voices of oppressed peoples.

In recent years, the influence of the Zapatista movement has attracted the interest of scholars and political activists alike. The Zapatista movement has been labeled as the world's first postmodern revolution. Scholars have marveled at how this movement on behalf of an indigenous and agricultural people, primarily Mayan Indians in the Chiapas region of southern Mexico, has successfully used the Internet as a means of promulgating global support (Cleaver 1998, Froehling 1997, Glusker 1998, Harvey 1998, Ford and Gil 2001). Meanwhile, political activists and social justice organizations around the world, particularly advocates of human rights and opponents of neoliberal policies such as NAFTA and the Multilateral Agreement on Investment (MAI), point to the effectiveness of the Zapatista movement as a stimulus for international grassroots activism. Harry Cleaver, University of Texas professor and creator of the popular "Zapatistas in Cyberspace"[1] Web page directory notes that "the influence of the pro-Zapatista mobilization has reached across at least five continents. Moreover, it has inspired and stimulated a wide variety of grassroots political efforts in dozens of countries" (1998, 622).

Indeed, the technology has enabled the Zapatistas to overcome the barriers of time, space, and borders. With the help of a highly organized network of activists, communiqués on the plight of people living in Chiapas were written in the Lacandón jungle and disseminated all over the world, despite the impossibility of finding an outlet let alone a modem in the remotest areas of southeast Mexico.

The Zapatistas use the Internet to agitate, enact their autonomy, create a collective identity, and, ultimately, generate worldwide support for their cause all the while maintaining protection against retaliation by the Mexican government. The support generated is not simply for the struggle for autonomy of a local, indigenous, agricultural people but is part of the mounting organized resistance against the international influence of neoliberal institutions, such as the World Trade Organization (WTO) and the International Monetary Fund (IMF). Ultimately, the Zapatista movement through cyberspace is both strategic and symbolic. Beyond obtaining the ability to globalize their otherwise local voices, they have created an alternative public sphere, a digitized "counterpublic"[2] that serves as a collective voice of people from diverse regions, cultures, and classes connected electronically. This global community linked by wires reinforces the Zapatistas' message for it is a symbolic and material representation of their egalitarian ideology.

In this chapter, I will discuss how access to media technology such as radio, television, and the Internet has transformed indigenous communities in both positive and negative ways. I will then explore the rise of the Zapatista movement, particularly how the Zapatistas have used Internet technology to mobilize their struggle, gain representation, and generate a collective voice composed of an intercontinental, decentralized, egalitarian coalition of human rights advocates. Finally, I will discuss the sociopolitical and rhetorical implications of civil disobedience in cyberspace, especially its potential to create counterpublics.

INDIGENOUS VOICES AND GRASSROOTS MEDIA

Over the past decade, media technology—whether it be radio, television, or computer—has increasingly been placed in the control of a small group of elite and powerful corporations dedicated to the goal of making a profit. Diversity and differences are underplayed as the same news and entertainment programming is broadcast around the world. Despite the growing homogenization of mainstream media, media technologies have been and continue to be used by oppressed minority and ethnic groups to preserve their culture, gain a public hearing, resist power, and provide alternative perspectives to those represented by corporate controlled networks. The influence of communication technology on indigenous communities is a topic that has attracted the attention of media scholars and anthropologists in recent years.[3] Indigenous groups whose members have been separated and culture diluted as a consequence of assimilation and government "development" initiatives, and whose voices are virtually absent in the mainstream media, have especially benefited from the ability of alternative networks to broadcast culturally distinct programming and transcend geographic space and borders. However, not every indigenous group seeks representation in the dominant public sphere, and the introduction of new technology to such groups can threaten the preservation of cultural traditions.

For indigenous groups who do seek political representation beyond their local community, the media provide crucial access to audiences. When denied access to having their voices heard, indigenous and other minority groups resort to civil disobedience and sometimes violence as a means of gaining a public hearing. In its January 1, 1994, uprising, for example, the Ejército Zapatista de la Liberación (EZLN, or Zapatista National Liberation Army) seized a government-run radio station in Las Margaritas. Although the radio station piracy played no role in the Zapatistas' revolt that day, it was used to broadcast messages from relatives and friends displaced by the ensuing clash with the Mexican military (Lawless 2000). In addition to seeking access to media establishments, whether by force or peacefully, groups also turn to establishing their own alternative networks free of influence from corporations and government.

Radio

Radio, one of the most accessible and inexpensive communication technologies, has played a significant role in sustaining indigenous culture as well as facilitating grassroots organizing. Within the jungles of southeast Mexico, internal EZLN communication between soldiers and leadership is made possible by using simple civil band or CB radio.[4] However, it is broadcast radio that enables a group to generate support from a community of listeners. Even radio stations limited to a short-range audience have potential to unite a community. Independent radio, according to Dorothy Kidd (2000), "is undergoing a worldwide revival, especially in some poorer and newly formed countries, and among populations such as women and indigenous peoples who have been left out of mainstream media" (86). The indigenous Maori in New Zealand, for example, broadcast programs on a Maori-run radio station to preserve their distinct culture and language (Browne 1996).

Radio stations representing indigenous and ethnic groups use short wave, Internet, or micro radio to program their own music and news, enabling them to maintain a sense of cultural identity and community, address their specific needs, and organize collective action. According to Lorna Roth (1993), phone-in, or talk-back radio, played a crucial role in the outcome of a land conflict between the Mohawk community and the governments of Quebec and Canada in 1990. Two small radio stations, one in the reservation of Kahnawake and the other in the territory of Kanehstake, provided these Mohawk communities information about the conflict as it unfolded, while telephone and fax lines helped generate national and international support. Because the range of Kahnawake's radio station reached beyond native territory in southern Quebec, nonnatives participated in the phone-in programs, thereby widening support for the land struggle beyond the Mohawk community. "Mohawk radio became a very powerful tool of communication," argues Roth, " because it offered associative and participatory links that enabled more thorough psychological identification between audiences and on-air hosts to take place than is probable with conventional radio services" (326). In particular, the oral medium of radio diffused perceived barriers arising from visual markers of race and ethnicity and allowed nonnatives to hear natives in their own voices. However, when the conflict ended, members of a nearby nonnative community, fueled by the public excitement generated during the Mohawk crisis, attempted to use the Kahnawake phone-in service to rally support for their own economic and political gain (Roth 326–27). Indeed, as the following discussion on television further demonstrates, while broadcast technology can be effective in building cohesion and organizing collective action within indigenous communities, indigenous cultures also become more vulnerable to appropriation by the dominant culture.

Television and Video

Television and interactive video provides an especially powerful mechanism for generating collective identity and action in its capacity to document the culture and beliefs of a group through a combination of visual and oral representation. Indigenous-run television networks that provide culturally relevant news and entertainment can be found in Australia, Brazil, Canada, and many other parts of the world.[5] In Australia, some aboriginal groups have reestablished cohesive communities by using interactive video, despite their dispersed population (Malcolm 1999, 481). However, it is important to recognize that the extent to which communication technologies like television are beneficial for indigenous communities is determined by whether an indigenous group has sovereign control over the content and accessibility of the technology.

For the Warlpiri in Australia, an aboriginal group whose cultural code determines who, what, where, how, and to whom information is communicated, the introduction of television in 1985 to their oral society was done with caution in order to maintain cultural integrity. As Eric Michaels (1994) explains, public communication for the Warlpiri "involves restricting access to performers and performances so that no one whom the social structure does not position in the correct kinship relationship can bear witness to any valuable speech or performance event" (30.1). Therefore, television threatened culturally prescribed rights to own, transmit, and receive information. Of course, with the use of satellite technology, the potential that restricted information such as rituals, songs, stories, and dances could be communicated to non-Warlpiri and that programs originating from outside the Warlpiri community (i.e., programs without regard for Warlpiri cultural codes) would become accessible and therefore dramatically alter their culture made the situation even more serious. In response to these challenges, the Warlpiri Media Association employs strategies such as "control of incoming television signals, control of self-representation through local video production in local languages, refusal to permit outsiders to film, and negotiation of coproductions that guarantee certain conditions aimed at cultural maintenance."[6]

The specific needs and conditions of a particular community determine the ethnographic implications of integrating television and other communication technologies into indigenous life. While maintaining cultural integrity has been the principal concern of the Warlpiri in integrating television technology into their community, other indigenous groups have strategically used television to gain political representation. Perhaps the most successful use of television by an indigenous group is the Inuit Broadcasting Corporation (IBC) established in 1982, supporting not only cultural preservation but also political representation. IBC programming has facilitated the creation of a socially cohesive Inuit cultural identity by featuring programs created by Inuit, presented in the Inuit language, Inuktitut, and that reflect Inuit values, such as appreciation for the land and consensus building (Madden 1992). The creation of Nunavut, a distinct Inuit political entity, in 1999 was in part a by-product of the reconstitution of Inuit identity and autonomy made possible by IBC broadcasting across vast and remote geographic distances in northern Canada (Madden 2000).

The Zapatistas have also taken advantage of television opportunities to publicize the conditions and needs of Mayan Indians. Although they do not run their own television network, it is not unusual to see the charismatic EZLN spokesman, Subcomandante Marcos, appear in television and print interviews, particularly in the United States and other countries outside Mexico where he is more sheltered from retaliation by the Mexican government. On the occasion of an interview or a public appearance, a Zapatista's identity is disguised by wearing a signature black ski mask, which offers a means of protection and is a striking visual symbol of the Zapatista's struggle. Subcomandante Marcos has been interviewed by journalists all over the world, including an appearance on an episode of *60 Minutes* in March 1994, just months after the NAFTA inauguration uprising.[7] The Zapatistas rely on journalists to gain access to television networks and they do so with caution to avoid revealing their location. Indeed, at this time, it is unlikely that we will see the establishment of a Zapatista television corporation since the EZLN has to shield itself from violent attacks by government and paramilitary forces[8]—a limitation that the EZLN has overcome by using the Internet. Of course, the influence of television as well as radio is inevitably limited by the availability of frequencies and channels. Internet communication, however, is not subject to the same constraints as these other technologies.

Internet

The potential of the Internet as a forum for community organizing and po-litical activism is magnified by the democratic nature of the technology with its ability to disseminate information to a global audience almost instanta-neously and to accommodate an unlimited number of servers and users. Rash (1997) argues that for grassroots organizations, the Internet is "an electronic life force that not only makes these groups function well but that may in fact make them possible" because of the efficiency of the technology (10). In-deed, the efficiency and speed of Internet communication is advantageous to social movement organizations who seek to keep one step ahead of the es-tablishments they oppose; for example, the protest amassed against the World Trade Organization in December 1999 in Seattle, Washington (which included a group of demonstrators wearing black ski masks signifying their support of the EZLN's stance against neoliberalism) and against the Interna-tional Monetary Fund in April 2000, was facilitated by interactions on the Web in not only planning the events, but also communicating up-to-the-minute written and video reports on the ensuing confrontation with police officers.

Despite the advantages of efficiency offered by electronic communication for oppositional groups, the price in terms of the potential for government surveillance and the sheer cost of access to the technology shatters any ide-alistic vision of democracy on the Internet. Placing data on the Web "allows much faster and more efficient invasion of privacy" (Grossman 1997, 167). The price in money, skills, and infrastructure is so high that a majority of the world's population will not experience any benefits from Internet technol-ogy in the foreseeable future (Warf and Grimes 1997). Moreover, the in-creasing influence of commercial interests on the Web undermines its po-tential as a participatory forum (Ford and Gil 2001, 206–7). Still, new technologies and the new possibilities for communication that come with them, have resulted in a shift of the political center, away from government and towards corporations, non-governmental organizations, and activist groups (Deibert 1998). Many social-movement organizations maintain Web pages, bulletin boards, and e-mail lists, providing viewpoints that counter that of the state. Greenpeace, People for the Ethical Treatment of Animals, School of Americas Watch, and Amnesty International are among the score of social movement organizations that maintain sites. And some indigenous groups are combining cable television and Internet technology. The Inuvik, a community in the Northwest Territory of Canada, began combining cable television with the Internet beginning in 1996.[9] Strategic use of information technology is beginning to play a critical role in preserving and revitalizing indigenous traditions, culture, and language (May 1998).

The Zapatista movement is arguably the first example of an indigenous movement that has successfully used the Internet to globalize its support. It has also taken advantage of radio and television to some extent, as noted above; however, the Internet has been undeniably central in launching and maintaining the Zapatistas' struggle as a globally significant phenomenon. The following section examines how the Zapatistas adopted the Internet as a vehicle for political action in a struggle that they claim has been ongoing for over 500 years.

ZAPATISTAS IN CYBERSPACE

The class symbolism appears incongruous: a movement on behalf of the rights of poor people living in a remote agricultural region of Mexico using the sophisticated technology of the Internet to promulgate support. Oliver Froehling comments: "The uprising offers the apparent contradiction of a high-tech medium brought to aid an insurrection of indigenous peasants who are hardly aware of its existence" (1997, 291). Moreover, the EZLN's presence in cyberspace can have the effect of drawing attention away from the harsh reality of the armed struggle fought on the ground. And, if we take into consideration the idolization of the movement's primary spokesperson, Subcomandante Marcos, as a postmodern Robin Hood and an international sex symbol, the Zapatista movement even appears glamorous.[10] However, despite the hype generated by the EZLN's media-savvy leadership, the Zapatistas' struggle ultimately concerns the serious matter of exploitation of indigenous people, lands, and resources.

On January 1, 1994, the day NAFTA went into effect, a ragtag army of peasants equipped with obsolete rifles, machetes, sticks, and stones protested the influx of cheap corn from the United States that would undermine the livelihood of corn farmers in southern Mexico by occupying five towns and over 500 ranches. At least 145 people died in the ensuing battle with state troops. The EZLN is a guerrilla army of indigenous peasants that has arisen in response to subjugation that has historical roots in the 1910–1919 army led by Emiliano Zapata.[11] The 1994 resort to use arms by the EZLN, an organization otherwise committed to promoting peace through nonviolent forms of civil disobedience, was a response to mounting adverse conditions. Peasants in Chiapas, comments Collier (1999), "have endured the same adversity that tropical frontiers pose for settlers from other areas—poor soils, unfamiliar and poisonous plants and animals, skin-burrowing insects, and parasitic diseases—and suffer opposition from ranchers who control the best land in the region" (37). Rather than embrace the country's diverse ethnic, cultural, and linguistic heritage, the Mexican government's policy has been to attempt to assimilate the indigenous population. Agrarian reform and the establishment of NAFTA only exacerbated the situation. Within the discourse of capitalism, with its emphasis on mass culture and the suppression of diversity, and with its commodification of human lives, indigenous peoples are relegated to the position of marginal Other, lacking an autonomous voice and serving the interests of the Mexican government and multinational corporations that benefit from their labor.[12] Zapatista communiqués posted on the EZLN Web site at www.ezln.org confirm that the long-standing issues of land tenure, indigenous rights, health care, education, and democratization are the focal points of their struggle.[13]

On the day of the January 1 uprising, the Internet was flooded with e-mail messages and communiqués from the EZLN, providing regular coverage of the battle as it was occurring, directly from the EZLN rather than secondhand journalists.[14] All EZLN communications were and continue to be sanctioned by the EZLN leadership, the Clandestine Revolutionary Indigenous Committee-General Command (CCRI-GC); however, they are usually written and signed by Subcomandante Marcos (Ross 1995, 13). The EZLN delivered its own firsthand reports to the press through an onslaught of postings and press releases that required the assistance of an organized network of volunteers living in Mexico and the United States. As Cleaver notes: "Although there is a myth that Subcomandante Marcos sits in the jungle uploading EZLN communiqués from his laptop, the reality is that the EZLN and its communities have had a mediated relationship to the Internet" (1998, 628). With the help of able volunteers, the Internet provided a means to deliver uncensored, eyewitness testimony to a global audience while protecting the whereabouts of the EZLN. All EZLN communications list the return address as "the mountains of southeast Mexico." The protection afforded by the technology, albeit with the invaluable help of volunteers, is significant because it allowed the EZLN to represent themselves in their own voice, without the inevitable distortion of information by the Mexican government and military. It enabled them to enact their goal of achieving autonomy, at least in cyberspace.

CYBER-AGITATION

The presence and exchange of pro-Zapatista information on the Internet served as an extension of the usual means of agitation via street demonstrations, rallies, and petitioning. The EZLN has been in existence since 1983, and therefore they were able to build upon an already established network of solidarity supporters. Zapatista communications, note Ford and Gil (2001), "circulated via Internet travels circuitously from peer to peer, collective and individual, with no predetermined patterns of access, editorial control, or outcome" (221). However, the early stages of information circulation were organized such that communiqués would travel via courier and appear in print within twelve hours of their arrival at various newspaper outlets in Mexico, and they were translated for Internet distribution by the next morning (Collier 1999, 13). The system established by the EZLN to disseminate information online began with a person living in Chiapas who would telephone or fax a message to someone outside the region. The person contacted would then put the message in Spanish initially on preexisting lists, then on a specifically formed Chiapas list.[15] Next, another person would translate the message to English, and then send it to subscribers of the list. Volunteers living near the United States-Mexico border and associated with the National Commission for Democracy in Mexico in El Paso, Texas, bought newspapers in Mexico and returned to the United States to translate and transmit them. The listserv and the official Web page were and continue to be used in conjunction with others, hosted mostly by students, professors, and activists, as a forum to discuss peace prospects, raise awareness, launch letter or e-mail writing campaigns, and promote local rallies for the Zapatistas. Postings have also been picked up on UseNet newsgroups whose audiences identify with the Zapatistas' egalitarian ideology, including environmental, humanitarian, and feminist groups.[16] A network of organizations "stands ready to mobilize e-mail and letter writing protest at any hint of military action against the Zapatistas," including the International Service for Peace (SIPAZ) and the Center for Economic and Political Research on Community Action (CIEPAC) (Collier 1999, 171).

An "official" EZLN Web page at www.ezln.org was constructed to provide a central location for updates on the conditions in Chiapas and the status of the EZLN attempts at negotiation with the government, with Marcos serving as the primary spokesperson.[17] The top of the page contains prophetic statements from Marcos, known for his dramatic, poetic, and ironic style, as well as a quote from William Shakespeare's Sonnet XXIII. Also appearing on the page are slogans such as "*¡Ya Basta!*" ("Enough is enough!") and "*¡Alto a la persecución!*" ("Stop the persecution!"). Visitors can choose to explore the site in Spanish, French, or English. The English links include an overview of the struggle in the Chiapas written by Marcos, a map of Mexico, and an essay sponsored by Food First—an American social-movement organization, indicating the significance and presence of outside support. Other important links include EZLN chronologies and declarations that provide examples of EZLN written rhetoric.

The rhetoric of the EZLN constructs the Zapatista struggle as an international effort of resistance against a history of subjugation. For example, the first of five "Declarations of the Lacandón Jungle," written by Marcos, contains explicit references to Mayan culture and casts the Zapatistas as participants in a chain of "five hundred years of struggle" against subordination and exploitation from the Spanish conquest to the current PRI regime. The document explicitly declares war on the Mexican Army, called for the repudiation of former President Salinas, and demanded the establishment of a transitional government. Marcos urges "Mexican brothers and sisters" and the "millions" of "dispossessed . . . workers, campesinos, students, honest professionals, Chicanos, and progressives of other countries" to unite in this effort. Such documents provide evidence of the rich symbolism used by the Zapatistas to represent their specific indigenous identity and, simultaneously, their attempt to identify with broader human rights and class struggles.

DIGITIZING AND GLOBALIZING ZAPATISTA IDENTITY

The visual layout of the page also provides insight on the EZLN's attempt to locate Zapatista identity in a historical narrative of oppression and create a broad network of support. Prominently displayed as wallpaper on the EZLN Web site is a tiled image of Emiliano Zapata. This visual image of Zapata is reinforced by text posted on the site. A February 1994 communiqué by Subcomandante Marcos states:

> For years and years we harvested the death of our people. . . . But the truth that traveled on the paths of the word of the oldest of the old also came hope for our history. And in their word appeared the image of one like us: Emiliano Zapata. And in it we saw the place toward which our feet should walk in order to be true.[18]

Similar prophetic language appears in an essay posted on the page entitled "Mexico 1998: Above and Below, Masks and Silence," also written by Marcos:

> While the supreme government gears up for war and tries desperately to bring together the winds from above, beastly growls, and spells in order to push the heavy sails of the ship of death, these indigenous Mexicans, who have added the name of Emiliano Zapata to their history, prepare in silence the justice and the dignity which will arrive in spite of their death (or perhaps because of it). (20)

Mythification, according to Arthur Smith, is a movement strategy that provides a group with a feeling of particularity by employing historical or religious symbolism as an instrument of change. By linking the current struggle to those of the past, the Zapatista movement presents itself as sanctioned and validated by history. In this sense, the Zapatistas' construction of identity is actually a "reconstruction." As Stuart Hall (1989) notes: "Cultural identities come from somewhere, have histories. But, like everything, which is historical, they undergo constant transformation. Far from being eternally fixed in some essentialised past, they are subject to the continuous 'play' of history, culture and power . . . identities are the names we give to the different ways we are positioned by, and position ourselves within, the narratives of the past" (70).

In the above quotation Marcos says "*these*" rather than "*we* indigenous Mexicans" for Marcos is *mestizo* (a person of mixed Spanish and Indian blood), a middle-class intellectual from Mexico City who is one of the few nonindigenous leaders who speak on behalf of the indigenous members of the EZLN. Even though the term "Zapatista" is constructed to draw attention to the rights and current needs of indigenous Mayans (all the while embedded in an explicit historical narrative), Zapatista identity is ultimately fragmented to allow for a plurality of supporters who can call themselves "Zapatista." By fragmentation, I am referring to the ways in which the term "Zapatista" is used as an inclusive label that represents a variety of people, classes, and cultures. The Internet plays a primary role in creating this fragmentation and, likewise, the plurality of voices represented by the term. The following paragraphs explore the construction of Zapatista identity as a collective subject whose meaning is symbolized through visual metaphors and enacted through a decentralized organizational structure.

Global interactive communication on the Internet enables the Zapatistas to conquer geographic space, as the Inuit have using cable television. However, whereas the Inuit have concentrated on creating social cohesion among the Inuit, the Zapatistas have emphasized solidarity among people of all races, ethnicities, classes, and genders, forging connections in both industrialized and developing countries. And, whereas the Inuit have used cable technology to create a centralized political body to represent their movement by forming Nunavut, the Zapatistas have used the Internet to develop a decentralized political body that encourages global, collaborative participation. One need not be a poor, indigenous, and agricultural person to call oneself "Zapatista." In exploring the range of Zapatista Web sites, in addition to the official EZLN page, this immediately becomes evident.[19] Anyone who identifies with the goal of eliminating the class injustices attributed to neoliberalism, or capitalism more generally, and who embraces a wide variety of alternatives for organizing social life, including cyberspace and collaborative models of organizations, is invited, or more specifically interpellated, to identify themselves as Zapatista. As George Collier explains (1999), the Zapatista revolt is not merely a Mayan Indian struggle, but a peasant one. Their revolution is national, not ethnic, and, internationally, the Zapatistas aim to end social injustice caused by neoliberal institutions. The highly visual rhetoric of the EZLN provides a material representation of their inclusive ideology through the combined symbolism of the black ski mask and the Internet itself as an intricately connected network of wires.

The black ski mask is an image that appears repeatedly among the score of Zapatista linked Web sites. One particularly provocative Web site image is featured on the popular Zapatistas in Cyberspace directory page and demonstrates the use of the masked and wired individual as symbolic of the EZLN's inclusive egalitarian ideology. The foreground of the picture features a person wearing a black ski mask with what appears to be two wires attached to the figure's forehead, linked to a small computer located near the mouth. On the left is a satellite and in the background appears a grid system, symbolizing connection. In the background on the right is a second figure, apparently holding up a torch that signifies truth and strength. The ethnicity and gender of both figures is somewhat ambiguous. The black ski mask, the signature symbol identifying one as Zapatista, has the effect of eliminating recognizable differences in physical appearance and, in turn, symbolizing unity despite difference. Just as the black ski mask is an identifiable sign of this movement on behalf of an indigenous agricultural people, the computer is a sign of a highly advanced, technologized culture—and typically that of the middle and upper class, not the culture of rural peasants. The ambiguity of the meaning of the masked image reinforces the Zapatistas' message by serving as a visual embodiment of their broad-based egalitarian ideology. Zapatista identity (that is, of those living in Chiapas) is primarily constituted along class, ethnic, and agricultural lines; however, the image of the black mask signifies an open, indeterminate, and pluralistic Zapatista identity with the wires emanating from the figure serving as a powerful visual metaphor of the interconnection between and among the pro-Zapatista collective.

The masked commander Marcos's *mestizo* ethnicity affirms this fluidity of Zapatista identity. While "the Sup," as he is affectionately called, gained immediate notoriety as well as hero status in the eyes of many Mexicans, including peasants and middle-class people throughout the country, by projecting the image of a Robin Hood defending the rights of the downtrodden against an unjust and repressive government. As a disguise, the black ski mask not only shields Marcos and other Zapatistas from being identified by the government or military, but it also masks differences among Zapatistas and symbolizes the antiauthoritarian structure of the movement. In his writings, he also uses the mask as a metaphor for how the neoliberal establishment ignores and disguises the human suffering it has created; he thus submits a call to "break silences and pull off masks." He primarily considers the signature black ski masks as symbolic challenge against authoritative rule:

> The main reason is that we have to be careful that nobody tries to be the main leader. The masks are meant to prevent this from happening. It is about being

anonymous, not because we fear for ourselves, but rather to avoid being corrupted. Nobody can then appear all the time and demand attention. Our leadership is a collective leadership and we must respect that. Even though you are listening to me now, elsewhere there are others who are masked and who are also talking. So, the masked person here today is called "Marcos" and tomorrow might be "Pedro" in Las Margaritas, or "Josue" in Ocosingo, or "Alfredo" in Altamarino, or whatever he is called. So the one who speaks is a more collective heart, not a single leader, or *cuadillo*. That is what I want you to understand, not a caudillo in the old style and image. The only image that you will have is that those who have made this rebellion wear ski masks. And the time will come when the people will realize that it is enough to have dignity and put on a mask and say that they too can do this. (Harvey 1998, 7)

The black ski masks are rich in meaning. While providing safety through anonymity and communicating strength through their threatening appearance, they also symbolize the collaborative and pluralistic structure of the movement. Note that one does not hide by wearing the mask, rather by taking it off. Furthermore, the mask symbolizes transformation. Wearing the ski mask legitimizes Marcos as a movement spokesperson for it symbolizes his own transformation from middle-class intellectual to crusader for indigenous rights. He strips away his old identity so that he may be considered equal with others who wear ski masks. By wearing the mask, movement supporters take on the collective identity, which is, in turn, enacted through the movement's decentralized organizational structure.

There is little information about the actual hierarchy within the EZLN. Marcos has all the characteristics we might expect of a charismatic movement spokesperson; however, as the title "Subcomandante" indicates, he is not the leader of the EZLN. The leadership is the CCRI-GC, a democratic committee of "eighteen representatives of four Mayan-language ethnic groups" (Collier 1999, 5). It is clear, however, that the EZLN is both a military and political body.

As a political body, the EZLN has attempted to present itself as part of an intercontinental network of resistance not only against neoliberalism, but also against all authoritative hierarchical structures insofar as they silence minority voices. As far as political decision making and organizing is concerned, the EZLN claims to have no central command or formal hierarchy. Their resistance to authoritative hierarchical structures is best demonstrated by the Intercontinental *Encuentro* (Encounter) for Humanity and Against Neo-Liberalism first held in July of 1996 and organized solely through Internet exchanges. Some 3,000 activists from five continents and forty-two countries traveled to the remote jungle of southeast Mexico to take part in the *encuentro* arranged and hosted by the EZLN (Froehling 1997, 303). This meeting resulted in the creation of a global network of activists that were not only connected electronically but in person. A second *encuentro* took place in Spain in 1997 with 4,000 people in attendance (Cleaver 1998, 630). The *encuentros* gatherings are significant because they indicate that it is possible for a pluralistic community formed in cyberspace to transfer itself successfully in the "real world." The Zapatista example of combined cyber and real world activism challenges Kolko, Nakamura, and Rodman's (2000) claim that "While the mediated nature of cyberspace renders invisible many (and in some instances, all) of the visual and aural cues that serve to mark people's identities IRL [in real life], that invisibility doesn't carry back over into 'the real world' in ways that allow people to log in and simply shrug off a lifetime of experiencing the world from specific identity-related perspectives" (4). The radically democratic structure of the *encuentro* parallels that of the Zapatista cyber community. It is perhaps a unique example of the creation and maintenance of at least the fiction of unity both online and off, enabling the generation of collective action, despite class, race, ethnic, and gender differences.[20]

The *encuentro's* structure is decentralized in its attempt to embody the Zapatista's egalitarian ideology (Cleaver 1998, 630). Both *encuentros* were planned in advance through exchanges on the World Wide Web. The proposal for the encuentros were distributed by e-mail and posted on Web sites. News of the *encuentros*, for example, was linked by a German Web site to a range of other struggles including the European March Against Unemployment, the strikes of the Liverpool dockers, and the campaign of undocumented Africans of St. Ambroise to obtain official papers from French authorities (Shultz 1995, 14). However, the extent of planning for the *encuentros* was limited. There were no scheduled speakers or panels; the stated purpose was for all to speak freely and listen equally. There was no prearranged agenda; rather those who attended it created as part of a bottom-up hierarchy. Volunteer groups were formed early on to facilitate the gathering. The participants coordinated food, shelter, and labor themselves. Participants returned to their own countries and home computers with the intent of implementing whatever plans were decided upon at the *encuentro* (Ruggerio and Duncan). For example, participants from New York City returned from the second *encuentro* and organized a teach-in entitled "Freeing the Media" in 1997. Subcomandante Marcos himself delivered a presentation in the form of a ten-minute video message where he discussed the importance of finding "open spaces within the mass media monopolies (to acknowledge news of social movements)" and the need to develop independent media outlets. Indeed, spatial metaphors provide a useful means of describing the potential of the Internet to provide a forum for disenfranchised voices.

A ZAPATISTA COUNTERPUBLIC

It is clear from my analysis thus far that the Zapatistas have been successful in harnessing the potential of the Internet to create a democratic forum in opposition to that of the government of Mexico. Through Web sites, e-mail exchanges, and other pluralistic discursive practices such as *encuentros* the Zapatistas, in effect, constitute an autonomous, separate, and distinct "counterpublic sphere." Nancy Fraser (1992) defines counterpublics as spheres of influence that expand the parameters of public discussion and function as "parallel discursive arenas where members of subordinated social groups invent and circulate counterdiscourse to formulate oppositional interpretations of their identities, interests and needs" (123). While the "parallel discursive arena" formulated by the Zapatistas is not limited to cyberspace, its presence in cyberspace made it possible for them to make known their self-ascribed identity, beliefs, and democratic organizational practices and invite international discussion with sympathetic others. Indeed, in an analysis of the potential for cyberspace to generate counterpublics, Palzcewski (2001) notes, "Counterpublics, as temporal, discursive, and even physical spaces, are not merely defined *by* identity but aid in the definition *of* identity."[21]

The existence of counterpublics, argues Fraser, expands the terrain of arguments available. She writes: "[I]nsofar as these counterpublics emerge in response to exclusions within dominant publics, they help expand discursive space. In principle, assumptions that were previously exempt from contestation will now have to be publicly argued out" (1992, 124). The Zapatista movement is a response to exclusion, and their use of the Internet has carved out a space to question the motives of neoliberal policies, deliberate, and even experiment with alternative political structures. As Cleaver points out, the networking of the Zapatistas "can already be seen as generative moments in the coalescence of a growing number of tightly knit global circuits of cyberspace communication and organization that threaten traditional top-down monopolies of such activity" (1998, 632). For example, the Mexican government suffered public embarrassment recently when a Chase Manhattan Bank memorandum encouraging the government to extinguish the Zapatistas was circulated on the Web. The dissemination of the document was quickly followed by fax campaigns and public demonstrations against the Mexican government's "toady to international capital" (Froehling 1997, 302).

Of course, the Mexican government has engaged its own effort in cyberspace to counter the Zapatistas' popular influence. For example, in 2000, the final year of the PRI's seventy-year political dominance, text posted on the Mexican government's Web page concealed its motivation to intimidate the Zapatistas.[22] The page claimed that the clash between paramilitary forces and local people in Chiapas existed only to enforce the rule of law, maintain order, and punish criminals, particularly those involved in drug trafficking. However, Vicente Fox, the new president elected under the National Action Party (PAN) in July 2000, has acknowledged the need to address the demands of Mexico's indigenous population and remove the military bases in Chiapas.[23]

THE INTERNET AND INDIGENOUS EMPOWERMENT

The Internet lends itself easily to creating counterpublics because of the potential it offers to carve out one's own territory, but cyber territories are not completely removed from the dominant public sphere. As Froehling comments: "The potentials of the Net are realized in articulation *with* other spaces and flows—the flow of money, goods, and bodies, for example—rather than in a struggle that constructs itself solely through some cyberreality" (emphasis added, 1997, 304). The Zapatistas are participants in a cyber campaign that can never replace the struggle that is occurring in Chiapas, but rather it serves to provide a forum and magnify it to the rest of the world as well as the Mexican government and neoliberal institutions they oppose.

The oppositional discourse of the Zapatistas on the Internet has influenced the negotiation process in the "real world"; that is, between the EZLN and the Mexican government—an example of the Internet's potential to "expedite access to the state" and "redefine relations to the state" (Palzcewski 2001, 24). After decades of simply ignoring the indigenous population in southern Mexico, the government began to participate, reluctantly, in negotiations with the EZLN and did so with the goal of stalling time to manufacture a military or paramilitary solution (Veltmeyer 2000). But, the fact that the Mexican government chose to negotiate with the EZLN at all, rather than rely solely on military means to squelch the movement, is in itself notable. Following the January 1994 uprising, public opinion in Mexico was clearly sympathetic to the EZLN's cause. Public demonstrations in Mexico City and other cities and an influx of human rights delegations from other countries led to the passage of the "Law for Dialogue, Reconciliation, and a Dignified Peace" in the Mexican Congress in March 1994 (Benjamin 1995, 4). Since then, the Zapatistas have continued to contribute to the political landscape in Mexico, receiving support from three million balloters in favor of passing the San Andres Accords on Indigenous Rights and Culture, a "'social pact' recognizing indigenous *pueblos* as having collective rights within a framework of autonomy" (Collier 1999, 162).

Ultimately, the Zapatistas presence in cyberspace is both strategic and symbolic. Web pages and e-mail exchanges provide firsthand accounts of their plight, disseminate it widely, and facilitate grassroots organization and action, while maintaining the EZLN's safety. Information technology has thus enabled them to successfully overcome the obstacles typically encountered by indigenous and disenfranchised groups. In turn, they have also created an alternative public sphere, a digitized counter sphere connected electronically as well as in person—both composed of a democratically formed collective of people from diverse regions, cultures, and classes.

The social implications of the Zapatistas' global effort, however, remain to be seen. The Inuit have been successful in using television to nurture their culture from within, resulting in the formation of Nunavut (Madden 1992, 2000). The Zapatistas, however, have used the Internet to venture outside Chiapas and Mayan culture, inviting the creation of a collective identity and international struggle that disregards space and borders. As an EZLN poster proclaims both in Spanish and English, "¡Nuestra Lucha Estyuya! Our struggle is your struggle!" Will the Zapatistas' emphasis on collective identity and action on a global scale, realized through Internet communication, undermine efforts to address the specific experiences of Mayan Indians living in Chiapas? In other words, will it lead to new forms of exclusion? Or will it build resourceful and influential global coalitions while preserving and celebrating cultural differences? More than likely, the answer is "yes" to all of these questions. However, as long as indigenous and disenfranchised groups have the ability to gain a forum for discussing their own experiences, needs, and culture, whether it is through access to information or media technologies, these matters of inclusion and exclusion that are inevitably addressed by all indigenous movements will hopefully achieve a state of healthy balance.

NOTES

1. The most comprehensive and regularly updated directory of Zapatista Web sites is Zapatistas in Cyberspace: A Guide for Analysis and Resources, hosted by the University of Texas and created by Harry Cleaver. See www.eco.utexas.edu/faculty/Cleaver/zapsincyber.html. Cleaver is the author of "The Zapatista Effect: The Internet and the Rise of an Alternative Political Fabric," *Journal of International Affairs* 5, no. 2 (Spring 1998): 621–40.

2. Rita Felksi explores the concept of "counterpublic spheres" in *Beyond Feminist Aesthetics* (Cambridge, Mass.: Harvard University Press, 1989) in a discussion about "critical oppositional forces" within society (166). Nancy Fraser elaborates on the notion of counterpublics in "Rethinking the Public Sphere," in *Habermas and the Public Sphere*, ed. Craig Calhoun (Cambridge, Mass.: MIT Press, 1992).

3. See Donald R. Browne, *Electronic Media and Indigenous Peoples: A Voice of Our Own?* (Ames: Iowa State University Press, 1996); Eric Michaels, *Bad Aboriginal Art: Tradition, Media, and Technological Horizons* (Minneapolis: University of Minnesota Press, 1994); and, James H. May, "Information Technology for Indigenous Peoples: The North American Experience," in *Digital Democracy: Policy and Politics in the Wired World*, ed. Cynthia J. Alexander and Leslie A. Pal (New York: Oxford University Press, 1998).

4. "Subcomandante Marcos; Leader, Spokesman of the Zapatista National Liberation Army of Mexico Captures the Heart of Impoverished Indians and the Attention of the Government," *60 Minutes*, Burrelle's Information Services, CBS News Transcripts, online at Lexis/Nexis, 13 March 1994.

5. See *Channels of Resistance: Global Television and Local Empowerment*, ed. Tony Dowmunt (London: BFI Publishing, 1993).

6. Marcia Langton, introduction, *Bad Aboriginal Art: Tradition, Media, and Technological Horizons* by Eric Michaels (Minneapolis: University of Minnesota Press, 1994), xxxiv and xxxv.

7. "Subcomandante Marcos; Leader, Spokesman of the Zapatista National Liberation Army of Mexico Captures the Heart of Impoverished Indians and the Attention of the Government," *60 Minutes*, Burrelle's Information Services, CBS News Transcripts (Online: Lexis/Nexis, 13 March 1994). The *60 Minutes* interview, conducted by Bill Bradley, aired again on August 21, 1994 and December 31, 1995 (online at Lexis/Nexis).

8. For a discussion on the conflict between the EZLN and the Mexican government from a pro-Zapatista perspective, see George A. Collier with Elizabeth Lowery Quaratiello, *Basta! Land and the Zapatista Rebellion in Chiapas*, rev. ed. (Oakland, Calif.: Food First Books, 1999) and John Ross, *The War against Oblivion: The Zapatista Chronicles 1994–2000* (Monroe, Maine: Common Courage, 2000). For an anti-Zapatista account sponsored by Rand Arroyo Center's Strategy and Doctrine Program of the United States Army, see *The Zapatista "Social Netwar" in Mexico* (Santa Monica, Calif.: RAND, 1998), online at www.rand.org/publications/MR 994.pdf/.

9. David G. Malcolm, rev. of *Digital Democracy: Policy and Politics in the Wired World*, ed. Cynthia G. Malcolm and Leslie A. Pal (New York: Oxford University Press, 1998).

10. Marcos's poems, political harangues, and short stories have appeared in newspapers, television news, and on the Internet. He is also the author of a controversial children's book, *The Story of Colors*, which was granted a National Endowment for the Arts award then retracted by the organization when they realized he was a leader of a rebel group. Marcos has also been known to pose for popular magazines such as *Mademoiselle* and *Vanity Fair*. Marcos dolls are in high demand in Mexico City. His physical appearance adds to his aura. A black ski mask is a permanent part of his uniform as it is for other EZLN members. Canadian filmmaker Nettie Wild explores his popularity and influence in her documentary about *A Place Called Chiapas*. In a *New York Times* review of the documentary, Marcos is described as "a shrewd manipulator of the media. When he calls for a convocation of journalists and observers, an international throng shows up for a gathering the filmmaker calls a 'post-glasnost revolutionary Woodstock'" (Holden 1998).

11. In this earlier movement for peasant autonomy, villages became centers of self-government not unlike the current organizing strategies of the Zapatistas. Zapata's army joined forces with Pancho Villa and rode victoriously into Mexico City in 1914. In 1919, the government assassinated Zapata. The government's ruling party has been in place ever since (calling itself the Institutional Revolutionary Party or PRI as of 1930) until the election of Vicente Fox in 2000. Fox was elected under a platform that promises to end the conflict in the Chiapas.

12. The emergence and development of the Zapatista movement, including its link to broad-based human rights efforts, can be viewed as an example of what Chantal Mouffe (1988) refers to as a "new democratic struggle" (89). New democratic struggles are resistances to subordination, which have arisen out of an opposition to capitalist rationale. The increasing commodification, bureaucratization, and massification of everyday life are seen by Mouffe as generating counterhegemonic struggles to resist the impersonal power of the market and the state (98–99).

13. The rise of the Zapatista movement as it relates to long and complex history of peasant subordination has been thoroughly explored by previous scholars. See Guillermo Bonfil, *Mexico Profundo: Reclaiming a Civilization* (Austin: University of Texas Press, 1996), James D. Cockroft, *Mexico's Hope: An Encounter with Politics and History* (New York: Monthly Review Press, 1998), Neil Harvey, *The Chiapas Rebellion: The Struggle for Land and Democracy* (Durham, N.C.: Duke University Press, 1998), June Nash, "The Reassertion of Indigenous Identity: Mayan Responses to State Intervention in the Chiapas," *Latin American Research Review* 30, no. 3 (1995): 7–41, and Donald E. Shultz and Edward Williams, *Mexico Faces the Twenty-first Century* (Westport, Conn.: Greenwood Press, 1995).

14. For a bound collection and chronology of EZLN communiqués and letters posted on the Web, see *Shadows of Tender Fury: The Letters and Communiqués of Subcomandante Marcos and the Zapatista Army of National Liberation*, trans. Frank Bardacke, Leslie López, and the Watsonville, California Human Rights Committee (New York: Monthly Review Press, 1995).

15. The lists that were already in place included those used as part of the effort to block the passage of NAFTA and raise awareness about the conditions of indigenous people in Latin America.

16. For a more detailed description of the role of the Internet in the EZLN's campaign, see Cleaver, Froehling, and Glusker.

17. The "About this Page" link to the page reveals that site is in fact not officially registered by EZLN; rather it was created by a volunteer with the permission of the EZLN. Indeed, as noted earlier, the necessity of shielding the EZLN from government retaliation is a matter of survival for this rebel organization. The anonymity possible with Internet communication certainly offers an advantage to all protest groups, especially those targeted as enemies by their own governments.

18. *Shadows of Tender Fury*, 137–38.

19. See Cleaver, *Zapatistas in Cyberspace: A Guide to Analysis and Resources.*

20. A unique aspect of the Zapatista movement's structure is its strategic inclusion of women. "During the 1910 revolution," according to Florencia E. Mallon, "the call for municipal autonomy that fired popular imagination contained the twin promises of a return to communal democracy and to familial solidarity (which often meant that all men would have authority over "their" women)" (1994, 99). But, the Zapatista movement that emerged out of Chiapas in the 1980s and 1990s is clearly aligned with the movement for women's rights. One example of the representation of women is found in the Clandestine Revolutionary Indigenous Committee's "Revolutionary Laws," which specify the equal treatment and equal access to health care, education, and employment, among other things. These laws were created after months of discussion with hundreds of women in dozens of communities and adopted in March 1993, ten months before the official EZLN uprising. Zapatista women demonstrate, serve in leadership positions, bear arms, fight, and wear ski masks along with men in the EZLN. Probably, the most known woman leader of the EZLN is Comandante Ramona. Donning a mask just like Marcos, she has often served as a representative of the EZLN in negotiations with the government. The inclusion and contributions of women further demonstrate the pluralistic tone of the Zapatista movement in its attempt to form coalitions with people of all classes and ethnicities. For further discussion, see Francie R. Chasen-Lopez, "From Casa to Calle: Latin American Women

Transforming Patriarchal Spaces," *Journal of Women's History* 9, no. 1 (Spring 1997): 174–91.

21. Catherine H. Palzcewski, "Cybermovements, New Social Movments, and Counterpublics," in *Counterpublics and the State*, ed. Daniel Brouwer and Robert Asen (New York: SUNY Press, 2001).

22. Online at www.presidencia.gob.mx/welcome/chiapas. Access to this page is no longer available.   •

23. A revised official government Web page reflects this shift in policy, although it remains to be seen whether the government follows through on its promises. See http://www.presidencia.gob.mx/?EXACTO=Chiapas&P=48&SubTupo=Exacto.

BIBLIOGRAPHY

Benjamin, M. 1995. "On the Road with the Zapatistas: Mexican Crackdown in Chiapas." *The Progressive* 59, no. 5 (May): 28.

Bonfil, Guillermo. 1996. *Mexico Profundo: Reclaiming a Civilization*. Austin: University of Texas Press.

Browne, Donald R. 1996. *Electronic Media and Indigenous Peoples: A Voice of Our Own?* Ames: Iowa State University Press.

Channels of Resistance: Global Television and Local Empowerment. 1993. Ed. Tony Dowmunt. London: BFI Publishing.

Chasen-Lopez, Francie R. 1997. "From Casa to Calle: Latin American Women Transforming Patriarchal Spaces." *Journal of Women's History* 9, no. 1 (Spring): 174–91.

Cleaver, Harry M., Jr. 1998. "The Zapatista Effect: The Internet and the Rise of an Alternative Political Fabric." *Journal of International Affairs* 5, no. 2 (Spring): 621–40.

———. Zaptistas in Cyberspace: A Guide for Analysis and Resources. Online at www.eco.utexas.edu/faculty/Cleaver/zapsincyber.html.

Cockcroft, James D. 1998. *Mexico's Hope: An Encounter with Politics and History*. New York: Monthly Review Press.

Collier, George, with Elizabeth Lowery Quaratiello. 1999. *Basta! Land and the Zapatista Rebellion in Chiapas*. Rev. ed. Oakland, Calif.: Food First Books.

Deibert, Ronald J. 1998. "Altered Worlds: Social Forces in the Hypermedia Environment." Pp. 23–45 in *Digital Democracy: Policy and Politics in the Wired World*, ed. Cynthia J. Alexander and Leslie A. Paul. New York: Oxford University Press.

Ejército Zapatista de la Liberación. Online at www.ezln.org.

Felski, Rita. 1989. *Beyond Feminist Aesthetics*. Cambridge, Mass.: Harvard University Press.

Ford, Tamara Villarreal, and Genève Gil. 2001. "Radical Internet Use." Pp. 201–34 in *Radical Media: Rebellious Communication and Social Movements*, ed. John D. H. Downing. Thousand Oaks, Calif.: Sage Publications.

Fraser, Nancy. 1992. "Rethinking the Public Sphere." Pp. 109–42 in *Habermas and the Public Sphere*, ed. Craig Calhoun. Cambridge, Mass.: MIT Press.

Froehling, Oliver. 1997. "The Cyberspace 'War of Ink and Internet' in Chiapas, Mexico." *Geographical Review* 87, no. 2 (April): 291–307.

Glusker, Susannah. 1998. "Women Networking for Peace and Survival in Chiapas: Militants, Celebrities, Academics, Survivors and the Stiletto Heel Brigade." *Sex Roles* 39, nos. 7/8 (October): 539–57.

Grossman, Wendy M. 1997. *net.wars*. New York: New York University Press.

Hall, Stuart. 1989. "Cultural identity and Cinematic Representation." *Framework* 36: 68–81.

Harvey, Neil. 1998. *The Chiapas Rebellion: The Struggle for Land and Democracy*. Durham, N.C.: Duke University Press.

Holden, Stephen. 1998. "Examining Mexico's Zapatista Uprising." *New York Times*, 4 November.

Kidd, Dorothy. 2000. "Grassroots Radio." *Whole Earth* 100 (Spring): 86.

Kolko, Beth E., Lisa Nakamura, and Gilbert B. Rodman. 2000. "Race in Cyberspace: An Introduction." Pp. 1–13 in *Race in Cyberspace,* ed. Beth E. Kolko, Lisa Nakamura, and Gilbert B. Rodman. New York: Routledge.

Langton, Marcia. 1994. Introduction to *Bad Aboriginal Art: Tradition, Media, and Technological Horizons*, by Eric Michaels. Minneapolis: University of Minnesota Press, xxvi–xxxv.

Lawless, Robert. 2000. Rev. of *Social Uses and Radio Practices: The Use of Participatory Radio*, by Lucila Vargas. *Journal of Third World Studies* 17, no. 1 (Spring): 274–76.

Madden, Kate. 2000. "Canadian Inuit: Reconstituting Culture, Reclaiming Autonomy." Div. on Voices of Diversity. Eastern Communication Association Convention. Pittsburgh, Pa. April.

———. 1992. "The Inuit Broadcasting Corporation Experience." Pp. 130–49 in *Mass Media Effects across Cultures,* ed. Felipe Korenny and Stella Ting-Toomey. Newbury Park, Calif.: Sage Publications.

Malcolm, David G. 1999. Rev. of *Digital Democracy: Policy and Politics in the Wired World*, ed. Cynthia J. Alexander and Leslie A. Paul. New York: Oxford University Press, 1998. *Peace Review* 11, no. 3 (September): 479–81.

Mallon, Florencia E. 1994. "Reflections on the Ruins: Everyday Forms of State Formation in Nineteenth-Century Mexico." Pp. 69–106 in *Everyday Forms of State Formation: Revolution and the Negotiation of Rule in Modern Mexico*, ed. Gilbert M. Joseph and Daniel Nugent. Durham, N.C.: Duke University Press.

Marcos, Subcomandante. 1997. Statement to the freeing the media teach-in. January 31–February 1. Online at http://artcon.rutgers.edu/papertiger/freemedia/marcos.html.

———. 1999. "Mexico 1998: Above and Below, Masks and Silences." *Ejercito Zapatista de Liberacion Nacional*. Trans. Irlandesa. Trans. Rev. Joshua Paulson. 19 October. Online at www.ezln.org/fzln980700b-eng.html.

May, James H. 1998. "Information Technology for Indigenous Peoples: The North American Experience." Pp. 220–37 in *Digital Democracy: Policy and Politics in the Wired World*, ed. Cynthia J. Alexander and Leslie A. Paul. New York: Oxford University Press.

México. 2000. Official Government Page. Online at www.presidencia.gob.mx/welcome/chiapas.

México. 2001. Official Government Page. Online at www.presidencia.gob.mx/ ?EXACTO=Chiapas&P=48&SubTupo=Exacto.

Michaels, Eric. 1994. *Bad Aboriginal Art: Tradition, Media, and Technological Horizons.* Minneapolis: University of Minnesota Press.

Mouffe, Chantal. 1988. "Hegemony and New Political Subjects: Toward a New Concept of Democracy." Pp. 89–101 in *Marxism and the Interpretation of Culture*, ed. Cary Nelson and Lawrence Grossberg. Urbana: University of Illinois Press.

Nash, June. 1995. "The Reassertion of Indigenous Identity: Mayan Responses to State Intervention in Chiapas." *Latin American Research Review* 303: 7–41.

Palzcewski, Catherine H. Forthcoming. "Cybermovements, New Social Movements, and Counterpublics." In *Counterpublics and the State*, ed. Daniel Brouwer and Robert Asen. New York: SUNY Press.

Rash, Wayne, Jr. 1997. *Politics on the Net: Wiring the Political Process.* New York: W. H. Freeman.

Ross, John. 1995. "The EZLN, a History: Miracles, Coyuntras, Communiqués: An Introduction." Pp. 7–15 in *Shadows of Tender Fury: The Letters and Communiqués of Subcomandante Marcos and the Zapatista Army of National Liberation*, trans. Frank Bardacke, Leslie López, and the Watsonville, California, Human Rights Committee. New York: Monthly Review Press.

———. 2000. *The War against Oblivion: The Zapatista Chronicles 1994–2000.* Monroe, Maine: Common Courage Press.

Roth, Lorna. 1993. "Mohawk Airwaves and Cultural Challenges: Some Reflections on the Politics of Recognition and Cultural Appropriation after the Summer of 1990." *Canadian Journal of Communication* 18: 315–31.

Ruggerio, Greg, and Kate Duncan. "On the Growing Free Media Movement: Recent Trends in Radical Media Organizing." *Z Magazine.* Online at www.lol. shareworld.com/zmag/articles/ruggeriooct97.htm.

Shadows of Tender Fury: The Letters and Communiqués of Subcomandante Marcos and the Zapatista Army of National Liberation. 1995. Trans. Frank Bardacke, Leslie López, and the Watsonville, California, Human Rights Committee. New York: Monthly Review Press.

Shultz, Donald E., and Edward J. Williams. 1995. *Mexico Faces the Twenty-first Century.* Westport, Conn.: Greenwood Press.

"Subcomandante Marcos; Leader, Spokesman of the Zapatista National Liberation Army of Mexico Captures the Heart of Impoverished Indians and the Attention of the Government," *60 Minutes*, Burrelle's Information Services, CBS News Transcripts, Online. Lexis/Nexis. 13 March 1994.

Veltmeyer, Henry. 2000. "The Dynamics of Social Change and Mexico's EZLN." *Latin American Perspectives* 27, no. 5 (September): 88–110.

Warf B., and J. Grimes. 1997. "Counterhegemonic Discourses and the Internet." *Geographical Review* 87, no. 2: 259–74.

Wray, Stefan. 1999. "On Electrical Civil Disobedience." *Peace Review* 11, no. 1 (March): 107–11.

The Zapatista "Social Netwar" in Mexico. 1998. RAND. Online at www.rand.org/ publications/MR 994.pdf/.

IV

GLOBALIZATION
AND GOVERNANCE

7

E-Capital and the Many-Headed Hydra

Nick Dyer-Witheford

INTRODUCTION

No concept is more central to current discussions of the Internet than that of "enclosure."[1] Ever since Raymond Williams pointed out the shared root of the words "commons" and "communications," critical theorists have found early capitalism's fencing in of collective lands a potent metaphor to describe and condemn the ever-expanding scope of corporate media power.[2] And as commercial interests occupy cyberspace, once conceived as an open domain of free information and virtual community, at amazing speed, many authors speak of "enclosures" to describe e-capital's advance on the digital territories of the Net.[3] But power quickly co-opts and neuters radical ideas. The mainstream liberal economist Lester Thurow recently wrote that "just as the Industrial Revolution began with an enclosure movement that abolished common land," so information capitalism requires "a socially managed enclosure movement for intellectual property rights."[4] Other market advocates invoke Garret Hardin's famous neo-Malthusian essay, "The Tragedy of the Commons," to legitimize the privatization of the Net. That essay argued that collective resources undisciplined by property relations are fated to overuse and neglect.[5] To restore a critical perspective to the "enclosure" analysis of e-capital, I therefore want to introduce another metaphor—that of the "many-headed hydra." This phrase comes from the title of Peter Linebaugh and Marcus Rediker's brilliant new study revealing the scope of rebellions against early industrial capitalism.[6] Drawing on their image of proliferating, clandestine, hydra-like revolt, I argue that twenty-first-century e-capital faces a similar multifarious opposition that seriously threatens the success of its futuristic enclosures.

129

THE "OLD" ENCLOSURES: PRIMITIVE ACCUMULATION

The "old" enclosures were an episode in English history in which a rural economy of village collectivity and peasant occupier-ship was destroyed in favor of large and increasingly commercial estates.[7] In the early phases, beginning in the late middle ages, landlords expropriated small farmers from scattered strips of land. In the later stages, which reached a climax in the eighteenth century, common lands by custom available for general use by a local community were fenced in or "enclosed." Villagers lost access to grazing, fishing, hunting, quarrying, fuel, building materials, and rights of way. An entire culture based on shared usage was annihilated and replaced by a new economy in which landlords developed estates as capitalist enterprises, selling the outputs as commodities on a growing world market. The Marxist tradition has analyzed the enclosures as the starting point of capitalist society, the basic mechanism of "primitive accumulation," which created a population of workers "free" from any means of self-support.[8] The evicted rural populations became paupers, vagabonds, and beggars, migrated across the oceans, resorted to soldiering, sailoring, or prostitution in the city, or, eventually were compelled to work for a wage in the new "manufactories"—thus providing the first proletariat for industrial capitalism.

Enclosure was thus not simply the fencing of common lands, but a complex, many-sided process with ramifying social consequences. It involved such elements as: the use of force with local militias, bailiffs and goon squads evicting and harassing common users and farmers; special legislation—most notably the Parliamentary Enclosures Act—investing this process with the force of law; large-scale hydraulic engineering to convert areas such as fens into arable lands, while driving off the hunting and fishing communities that inhabited them; innovations in agricultural production, such as new forms of crop rotation, or the introduction of sheep farming and crofting in Scotland or cattle grazing in Ireland; the building of highways—turnpike roads—which carried the new agricultural commodities to towns and ports, traversing and cutting across remaining commons in the process. Enclosures were integral to a burgeoning European colonialism: They provided the displaced human material for immigration, and imperial armies and navies; finances for agricultural "improvements" often came from the colonies, through the slave, sugar, or coffee trade, while, conversely, the model of privatized land ownership was "carried across the Atlantic, to the Indian sub-continent, and into the South Pacific by British colonists, administrators and lawyers."[9] Enclosure was intimately related to the emergence of new intellectual disciplines and discourses such as Malthusian demographics and classical political economy, whose object of study was the new quantum of dispossessed labor-power it created.[10]

Enclosure also required a new regime of social discipline, surveillance, and criminalization including the witch-hunting of commons dwellings and using women, poor laws, antivagrancy legislation, workhouses, and the first steps in the formation of an internal state apparatus of thief-taking and policing to monitor, confine, and punish the potentially unruly population evicted from the land.[11] This was important, because enclosure provoked opposition. The fencing in of commons met with responses ranging from appeals, petitions, and lobbying of Parliament to direct uprising and riots, mobbing of surveyors, destruction of records, sporadic and clandestine arson, fence breaking, poaching, and systematic trespass. Antienclosure sentiment provided the background for the early-nineteenth-century revolts of impoverished rural laborers, who adopted the collective name of "Captain Swing" with which to identify their anonymous attacks on landlords and agribusiness. Their insurrections ran parallel to the more famous machine-smashing uprisings of "Ned Ludd" against the destitution caused by early capitalist machinery. The hostility incited by enclosure, occasionally flaring into overt form, constantly burning underground, provided a context within which various forms of crime—such as highway robbery on the new turnpike roads—would be celebrated as acts of popular resistance in a smoldering land war.[12]

But our knowledge of the antienclosure movement has leaped forward with the recent work of Linebaugh and Rediker on the "hidden history of the revolutionary Atlantic."[13] Marshaling original research from archives in the Americas and Europe, the authors show how in the seventeenth and eighteenth centuries early capitalism's "primitive accumulation" was met by dozens of organized rebellions in both England and its New World colonies. The subjects of these revolts were extraordinarily diverse—dispossessed laborers, sailors, slaves, pirates, market women, and indentured servants. But they repeatedly came together in combinations, from Digger communes to the maroon settlements of slave and settler runaways, that crossed what later became sedimented divisions of race, gender, and class. This motley array of revolutionaries was the human residue of the enclosures—"commoners." For many, the deracinating violence of eviction from the land was the catalyst to insurgency. For most, the still living memory of common lands was a constant reference point in resistance to emergent capitalism. Aghast at the recurrence of these outbreaks, the rulers of the day spoke of the rebels as a "hydra" whose regenerative powers resisted their own "Herculean" attempts at decapitation. Eventually, they did succeed—by bayonet, execution, torture, imprisonment, and deportation—in suppressing their risings. Yet many of the ideas and experiments of the early "commonist" rebels fueled both the American and French Revolutions, and went on to bleed into the revolutionary movements of the twentieth century. This is the history informing our account of "new" cyberspatial enclosure.

THE "NEW" ENCLOSURES: FUTURISTIC ACCUMULATION

In the case of the Internet, there is no original moment of "common" posses-
sion. The story is more complex—a cycle of appropriations and reappropriations. As is well known, the linking of computers and telecommunications
was pioneered under military auspices, initially as part of the U.S. nuclear war
fighting preparations. Later, the network was used to connect the supercomputing centers vital to Pentagon research. But the techno-scientific workers
employed in the sites of the military-academic-industrial complex—faculty
and especially graduate students—extended the network far beyond its original scope, using it for nonmilitary research, creating news groups and games,
and designing successive layers of additional operations connecting into the
main backbone. Systems managers, enchanted by the technological sweet-
ness of the results and keen to sustain the involvement of brilliant free labor,
tolerated this accretion of self-generated services. Soon, as Peter Childers and
Paul Delany put it, "the parasites had all but taken over the host."[14]

Like the destruction of the terrestrial commons, the enclosing of cyberspace
was a complex, multilayered process. Just as the enclosures of eighteenth-
century England—"free market" rhetoric notwithstanding—required state
support, so did those of late-twentieth-century America. This was primarily
the work of the Clinton-Gore administration. The 1992 National Information
Infrastructure initiative—the famous "information superhighway" plan—
affirmed government backing for rationalizing and extending publicly subsidized but privately owned digital networks. The 1996 Telecommunications
Act made clear this process would occur within a context of media marketization, privatization, and deregulation. Within this overarching framework a
series of incremental initiatives eroded the public status of the Net. One was
the switch in 1993, from the first come, first served registration of Internet addresses to the commercial sale of domain names. This was widely referred to
as a "sale of virtual land" and was accompanied by extensive "cyber squat-
ting," as people registered desirable addresses speculating on their resale
value. Even more critical was the privatization of the Net backbone. In 1991,
under mounting corporate pressure, the National Science Foundation, the
U.S. government agency responsible for running the Net, lifted restrictions on
its commercial use.[15] By 1995 the high level networks that structure its coordinating architecture were transferred from the ownership of the National Science Foundation to a handful of telecommunication companies.

These high-level policy shifts, though largely imperceptible at the level
of the individual user, set the scene for changes that cascaded down
through every level of the Net. The enclosure process moved by a series of
invasive entrepreneurial initiatives, which, since they have been widely
analyzed elsewhere, can be briefly summarized here:[16] the commercialization of online service provision, first through attempts at sanitized propri-

etorial networks such as those of CompuServe or MSN, then by direct connection to the Net through thousands of "mom and pop" ISPs whose numbers were then—in a familiar story of industry concentration—being whittled down by the power of the giant telecommunication and cable conglomerates; an influx of media providers seeking to create virtual infotainments such as online journalism, network gaming, and TV-style "Webispodes"; human wave assaults of marketers experimenting with banners, spots, buttons, spam, interstitials, advertorials, search engine retrieval ranking, "free" advertising-supported connections, e-mail and even computers, and viral-marketing techniques; an explosion of e-tailing hype brought vendors of pornography, groceries, financial services, travel, natural gas, and Nazi memorabilia swarmed to online selling, drawn by prospects of geography-transcending markets, reduced staff and space costs, opportunities for targeted advertising and information gathering, illusions of low start-up costs, and dreams of disintermediating outmaneuver of dominant rivals.

Crucial to both e-advertising and e-selling was the process of portalization that ordered and disciplined the chaotic ebb and flow of Net activity. Net use was channeled through high profile gateways constructed around search engines, or the sports, news, and entertainment sites of major corporations, attracting users by the vigorous cross-promotions on their corporate owners, and directing them to the sites of subsidiaries, corporate allies, and paying clients. Even more important was the use of benignly named Web "cookies" to construct a regime of commercial panopticism, monitoring cyberspatial activity with surveillance methods invisible to average users and dissolving the integrity of the "personal" computer by a routine infiltration of hard drives with tracking programs delivered from external sources. The gathering of information from these sources, either for a company's own marketing purposes, or for sale to other concerns, rapidly became a central part of the Net economy. But primary to all these enclosure operations was a sustained drive to consolidate intellectual property in a digital environment. This involved a two-pronged attack. Exclusionary technological innovations—such as commercial encryption, digital watermarking, and, eventually, hard-drive installed antipiracy devices—built up increasingly formidable "copyright management infrastructures." And changes to the law, such as the Millennium Digital Copyright Act, imposed punishment and fines for attempting to circumvent such measures. Revising and enforcing copyright law for Net distributed texts, games, and music became a priority for corporate lawyers, and—as we will see in more detail later—the hunting down of digital transgressors a major preoccupation of state security forces.

Although every kind of business leaped to establish e-presence, there was quickly visible a central core of commercially developed virtual estate,

owned by what Roberto Verzola describes as the "cyberlords"—"the proper-
tied class of the information society, [who] control either a body of information or the material infrastructure for creating, distributing or using information."[17] A triadic core of oligopolistic interests dominated these holdings.
First were the major computing software companies—preeminently the information age's favorite predatory monopolist, Microsoft, whose tightly cou-
pled control of operating systems, software applications, and net browsers
gave it a position of exceptional power. Second were the giant carrier companies, most notably the telecommunications and cable companies,
ATT/TCI, Time Warner/AOL, and various Bells, vying to control the wired
and wireless channels running into domestic homes. Third were the mam-
moth content providers, mainly established conglomerates of the infotain-
ment business, such as Time Warner/AOL (again), Disney, Viacom, News
Corporation, and Vivendi/Universal, who believed that their supremacy in
traditional media—film, television, music, journalism—could, if supple-
mented by judicious investment in new media such as video games and Web
start-ups, be translated into cyberspatial dominance. Within this triadic sector mergers and alliances proceeded pell-mell, as all parties aim to win strategic position vertically integrating control of software, carriage, and the content. At the same time the new corporate entities constructed from these
fusions are reaching out to absorb the most important specifically Net-based
commercial operations—particularly search engines and ISPs. This process
is in many ways chaotic and contradictory. Corporations do not know which
of their cyber-ventures will prove truly profitable, and are engaged in an expensive and speculative process of option covering and preemption in
which billions are wasted in failed gambles. There are vicious competitive
conflicts—between Microsoft and its software rivals over digital standards,
between carriers and content providers over intellectual property right
protections—even while these same companies are simultaneously involved
in deeply collusive arrangements. But the net result is a dizzying process of
dynastic corporate marriage, liaison, and procreation, generating a set of
new corporate christenings—Time Warner/AOL, Disney/Infoseek, AT&T/
TCI, NewsCorp/ MCI /World Com—whose hyphenation is worthy of an
older terrestrially landed aristocracy.

   As the terrestrial enclosures were justified by classical political economy,
so cyberspatial enclosures generate their own legitimating discourses. The
theory of the "new economy" is a high tech rejuvenation of Adam Smith's
doctrine of market supremacy. Net and the Market are presented as "essentially similar entities, inseparable and self-regulating . . . electrifying each
other in a reciprocal embrace."[18] The Net creates conditions of digital abun-
dance, lowers costs of market entry, and creates the condition of perfect information between buyers and sellers on which the operations of the "invisible hand" were premised, bringing into being the "friction free capitalism"

celebrated by Bill Gates as fulfilling Smith's dream of "perfect competition."[19] Alienating work, class conflicts, crisis of the business cycle, and ecological destruction are the fading legacies of the old smokestack era. Now, in its digital incarnation, market society is set for an era of unprecedented growth and prosperity—the "long boom"—a period so expansive and exciting as to amount to a whole new epoch of civilization, "A world so different its emergence can only be described as a revolution."[20]

Despite such hyperbole, there is no doubt that in a very few years e-capital has transformed the composition of cyberspace. In 1991 there were only some 181,361 ".com" hosts, 12 percent of the total, lagging just behind the 13 percent of ".edu" sites associated with universities, research institutes, and schools. In 1995 "dot.coms" were not only some ten times as numerous—1,829,119—but also accounted for 31 percent of all hosts. In 2000 there were a staggering 32,696,253 commercial sites—35 percent of the total.[21] In 1993, 1.5 percent of World Wide Web sites had the ".com" suffix, by 1995, 31.3 percent, and by 1997, 62.6 percent.[22] According to the OECD two-thirds of Internet traffic consists of internal data transfers within corporations.[23] Even these figures may understate commercial presence. A 1999 study of Web server content in the journal *Nature* reported 1.5 percent of its sampled pages as "pornographic," 2 percent as "personal," 3 percent as "health information," 6 percent involving "scientific or educational" material, and 83 percent as "commercial."[24]

But to present the digital world simply as subject to monolithic corporate dominance would be wrong. Net-enclosure is a troubled project. E-capital is encountering resistances and alternatives—lines of fight and flight. Some arise from the commons traditions of the Net's early academic/anarchic phase. At the same time as these practices, almost antediluvian in Net-time, are being modified, new subversions spring up from generations who have grown within cybercapitalism's digital culture, but experience contradictions between its abundant potentiality and actual exclusions and banalities. Emerging in cyberspace, alongside and against the e-enclosers, are collectivities who, rather than accepting the digital law of value defy its rules. The metaphor of the serpentine "hydra" is appropriate to describe these activities, for they are proliferating, decentered, and sinuously circuitous. When one head is lopped off a hydra, another grows; on the Net, anticapital may be quickly suppressed, but also regenerates and alters very fast. But since the original hydra started off with seven heads, we will inventory seven major subverters of e-capital: hackers, pirates, free software creators, universal and open access movements, cyberactivists, and hacktivists.

Hackers

As so often before, new forms of conflict appear first under the guise of criminality and delinquency—in this case, as "hacking." Just as in the eighteenth century poachers and highwaymen were celebrated as defenders of the rights and prerogatives of rural common dwellers against the encroachments of a new commercial order, so too twenty-first-century hackers embody—even if in twisted, individualized ways—a resistance against the enclosure of the Net. For the sake of convenience we will define three stages in the history of hacking— the phases of "the ur-hackers," "the hacker elite," and "mass hacking."[25]

It is generally recognized that the pejorative use of the term "hacking" marks the criminalization of activities once considered legitimate and vital for the development of computer networks. The ur-hackers were young programming wizards whose unauthorized but accepted experimental computer play was crucial to the work of advanced digital centers such as the Massachusetts Institute of Technology in the late 1960s and the 1970s. In this period "hacker" meant simply a computer virtuoso, a sense retained by *The New Hackers Dictionary* when it defines a hacker as someone "who enjoys exploring the details of programmable systems and how to stretch their capabilities; one who programs enthusiastically, even obsessively."[26] The ur-hackers were paradoxically situated. Elite employees of the military-industrial complex, many were disaffected by Vietnam and Watergate, and committed to the idea that computers were an empowering and democratic technology. Their idealism was encapsulated in the "hacker ethic," of which the most famous slogan is "information wants to be free."[27] No more explicit repudiation of commodification—a late-twentieth-century version of "property is theft"—could be imagined.

Indispensable as the invention-power of ur-hackers was to the creation of the Net, their creed was doomed to collide with the cybercapital. Hackers ignored digital fences, trespassed on enclosed territory.[28] Sometimes they poached or stole. The computing community distinguished "hackers"—who explore—and "crackers"—who steal. Even many "crackers" rejected the robber label, arguing that reproducing information without removing it from the original owner could not be theft. To the enclosers, however, these distinctions were arcane: "hacker" came to cover any sort of electronic trespass, and was defined as a new category of criminal delinquency, for whom new penalties, legal detection, prosecution, offenses, countermeasures, and punishments had to be devised and enforced in a mounting war over digital property rights.

Hackers rationalized their actions by arguing that information cannot and should not be owned; that its copying deprived no one; that their actions liberated digital knowledge from self-interested restrictions of corporations and governments; that the databases of these powerful institutions constituted a threat to individuals; that for-profit privatization of information slowed down invention; and that their incursions were a way of promoting technological development. From this point of view, hacking was a public-spirited activity, an attempt to realize the potential wealth of information technologies currently held prisoner by capital and state. Even opponents were not immune to a grudging respect for these arguments. In one famous incident Dorothy Denning, a leading academic computer security expert, issued a report that declared:

> Hackers say that it is our social responsibility to share information, and that it is information hoarding and disinformation that are the crimes. The ethics of resource and information sharing contrast sharply with computer security policies that are based on authorization and "need to know." The discrepancy raises an interesting question: Does the hacker ethic reflect a growing force in our society that stands for greater sharing of information?[29]

This sympathetic characterization attracted torrents of criticism from Denning's establishment colleagues and she subsequently repudiated it in favor of a more negative appraisal.[30] But the incident showed how hacking crystalized disquiets about the emergent forms of info-property, even among some of its professional defenders. Such tremors of doubt did not, however, halt the determination of authorities to crush the hacker elites— a task that was increasingly imperative as the Internet became ever more central to the information economy. New legal and investigative weapons were forged. In the United States, the Secret Service was given jurisdiction over computer fraud in 1984 by the Comprehensive Crime Control Act; the Computer Fraud and Abuse Act of 1986 removed legal obstacles to prosecuting unauthorized trafficking in computer passwords; and the Computer Emergency Response Team (CERT), based at Carnegie Mellon University, was formed in 1988 by military agencies to investigate the growing volume of hacker attacks. In 1990, suspecting, incorrectly, that hackers had caused a nationwide crash of AT&T's long distance system, the FBI, Secret Service, and other federal and local law enforcement agencies launched Operation Sun Devil. A massive sweep closed in on a small network of hackers who had circulated a purloined file describing the 911 emergency phone systems, in an operation that included early morning gunpoint arrests in suburban homes, the apprehension of dozens of suspects, and the impounding of hundreds of computers.[31]

The only major trial that resulted—that of "Knight Lightning"—fell apart when it was demonstrated in court that the allegedly stolen information was publicly and cheaply available. The most immediate consequence of the crackdown was to persuade many Net users that cyber-police might be as big a problem as hackers, and catalyze the formation of the civil libertarian Electronic Frontier Foundation. Nonetheless, the long-term effect was to chill the hacker community. Other influences—aging and the advent of family responsibilities, the increased use of the Internet to track intrusions, and above all the implosive effect of spectacular publicity, which resulted in the swamping of formerly select bulletin board systems, IRC and Usenet news-groups with hacker "wannabees"—marked the passing of the hacking elites. Many of their members passed into the burgeoning computer security business, neatly illustrating a symbiotic relationship between criminals and privatized police that would have been appreciated by eighteenth-century thief-takers.

But though the hacker elites thinned out, hacker intrusions did not. Although hacker activity is hard to track, largely because businesses are reluctant to admit vulnerability, all evidence suggests that the 1990s saw the inauguration of an era of "mass hacking." In part this occurred simply because the online population was increasing, in part because e-capital presents an ever-expanding target for systematic crime, fraud, industrial espionage, and political dissent. In a survey of more than 1,000 companies done by Ernst and Young in the late 1990s, 20 percent reported financial losses from unauthorized computer break-ins by hackers, competitors, or employees.[32] Figures from CERT—which receives notification of only a tiny fraction of total hacker attacks—show a steady escalation from eight "incident reports" in 1988 to 252 in 1990, to 2,412 in 1995, 9,859 in 1999, and more than 15,000 in the first nine months of 2000.[33]

Among the most recent and, to e-capital, most disturbing manifestations of mass hacking are "denial of service" attacks. These are a form of hacking that do not just trespass or remove information, but cripple and disrupt organizations, using software tools that swamp the target server with spurious requests for information. These attacks are extremely difficult to stop, and relatively easy to launch. The software tools used by "scrip hackers" are ready-made and distributed on the Net. In June 1999, Ray Kammner, director of the National Institute of Standards and Technologies, told a U.S. congressional subcommittee that "at least 30 computer attack tools were written and published on the Internet per month," and that one popular Web site had over 400,000 unique visitors per month downloading attack tools.[34]

In February of 2000 major portals such as Amazon, Yahoo, eBay, E-Trade, ZDNet, CNN.com, Buy.com, and Excite were hit by massive assaults using tools such as Tribal Flood Network (TFN) that allowed a single computer user to coordinate assaults from hundreds or thousands of places at once, co-opting other systems as unknowing "zombie" perpetrators. A momentary panic hit e-commerce stocks; the FBI launched high-profile investigations; and the White House acknowledged the incident as a serious crisis. Much of the discourse about these attacks focuses on the personal motives of the perpetrators. But in a way this is beside the point: regardless of whether scrip hackers act from adolescent angst or political principle, they respond to a situation in which the face of power, and presiding authority in the digital world—and hence the primary target for all expressions of dissent—is clearly and manifestly commercial. Denial of service attacks represents the negating power of a hacker tradition whose dream of free information flows is violated by the commodification of the Net. They are the equivalent to the arson, fence breaking, livestock maiming, and rick burning that so often met terrestrial enclosures. But there are other offshoots of the hacker tradition that are both more creative, and perhaps in the long term more threatening to Net capital, and it is to their examination that we now turn.

Pirates

"Piracy" is the term today used to describe illicit distribution of software, either for free or as part of black market networks. Historically, pirates are known as romantic but dastardly and bloody seagoing villains preying on legitimate merchant trade. Linebaugh and Rediker, however, argue that eighteenth-century pirates were often a maritime wing of early anticapitalist rebellion, informed by revolutionary ideas of radical republicanism and democracy, often releasing the human slave cargoes they captured, and intimately connected to mutinous refusals of tyrannical discipline in the imperialist navies.[35] It is therefore only fitting to consider whether there may be more to the activities of contemporary digital pirates than just the criminal delinquency with which they are charged by today's captains of e-commerce.

Piracy of copyrighted and patented works is nothing new. It is part of the history of many media—printed texts, recorded music, videotapes, and satellite television, a clandestine shadow-world that obstinately follows the attempt to enclose information in commodity form. But nowhere has it exploded as it has on computer networks. Ken Wasch, the president of the Software Publishers Association, acknowledges, "computer software is the only industry in the world that empowers every customer to become a marketing subsidiary."[36] The reproduction of digitized works is fast and virtually cost free, a matter of point and click, and the Net makes the global distribution of digital copies, in a way that completely confounds national judicial boundaries, nearly instantaneous. Much of this illicit activity is folded back into commodity form through the black market. However, what is remarkable is that so much corporate effort—in technological design and legal activity—is today being exercised to restrict what the media corporations ostensibly promote, that is, the literally free flow of information.[37]

Antipiracy organizations like the Software & Information Industry Association, and Business Software Alliance say that some 38 percent of programs loaded on computers worldwide are pirated, estimate more than $5 million worth of code is cracked and uploaded daily to the Net, and claim total industry losses at $11 billion annually.[38] These figures are based on the premise that every pirated piece of software represents a lost sale, an assumption

that is, to say the least, implausible.[39] Nonetheless, there is general agreement that piracy of this kind is a major part of the global information economy—particularly in the areas of office software, video and computer
games, and music. Although industry denunciations tend to lump all forms
of illicit copying together, it is a complex phenomenon that involves several
distinguishable, though overlapping, practices. It has been estimated that
one-third of piracy is "garden variety unlicensed copying"; one-third "Far
Eastern-style counterfeiting," and one third "warez" networks, driven by
bragging rights and barter economies.[40]

"Garden variety" piracy involves the exchange of software between
friends or from work. It also includes "softlifting" practices by businesses,
where a company buys one copy of a computer program and then uses it on
four different computers within the organization. This is amongst the most
common type of piracy, and it involves many legitimate busineses; for example, it's commonplace for 3-D animators and modelers to use pirated,
cracked, or at least unlicensed copies of their office software at home, for
overtime or experimentation.[41]

Much more dramatic, and more publicly stigmatized, however, are
"warez" groups—online networks for the distribution of "cracked" software
organized through BBS, Usenet news groups, and IRC chat forums. In the
1990s, the most prestigious pirate groups—Razor 1911, DOD, Pirates With
Attitude, the Inner Circle—were "tightly knit clubs whose members have
known each other for years."[42] Pirate bulletin boards such as the Pits and Elu-
sive Dream operated with as many as twenty-three incoming phone lines.
Some BBS operate on a commercial basis. However, the true "warez" culture
is a nonprofit venture.

> Warez crackers, traders and collectors don't pirate software to make a living:
> they pirate software because they can. The more the manufacturers harden a
> product, with tricky serial numbers and anticopy systems, the more fun it be-
> comes to break. Theft? No, it's a game.[43]

"Warez" may be offered as gifts—"testimony to the power and stature of the
giver" or as part of an intricate barter economy operating through select groups
where membership is dependent on a demonstrated ability to contribute to the
collective store.[44] On the boards of major "warez" networks such as Inc.,
TDT/TRSI (The Dream Team/Tri Star Red Sector Inc), Razor 1911, and The
Humble Guys could be found "zero hour" software—available at the same
time, or before it became available in stores, complete with manuals and full
downloading instructions supplied from sources within the developer or pub-
lisher, perhaps from employees who had a test copy, and complete with "crack
fixes"—patches to remedy problems in the pirated product.

There is a blur between warez and commercial pirating. Committed to a virtual gift economy as they may be, warez pirates cannot guarantee their trophies do not end up somewhere on the planet bundled on a black market CD.[45] But while warez networks are clustered in North America and Europe, the centers for commercial piracy are in the so-called developing world. The largest losses are attributable to operators in China, the Russian Federation, Taiwan, and Hong Kong. Much of the product is shipped through Hong Kong and Paraguay for reshipping to countries all around the world. In all, IDSA accuses fifty-five countries of either aiding counterfeiters or not establishing or sufficiently enforcing adequate protections against theft of intellectual property.[46]

The most notorious of these black market zones is the Far East, with Hong Kong as distribution hub. The notorious Golden Shopping Centre in Shamshuipo, "a grimy backwater in Kowloon," contains "several hundred small shops selling all sorts of computer paraphernalia."[47] While some of these stores stock original packaged software, neighbors with illegal copies undercut them for a tenth or less of the price. The Hong Kong Customs and Excise raids, confiscates stock, and prosecutes offenders. But this does not squash the trade, much of which is in the hands of the infamous "triad" criminal gangs, so that "detectives hired by software firms often receive death threats."[48] At one time it was believed that corporations' best chance of squashing pirates lay with Hong Kong's integration into China, and the imposition of authoritarian state socialist discipline. But this hope has faded as the liberalization of China's economy spawns its own thriving bootleg businesses. Beijing has its own "Thieves Alley" where software pirates congregated. In 1995, China and America teetered on the edge of trade war over the counterfeiting of software, music, and video. Eventually, the Beijing government agreed to crack down and closed many of the plants. Many, however, believed that the only effect was to push production deeper underground— or even into the clandestine private software factories of the People's Army and other state agencies.

Within North America, software, film, and music industry groups wage a highly publicized war against piracy. One front is waged technologically, through systems of electronic watermarking, encryption, use-limited software, and other "digital property management systems" that provoke hackers and crackers to ever create feats of technological ingenuity in an ever-escalating spiral. But behind this digital arms race also stand the powers of the U.S. state. In 1997 President Clinton signed into law the "No Electronic Theft Act," which closed a legal loophole for pirates by making it a criminal offense to possess or distribute multiple copies of online copyright material, whether for profit or not. The act was strongly backed by the software and entertainment industries but opposed by science and academic groups.[49]

The Digital Millennium Copyright Act followed in 1998, criminalizing the circumvention of antipiracy measures built into most commercial software, and outlawing the manufacture, sale, or distribution of code-cracking devices. The bill also resolved conflicts between the carrier and content sectors of information capital about intellectual property protection by limiting Internet service providers from liability for simply transmitting copyright-infringing information, while establishing an expectation that they will remove illicit material from users' Web sites.[50]

In an astute analysis David Tetzlaf has pointed out that there is both more and less than meets the eye in this antipiracy campaign.[51] Despite their high-minded law and order rhetoric, organizations such as the Business Software Alliance and the Software Publishers Association are for-profit ventures that obtain revenues from damages won in civil court cases. Their repeated rhetorical assaults against "warez" pirates obscure the fact that the major part of their income comes from cases won from corporate softlifters.[52] Most "warez" traders get away uncaught, and most antipirate organizations are content to denounce such freebooters as demonized and semimythological enemies whose evil reputation legitimates a far more mundane story of intrabusiness bickering. In Tetzalf's view capitalism's "piracy problem" is ultimately not so much about real risks to profits as about enforcing a general ideology of panoptic surveillance:

> In order to territorialize the Internet in the service of corporate capital, the system will need to generate new forms of warranting and location technologies applied to the purpose of generating social control within virtual space.[53]

But although Tetzalf is surely correct about the ideological consequences of the antipiracy crusade, this does not preclude real possibilities of market disruption as a result of large-scale copyright violation. His paper was written before the "download rage" of Napster, Gnutella, Free Net, and other peer-to-peer networks. The late 1990s have seen the arrival not only of "mass hacking," but also of "mass piracy," enabled by the combination of digitally formatted MP3 music—which appeared in 1998—with distribution networks that in varying degrees eliminate the need for copies to be stored on a monitorable central server. While some of these peer-to-peer networks—like Napster—were created as commercial applications, others—such as Free Net—were designed as political projects with the explicit intention of destroying both state censorship and commercial copyright. And while the music business has been the first to feel the impact of peer-to-peer piracy, many of the networks that are now following Napster have the capacity to distribute a much wider variety of digital entertainment products, including film and games. The adoption of these systems as a central component of North American youth culture presents a grassroots expansion of the digital commons and, at the very least, seriously problematizes current plans for their enclosure.

It would of course be naive to interpret the turmoil in the music oligopoly as a token of imminent capitalist collapse. The recent deal between Bertelsmann and Napster strongly suggests that commercial providers will strive to domesticate peer-to-peer copying, as they have with previous reproduction technologies from vinyl records to videocassettes. But "download rage" does indicate the Net may not be as easily commodified as some have believed. In the 1990s, neo-Marxist theorists such as the Schillers proposed that "alternative" uses of Internet simply repeated patterns characteristic of earlier generations of communication technologies, where an initial openness was quickly sealed off by the forces of commodification.[54] What the "Napster revolution" suggests, however, is that the very dynamism of the capitalism's "perpetual innovation" economy maintains a state of constant turbulence in which windows of opportunity open and close very fast, and which promise intellectual property owners little except an ongoing escalation of technological measures and countermeasures between owners and pirates. As important as the sheer technological capacity is the issue of ideological legitimacy: the immediate effect of the music industry's suing of Napster was to double the number of subscribers, taking it from 17 to 38 million in a matter of months. Peer-to-peer networks thus appear as the product of a generation socialized within the "third nature" of information capitalism, for whom the potentialities to freely reproduce and circulate digital information are a taken for granted, normalized component of their environment.[55]

There is therefore good reason to suspect that "friction-free markets and friction-free piracy run in tandem."[56] Conventional wisdom is that pirates are parasites who, by lowering industry profits, sap the innovative energies on which digital development depends. But this proposition can be reversed: It may be the illicit users of computers and telecommunications who most fully realize the possibilities of the information age. In their embrace of unrestrained digital reproduction and dissemination, pirates exploit to the full the potentials of a digital technology whose capacities for reproduction and instantaneous distribution legal business must in fact hobble to preserve the form of commodity production and exchange. The irony is that e-businesses have also encouraged and created the preconditions for the digital "gift economy" they now find so problematic. Companies from id games to Netscape have inaugurated varieties of freeware strategies, releasing important parts of their software gratis, hoping this will create an expanded market for full or recent versions, services, manuals, and spin-off products.[57] In this way, the Net "gift economy" can be contained within—and indeed propel—e-commerce, existing as a supplement to dot.com capitalism. But the danger of this strategy, from the corporate point of view, is that the "supplementary" world of free and uncommodified digital activity may, by a classic deconstructive reversal, become the main event—that the genie of "free goods" will refuse to stay in the bottle, waiting to be summoned up only as and when required, and instead escape and take on a life of its own, going on its way, throwing the bottle over its shoulder.

Free Software

While pirates "liberate" digital productions from commercial control, another offshoot of hacking ethic takes things a step further—by creating "free software." This is the thrust of what is now generally known as the "open source" programming movement, whose activities are assuming an increasingly prominent, and paradoxical, position within the digital economy. Open source is software for which the source code—the core programming that controls the basic operations—is publicly revealed, enabling users to produce their own revised, improved, or refunctioned versions. These new versions are then in turn available for further user modification. In conventional commercial logic source code constitutes the most basic asset whose protection makes possible the extraction of technological rents from users. Open source thus works by logic of "disclosure" diametrically opposite to that of proprietorial "enclosure."[58]

As Nathan Newman has argued, open source software is not really new. The programming that drove the explosion of the early computer industry and the development of the Net was in effect open source—produced by government-funded agencies, according to shared standards, and circulated noncommercially within an academic ethos of open information sharing. This was the context that generated the TCP/IP protocols, Unix, Gopher space, World Wide Web, Mosaic, and many others of the indispensable digital building blocks of the Net. Only from the mid-1990s, as the U.S. government succumbed to neoliberal ideology and gradually withdraw its presence and funding, was the door opened for corporate players such as Microsoft and Netscape to fragment the technological culture of the Net by the development of proprietary, competing, and incompatible software programs, "programs whose coding was kept secret and whose operating protocols were not public or standardized."[59]

The anticommercial tradition was however kept alive by a group of programmers, the Free Software Foundation led by Richard Stallman and founded in 1984. This group responded to the fragmentation of UNIX into competing proprietorial versions by developing an open source alternative, GNU. The GNU Manifesto, one of the most important documents of the cyberspace antienclosure movement, rejected the privatized appropriation of the fruits of a collective, and cumulative programming culture.[60]

Stallman and his colleagues defined free software as a matter of liberty, not price: "free speech," not "free beer."[61] The concept refers to the users' freedom to run a program for any purpose, copy, distribute, study how it works, change and improve it. This is the principle of "copyleft." To protect this principle, the GNU developers invented the General Public License, which guarantees that every user of software made under its auspices has the right of unconstrained use, copying, modification, and distribution and forbids anyone curtailing these rights for other users or seeking their surrender of them. "Copyleft" and the GPU can be seen as an attempt to formally legalize the principles previously observed by custom in the early Net commons.

GNU itself encountered a series of developmental problems and never fully realized the promise Stallman and the FSF had hoped for. But by the mid-1990s, two other examples of open source were becoming famous: Linux, the operating system elaborated out of the GNU experiment by Finnish programmer Linus Torvald, and the Web server Apache. By early 2000 Linux had hopped over competitors to become the second-most-popular operating system for server computers after Windows NT.[62] Apache commanded nearly 60 percent of the Web server market. Open source programs are "emerging as not just inexpensive but also more robust and dynamic alternatives to commercial software," and are particularly popular in developing countries where the costs of proprietorial software is often prohibitive.[63]

The free software movement is a product of the hacker ethic, and, as always within that diverse tradition, its emergence reflects a variety of agendas. For Stallman, the FSF and other like-minded groups such as the League for Programming Freedom, it is the expression of a principled critique of corporate ownership. Others see collective production as a preventative against the introduction of hidden surveillance features in proprietorial software packages: "it enables users to look under the hood to find out what's going on. . . . If there's anything funny, word will go out like lightning."[64] But many advocates also see pragmatic advantages over proprietorial practice. By harnessing the collective intelligence of thousands of users as codevelopers they claim to actually have increased efficiency in both debugging and evolving software. Eric Raymond terms this the discovery of an "inverse commons."[65] This, he says, is a reversal of Hardin's argument about "the tragedy of the commons." Hardin posited that collective ownership of resources without the incentives for protection provided by private property results in systemic overuse and neglect.[66] But, Raymond argues, in software development this dynamic is turned on its head, as collective ownership of source code results in greater productivity.

Paradoxically, in the late 1990s "open source" became increasingly attractive to the very corporate culture it initially opposed. The catalyst was Microsoft's escalating hold on operating systems, applications, and browsers. Confronting Gates's juggernaut, commercial competitors sought ways to escape being enclosed within its vertically integrated software empire. One of the first was Netscape, which, having played a key role in destroying the common standards computing culture, found itself being overwhelmed by Microsoft in the "browser wars." In an attempt to fight back, it took a leap beyond "freeware" and released the "Mozilla" source code for its Navigator browser, hoping to win both users and programming know-how to its cause. Although this was only a partial success, other Microsoft competitors, such as Sun and Corel, entered into rapprochement with Linux. Microsoft's rivals are now attempting to ingest what was initially an anticorporate logic to avoid being swallowed by that most characteristically capitalist entity—a large, aggressive monopolist. As so often the market is trying to get energy from the assimilation of the resistance it evokes, absorbing "open source" in order to protect itself from self-induced implosion.

This commercial attention led a split within the free software movement between "purists," represented by Stallman, and "pragmatists," whose most famous spokesperson is Raymond. Whereas the purists are anti-corporate, the pragmatists are prepared to pursue symbioses between open source and for-profit programming. Purists continue to use terms such as "free software" and "copyleft," while pragmatists prefer the less militant sounding "open source." The most famous example of pragmatist practice is the company Red Hat, one of a number of commercial ventures that aims to make money from Linux by providing packaging of and support for software that can be obtained free on the Net. The outcome of this interaction between commercialization and free software is, however, uncertain. One obvious prospect is the corruption of the open source movement. As Newman points out, "commercial interest runs the risk of a re-privatization, a fracturing into corporatized versions." He suggests that in order to prevent this there is a need for government to reenter the fray, by throwing the billion-dollar weight of its software "research, purchases and implementation" behind open source. But even in the meantime, open source is providing a striking example of collective, voluntary work effort that in many ways contradicts claims about managerial leadership, hierarchy, and command-and-profit motive.

Access—Universal and Open

Hackers, pirates, and open-source activists are technologically adept subverters of the digital enclosures. Partly alongside, but also often separate from, their challenges runs another line of contestation—struggles about access. Access politics are about who is in cyberspace and who is out, who is connected, on what terms, by what architectural processes of inclusion and exclusion. Such struggles might at first sight seem a world apart from those of, say, open-source activists. They tend to be fought out not in romantic digital deeps of cyberspace, but in the tedious and mundane processes of regulatory bodies and government budgetary decisions. And they involve movements by—or more often on behalf of—the poor and marginalized, those who "fall though the Net," the digitally excluded who, by definition, usually lack the skills for elaborate hacks and piracies.

But movements at the "high" and "low" end of digital empowerment share a rejection of the logic of corporate enclosure and commodification. Access struggles involve, and may be led by, information sector workers and professionals—librarians, computer scientists, or telecommunications trades unionists—who for political or ethical reasons, or even out of enlightened self-interest, champion widespread public access to the Net. Indeed, just as digitalization, by creating a common medium for capitalist transactions drives toward the convergence of distinct industries, so it creates a momentum for what Jim Davis terms a "popular digital convergence" among different sectors of social labor.[67] Organizations that fought separately for community access to cable television or the employment conditions of phone workers or the artistic rights of musicians and writers now find in their common concern around the "highway" a "new, practical basis for working together."[68]

Foremost among access struggles are challenges to the "digital divide." One weakness with the "commons" metaphor for the Net is that access has always been predominantly a prerogative of the privileged. Even in its noncommercial phase, the Net has been a domain of the affluent, the educated, and, until very recently, mainly of men. The majority of the population, even in North America, let alone globally (where the divide becomes a gaping abyss), has been fenced out from the world's most technologically advanced communication system. So in this area the struggle against enclosures cannot be construed as an attempt to preserve an already achieved state of commonality, but should rather be seen as a project of realizing a glimpsed but unfulfilled potential that marketization threatens to withdraw.

To say that commercialization menaces the potential for a more inclusive Net might seem perverse, for in many ways it has actually expanded connection rates. Throughout the 1990s, the aggressive marketing of ISP services and the prodigious advertising hype about the benefits of connection extended use went well beyond the boundaries of the highly educated or techno-savvy. But such market growth occurred most rapidly among the affluent—the potential e-shoppers, online information subscribers, the pay per use gamers, or Web TV watchers most eagerly targeted by virtual capital. For lower income sectors, the price of computers and connections remained a major barrier to Net access, while deregulated carrier companies had little or no incentive to lay massively expensive infrastructures to the neighborhoods of the urban poor or too sparse and scattered rural communities.

Opposition to this situation produced a host of access movements and initiatives, attempting to lower costs of connection, fighting corporate "redlining" of unprofitable communities. In 1993 a coalition called the Telecommunications Policy Roundtable (TPR), including Computer Professionals for Social Responsibility, the American Libraries Association, the Electronic Frontier Foundation, the Centre for Media Education, the National Writers

Union, and some sixty other groups formed around issues addressing corporate colonization of the Net. It adopted a set of principles urging creation of a network based on universality of access. This was defined not only in terms of availability of connections (with full service to homes, workplaces, and community centers), but also of low pricing, the provision of subsidized hardware, software, and training, and enabling all users to act not just as consumers but as producers with "the option to generate new information as well as publish that information through the network." While TPR conceded commercial interests a major role in the construction of the networks, it insisted on preservation of "diversity of content."[69] A central aspect of any information infrastructure would be the development of a "vital civic sector," constituting "public spaces" for discussion, governmental interaction, distribution of free software, and "the spontaneous development of communities of all kinds" among "groups . . . of people who want to discuss issues concerning their neighborhood, worksite, nation or planet."[70]

According to Pat Aufderheide, the activities of TPR and other public interest groups played an important role in policy debates over the "information highway" as a counterforce against the dominant corporate interests.[71] Their influence was reflected in the Clinton-Gore administration's decision to make the digital divide one of its top social policy issues. From 1995 onwards the U.S. government's National Telecommunications and Information Administration produced a series of studies showing the digital exclusion of a significant sector of the population—rural dwellers, low-income groups, and Blacks and Hispanics. While overall access rates were increasing, the disproportional concentration of growth among the wealthy meant that the digital divide between the highest and lowest income groups was actually widening.[72]

One of the concrete results of this policy direction was the introduction of the "e-rate," a federal program that helped connect schools and libraries in low income areas to the Internet by subsidizing start-up costs and discounting telecommunications rates. This measure, which has been described as "the only major public interest provision of the 1996 Telecommunications Act" became the focus of protracted battle, as telephone companies such as AT&T and Bell Atlantic, aghast at lost revenue and fearing it was the thin edge of further regulatory requirements, lobbied to roll back the e-rate, while organizations of librarians and teachers fought to hold it in place.[73] At the same time, the Telecommunication and Information Infrastructures program has since 1994 directed substantial funds to nonprofit and community organizations. The combination of federal funding with grassroots organizations, neighborhood networks, and community access centers has in fact constituted a set of digital public works that is in some ways reminiscent of aspects of the 1930s New Deal policies. In 2000 the Clinton administration reinforced this policy with the "click start" program, allocating vouchers to assist computer purchases by poor families with children.[74]

Such policies have obviously not prevented corporate sector hegemoniz-ing network development, and indeed they are (except for the "e-rate" pro-vision) very agreeable to e-capital, which has no objection to having its po-tential consumer base enlarged providing someone else pays for it. Critics have condemned the "click start" program for subsidizing sales by large com-puter firms, while ignoring the issues of online public service content.[75] Pro-grams to extend broadband connections to low income groups have also drawn fire for giving subsidies to telecommunications carriers rather than di-rectly to citizens or communities.

On the other side of the political spectrum, neoliberals deny the need for any government intervention to address digital divide issues, claiming that the prob-lem will be met by a market-driven reduction in computer and communication costs. Their criticism has been bolstered by the latest NTIA figures on access rates, which show a very sharp leap in the last year—from 26.2 of households with from-home Internet access in December 1998 to 41.5 percent in August 2000.[76] However, even if one accepts the validity of these dramatic figures, which are at odds with other surveys, it is apparent that there remain massive discrepancies across classes, with 77 percent of households with incomes over $75,000 having from-home access, compared with only 34 percent of those making between $25,000 and $35,000 and 12.7 percent of those with annual in-comes of less than $15,000.[77] In the light of these persisting class divisions, there is evidently a continuing need for social and community groups to fight for public programs that, however partially, counteract the extremes of e-stratifica-tion generated by a pure digital market.

At the same time, however, e-access activists have become increasingly aware that the mere quantitative count of individuals and households con-nected to the Net obscures important qualitative issues about what people are being connected to. These concerns have increasingly focused around another "commons" issue—that of "common carriage." Common carriage is a principle of telecommunications regulation that asserts ownership of com-munication channels should be separated from control of the content trans-mitted through those channels. The aim is to prevent companies that control the wired or wireless connections to a system from monopolistically dis-criminating in favor of their own informational products, or against those of competitors or critics. In the United States, preservation of "open access" has become the focus of political mobilizations. Alliances of public interest groups and media activists are fighting on a city-by-city basis for "open ac-cess" requirements to be included in cable franchise agreements. At the time of this writing, these coalitions have won one success—in Portland, Ore-gon—that is being contested in court by AT&T. Other municipal decisions are pending; and a coalition including the Center for Media Education, Com-puter Professionals for Social Responsibility, the Consumer Federation of America, and the Consumers Union are pressing for national level regulatory action. The outcome of these initiatives remains uncertain. But both "universal access" and "open access" movements are critical components of defiance against digital enclosures. All these contest information capital's tendency to stratify and fragment the Net according to its classificatory logic of demographic tiring and exclusion, and attempt to compel it to realize the rhetoric of "universal" connection to which its advertising propaganda shamelessly appeals.

Cyberactivism and Hacktivism

Ultimately, however, contesting Net enclosure involves not just software design, intellectual property, and network architecture, but also, and crucially, issues of content—of what kinds of communication, shaped by whose interests, and shared amongst what publics will be circulated within it. This brings us to the most explicitly politicized head of the oppositional hydra, that which bears the name "cyberactivism."

The Net has been intrinsic to the worldwide expansion and intensification of market relations euphemistically referred to as "globalization." Whoever today says "globalization" says also "communication," for the emergence of this new world order depends on nomadic corporate maneuver, the deterritorialization of capital from old centers to new zones of investment, and the systematic subversion of national sovereignty by the electronic flows of transnational financial markets—all of which would be unthinkable without telecommunications and computer networks. It is at this point that the issue of cyberspatial enclosure reencounters that of terrestrial enclosures. For despite its high-tech sheen, seen in planetary scope, and especially in the developing world, the activities of twenty-first-century business seem like nothing so much as an accelerated and expanded recapitulation of the brutal logic of original accumulation. The "old" enclosures have never stopped. Dispossession of peasants and subsistence dwellers is an ongoing capitalist process, a distant memory in Europe and North America, but a contemporary reality in Latin America, Asia, and Africa, where the eviction of farming or tribal land dwellers by modern agribusiness contributes to the creation of a vast Third World proletariat flooding into shanty towns and sweatshops and brothels from Guatemala City to Bangkok to Lagos. And there is a connection between the new, digital enclosures and the continuation of the old, terrestrial ones. For the reach and speed of global communication is vital to an intensification and expansion of the world market, today known as "globalization," that lies behind so many of today's land wars, in India, Nigeria, or Mexico.[78]

The Midnight Notes Collective, for example, describes this process of corporate globalization as a Pentagon of Enclosures, involving five processes: first, ending communal control of the means of subsistence (capitalizing land ownership and agricultural production in Asia, Africa, and Latin America); second, seizing land for debt (making such "reforms" a precondition for countries seeking loan relief from the IMF and World Bank); third, the creation of a new mobile and migrant proletariat, based on the dispossession of peasants and indigenous people; fourth, the destruction of state socialism in Russia, China, and elsewhere; and fifth, new ecological predations, from hazardous waste storage to biotechnological reappropriation. There is, as we have seen, one more point to add to this infernal diagram, making it a malign hexagram: the enclosure of the means of information by corporate media empires, making the dislocation and suffering caused by the other five aspects of enclosure invisible and incommunicable.[79]

This process has, however, generated its own opposition. If resistance to enclosures in cyberspace is hydra headed, its terrestrial equivalents have been doubly or triply so, involving a truly motley array of labor groups, environmentalists, social justice groups, antisweatshop activists, indigenous peoples movements, and cultural diversity defenders mobilized by a shared rejection of a corporate monoculture and market-driven race to the bottom degradation of wages, working conditions, and environment. Appearing first as a series of sporadic and localized neighborhoods of survival and communities of resistance, these struggles are generating a series of connections, contacts, coalitions, and networks of cooperation. As Peter Waterman points out, these movements appear to have "no international headquarters, no organization, . . . no obvious terrain of battle," but "alternatively, one could say that they have many headquarters, many organizations—and many terrains, forms and levels of struggle."[80] Such insurgencies are characterized by their opponents as antiglobalization movements. But though some are driven by nationalisms, fundamentalisms, and other localized protectionisms, many others see themselves rather as part of what they variously call "a new internationalism," "alternative globalization," "globalization from below," or "the other globalization"—a movement that embraces transnational trade and cultural intercourse, but within a framework that respects labor, social and environmental standards, and cultural heterogeneity.[81]

Paradoxically this process has proceeded by means of the very worldwide communications system formed to facilitate the operations of the market. The use of the Net to create what Harry Cleaver has termed an "electronic fabric of struggle" has been a signal feature of the movements against neoliberalism in the 1990s.[82,83] Even a rapid survey reveals a remarkably wide variety of green, feminist, social justice organizations, adbusters, culture jammers, and trade unions using the Internet to bypass the filters of the information industries, speed internal communication, send out "action alerts," and connect with potential allies. Major activist Web sites such as Z-Net, A-Infos, or McSpotlight are now central resources for counterinformation—the antiportals of the new movements against corporate power.

This making of an electronic fabric of struggles has interwoven in complex ways with the struggles over the making of the electronic fabric—the universal and open and access movements we have already described. Thus cyber-organizing has included the construction of independent networks that inter-face with the Internet but are entirely devoted to social activism, like the Association for Progressive Communications, which arose in the mid-1980s from the coalition of Peace-Net, Eco-Net, and Conflict-Net and now constitutes a global computer system dedicated to peace, human rights, labor, and environmental issues. Although, like all Net exchange, cyberactivism is heavily concentrated within the communication hubs of the developed world, it has also in some re-markable instances created truly world-spanning connections.

Take, for example, the "Battle of Seattle," the five-day confrontation in De-cember 1999 between the World Trade Organization and the forces of "al-ternative globalization." While protesters contested control of the streets with police under martial law conditions, in cyberspace the forces of dissent were "far more savvy and net organized than their opponents." The WTO Civil Society site, for example, offered a daily calendar of events, online chat rooms, briefing on trade issues broken down by economic sectors, and live video links to events. Seattle also saw the use of "hacktivism." WTO oppo-nents using the name "the electrohippies collective" hosted a "virtual sit-in" to jam the WTO's Internet servers, while other activists constructed a bogus WTO site—www.gatt.org rather than www.wto.org—mimicking its logos and typeface, but announcing "The WTO's purpose is to broaden and en-force their will against democratic governments" and including links to other groups opposed to the talks.[84] This type of practice had been pioneered in the Electronic Disturbance Theatre in 1998, when activists supporting the Zapatista movement organized the "flooding" of the Mexican government's Web sites.[85] Similar tactics had also been used by Strano Network to organize a "netstrike" against the French government in 1995 to protest its economic and nuclear weapons testing policies. Since the Seattle protest, the electro-hippies and/or EDT have used it in protests against genetically modified foods, targeting the U.S. Department of Agriculture, against the FBI, and against the White House in protest of economic sanctions and air strikes against Iraq.

For the organizers of these events, they are cyberspatial equivalents of ter-restrial civil disobedience—manifestations that depend for their legitimacy on the mass nature of the protest. (EDT estimates 10,000 people from all around the world participated in their digital support of the Zapatistas.)[86] The spectrum of hacktivism also, however, includes more individual hacking feats, involving the penetration, defacement, alteration, or disruption of the Internet sites of political opponents: Actions of this type were launched against the Web sites of the Indonesian government, protesting its occupa-tion of East Timor and against Indian nuclear agencies for the weapons tests.

There also was a series of hacking feats by Chinese dissidents and the hacker group the Cult of the Dead Cow against the Chinese government's violation of human rights.

Hacktivism is controversial within social movements. While some see it as a logical and legitimate extension into virtual realms of tactics already accepted "on the ground," others fear that it will be seen as a cyber-vandalism that discredits the causes it is associated with, or that it will provoke and legitimate responses that jeopardize the prospects of using cyberspace for organizing and circulating information. [87] Such a response could take the form of official "law and order" crackdown, of the sort that now appears in train following the anticommerce "denial of service" attacks we discussed earlier. It could also take the form of clandestine and anonymous attacks and counterattacks between "red" and "white" hacktivists and counter-hacktivists disrupting each others' sites in spiraling escalations—a pattern that already began to emerge in conflicts around East Timor.

It seems likely that computer-networking will continue to be crucial to new antienclosure combinations. Cyberspace is important as a political arena, not, as some postmodern theorists suggest, because it is a sphere where virtual conflicts replace struggles "on the ground," but because it is a medium within which terrestrial struggles can be made visible to and linked with one another. The sharing of lists-serves and discussion groups by labor, environmental, feminist, and indigenous groups implicitly asserts these movements' interconnections even while participants may still be searching for the explicit formulation of the political basis for such links. In combination with other autonomous media, such networks provide a channel within which a multiplicity of oppositional forces, diverse in goals, varied in constituency, specific in organization, can, through dialogue, criticism, and debate, discover a new mode of autonomy and alliance that does not depend on the directives of a vanguard party, but rather arises out of the transverse, transnational connections. In this sense, cyberspace is a potentially recompositional space in which the atomization that information capital inflicts on socialized labor can be counteracted. [88]

E-capital may contain hackers, pirates, and open-source activists and even harness them to new business models, as long as such transgressions remain disconnected from more mundane social movements. But the surge of cyberactivism and hacktivism shows the networks on which e-capital relies for the lightning fast circulation of commodities are not only vulnerable to disruption, but can also circulate the struggles protesting the unequal allocation not just of digital but physical goods—food, water, housing, medicine, a clean environment. And in these struggles, reflexively, the organization of the Net, its architecture, its software and carrier regimes, themselves increasingly becoming a target of critique and mobilization amongst groups seeking more generous, just, and common resource distribution than those of the world market.

HERCULES.COM VERSUS THE SERPENT

In its short history, the Net has become the terrain and the prize in a series of complex, fast moving contestations. Moving from the military system of the 1970s, to the academic network of the 1980s, to the populist virtual community of the early 1990s, to the drive to e-business, it has developed in a rapid sequence of appropriations and reappropriations. Today, it is an arena where e-capital's attempted enclosures tangle untidily with a molecular proliferation of activists, cyber-creators, and hackers whose projects are characterized both by a diverse singularity of interests and by a common rejection of the dominant lines of digital commodification.

What will be the outcome?[89] Let us consider three predictions. One is liberal coexistence. Paul Starr, writing on the "electronic commons," concedes that "the big corporate media will almost certainly dominate mass entertainment and commerce on the Web," but argues that the continuing stream of digital creation by individuals, nonprofit organizations, and publicly funded agencies (universities, libraries) ensures a growing repository of uncommodified, socially useful information.[90] Even commercial interests will contribute by offering free content and software to attract eyeballs to advertisements and future customers for services and new versions. This expanding commons—the "new public works"—will constitute a "broad expanse" of "information and communication available for free or at minimal cost." Why should the influx of e-commercialization harm the kind of public and nonprofit functions the Net is serving, Starr asks, since "there will be still an electronic commons, and it won't be hard to get to."[91]

But there is every reason to expect that Starr's "new public works" will rapidly become the target of profit-driven encroachment. This is the second scenario, generally foreseen by neo-Marxist political economists. Edward Herman and Robert McChesney, for example, while admitting there will always be a penumbra of "alternative" activities on the Net, predict these will be displaced by an increasingly central corporate presence, whose deep pockets, brand recognition, and control over crucial navigation tools garner the vast majority of Web traffic.[92] Their vision of enclosure is that of a "web within the Web" where "the large scale media firm websites and some other fortunate content producers are assured recognition and audiences, and less well endowed websites drift off to the margins." The Net will resemble not so much broadcast radio or television, with a limited number of channels, but magazine or book publishing. Assuming no explicit state censorship, anyone can publish, "but the right to do so means little without distribution, resources and publicity." Marginalized areas will continue to be a "vital tool for political organizing," but the Net's "dominant trajectory" will be "as a commercially driven entertainment vehicle."[93] In this view, most of the alternative social and political hopes associated with the digital world will reveal themselves as chimerical once the corporate world overcomes it uncertainties, passes through a phase of experimentation, and perfects its techniques of e-accumulation. And this perspective, while articulated from a critical position, probably precisely mirrors the hopes and expectations of most e-capitalists. But there is also a third possibility. In an audacious departure from Marxian gloom, Richard Barbrook has recently argued that the logic of "enclosure" is actually being defeated by the counterforces of "disclosure." While the official ideology of post–Cold War North America is a triumphal celebration of the free market, millions of its inhabitants in their daily practice are pragmatically apolitically creating "cyber-communism." They are "engaged in the slow process of superseding capitalism" by the circulation of free music, films, games, and information.[94] Ease of digital reproduction is warping and blasting holes in the fabric of intellectual property, through the perpetual value-hemorrhage of piracy and a plethora of open-source activity that makes obvious the inadequacy of private property to the conditions of digital production.[95] In the ultimate contradiction between forces and relations of production, the makers of e-commerce have created an infrastructure for the free circulation of decommodified e-goods: "dot.com" is generating "dot.Communism."[96]

Barbrook's dialectic may strain credulity, but it would be wrong to discount it entirely. The e-commerce meltdown of 2000/2001, which saw the Nasdaq lose half its value in a year, shows that enclosing the Net is far from a done deal. The transformation of "dot.coms" to "dot.bombs" is customarily attributed to the delirium of e-entrepreneurs bemused by their own advertising hype. But behind this failure to realize wild expectations lie the hydra-like resistances and recalcitrancies we have described. Underlying the burnout of virtual capital are nagging fears the Net may actually be intractable to the commodity form: that people will buy in a networked environment where they are used to free experiences, or worried about hacking and privacy breaches; that profits will be sapped by piracy; that markets constrained by digital divides will not be large enough; that transnational expansion will be stalled by "backlash" against globalization. Such uncertainties are then magnified as a perverse result of the very capacities promoted by e-capital. One cause of e-commerce turbulence is the activity of millions of investors connected through online brokerages and day traders. Popular digital participation, inserted into a market framework, manifests as an intensification of individualistic speculation and competitive behavior. One side of this is the collective euphoria—an "irrational exuberance"—that has buoyed up high-tech markets. But the other is a panic capitalism, jittery, nervous, possessed by fears it cannot deliver on its promises, and that the system that seemed to have the planet in its hand holds only a bubble.

Such tremors may be the familiar shakeout in a cycle of business consolidation: No one should underestimate the recuperative resilience of capital.

But if the e-commerce project does seriously falter, it may, by default, open a space for their emergence of a counter-agenda for the Net, which melds the concerns of terrestrial and cyberspatial antienclosure activists. Elements of such an agenda already exist in manifestoes such as the "One Planet, One Net" statement of Computer Professionals for Social Responsibility; the Bellagio Declaration on intellectual property rights issued by cultural anthropologists, software creators, indigenous peoples movements, and antibiotech activists; and the statements on the "right to communicate" arising from international social movements.[97] But even more importantly, the components of such an incipient communication commons are, as we have seen, daily practiced by millions of people.

Some ingredients in such a "commons" project could be: reforms to Net governance to make it truly representative of the global populations it nominally serves; publicly funded, tax-supported national and international extensions of infrastructures and access provisions beyond the scope afforded by market priorities; revisions of intellectual property regimes giving greater recognition to collective processes of knowledge and culture formation and less to corporate ownership; the widespread adoption of nonproprietorial open-source software standards; and civic guarantees of bandwidth and resources to public sector and social movement groups to preserve and expand digital commons.

The Herculean power of e-capital, with its magic armaments and muscular bankrolls, is encircled by snaking, multiheaded, cyberspatial subversions. Hercules is destructive, decapitating, and cauterizing everything that escapes the boundaries of profit. But the power of creativity lies with the serpent, for the hydra is generative, multiplying options and possibilities outside the boundaries of the existent order, and renewing itself from apparently fatal wounds. Three hundred years ago, the array of proletarians, runaways, pirates, maroons, disaffected officers, and mutinous soldiers and sailors who revolted against the first enclosures were crushed. Today, somewhere at the meeting place of hackers, pirates, free software creators, coder collectives, universal and open-access campaigners, and cyberzapatas and guerrillas with hotmail, a new "commonism" may be born. Past struggles are enclosed in the finality of historical defeat, but the future, though not made under conditions of anyone's choosing, remains open.

NOTES

1. This chapter is deeply indebted to the work of my friend and colleague Dorothy Kidd, whose "Talking the Walk: The Communication Commons amidst the Media Enclosures," Ph.D. dissertation, Simon Fraser University, 1998, has colored my whole thinking about "enclosures" and "commons."

2. Raymond Williams, *Keywords: A Vocabulary of Culture and Society* (New York: Oxford University Press, 1976), 70–73; Dallas Smythe, *Dependency Road: Communications, Capitalism, Consciousness, and Canada* (Norwood, N.J.: Ablex, 1981); Vincent Mosco, *The Pay-Per-Society: Computers and Communication in the Information Age* (Toronto: Garamond, 1989); Herbert Schiller, *Culture Inc. The Corporate Takeover Public Expression* (New York: Oxford University Press, 1989).

3. Ronald V. Bettig, "The Enclosure of Cyberspace," *Critical Studies in Mass Communication* 14 (1997): 138–57; Harry Cleaver, "The 'Space' of Cyberspace: Review of Miller's 'Women and Children First: Gender and the Settling of the Electronic Frontier,'" *Women and Performance* 17 (1995), online at www.echonyc.com/~women/Issue17/; Donald Gutstein, *E.Con: How the Internet Undermines Democracy* (Toronto: Stoddart, 1999), 135–39; James Boyle, *Net Total: Law, Politics and Property in Cyberspace* (forthcoming), sections available online at www.law.duke.edu/boylesite/; and Marita Moll and Leslie Reagan Shade, eds., *E-Commerce vs E-Commons: Communications in the Public Interest* (Ottawa: Canadian Centre for Policy Alternatives, 2001).

4. Lester C. Thurow, "Needed: A New System of Intellectual Property Rights," *Harvard Business Review* (September–October 1997): 101.

5. Garret Hardin, "The Tragedy of the Commons," *Science* 162 (1965): 1343–48. See also Garret Hardin and John Baden, eds., *Managing the Commons* (San Francisco: W. H. Freeman, 1977). For free market treatment of the "tragedy," see George Gilder, *Telecosm: How Infinite Bandwidth Will Revolutionize Our World* (New York: Free Press, 2000).

6. Peter Linebaugh and Marcus Rediker, *The Many-Headed Hydra: Sailors, Slaves, Commoners, and the Hidden History of the Revolutionary Atlantic* (Boston: Beacon, 2000).

7. Sources for the section, in addition to those cited below, include Kidd; Linebaugh and Reddick; E. P. Thompson, *The Making of the English Working Class* (London: Gollancz, 1965); Robert Allen, *Enclosures and the Yeoman* (Oxford: Clarendon, 1992); J. M. Neesen, *Commoners, Common Right, Enclosures, and Social Change in England 1700–1820* (Cambridge: Cambridge University Press, 1993); Mathew Johnson, *An Archeology of Capitalism* (Cambridge: Blackwell, 1996).

8. Midnight Notes Collective, "The New Enclosures," *Midnight Oil: Work, Energy, War 1973–1992* (Brooklyn, N.Y.: Autonomedia, 1992), 318.

9. E. P. Thompson, *Customs in Common* (London: Merlin, 1991), 107.

10. See Michael Perelman, *The Invention of Capitalism: Classical Political Economy and the Secret History of Primitive Accumulation* (Durham, N.C.: Duke University Press, 2000).

11. On the relation of enclosures to witch-hunting, see Silvia Federici, *Caliban and the Witches* (New York: Autonomedia, 1997), and "The Great Witch Hunt of the Sixteenth Century," *Maine Scholar* 1, no. 1 (1988): 31–52; Jane Humphries, "Enclosures, Common Rights, and Women: The Proletarianization of Families in the Late Eighteenth and Early Nineteenth Centuries," *Journal of Economic History* 50, no. 1 (1990): 17–42; Anne Llewellyn, *Witchcraze: A New History of the European Witch Hunts* (San Francisco: Pandora, 1994).

12. Pete Linebaugh, *The London Hanged: Crime and Civil Society in the Eighteenth Century London* (London: Penguin, 1991), 184–218.

13. Linebaugh and Rediker, *The Many-Headed Hydra.*

14. Peter Childers and Paul Delany, "Wired World, Virtual Campus: Universities and the Political Economy of Cyberspace," *Works and Days* 23, no. 4 (Spring/Fall 1994): 61–78, online at www.sfu.ca/~delany/wkndays.htm. See also Michal Hauben, "The Social Forces behind the Development of Usenet News," *Amateur Computerist* 5, nos. 1/2 (1993): 13–21: and Bruce Sterling, "A Short History of the Internet," *Magazine of Fantasy & Science Fiction,* February 1993, n.p, and by Katie Hafner and Matthew Lyon, *When Wizards Stay Up Late: The Origins of the Internet* (New York: Simon and Schuster, 1996).

15. PBS "Life on the Internet Timeline," at www.pbs.org/internet/timeline/index.html.

16. Robert McChesney, "So Much for the Magic of Technology and the Free Market: The World Wide Web and the Corporate Media System," in *The World Wide Web and Contemporary Cultural Theory,* ed. Andrew Herman and Thomas Swiss (New York: Routledge, 2000), 29.

17. Roberto Verzola, "Cyberlords: The Rentier Class of the Information Sector," in Josephine Bosma et al., eds., *Readme! Filtered by Nettime: ASCII Culture and the Revenge of Knowledge* (New York: Autonomedia, 2000), 92.

18. K. Patelis, "The Political Economy of the Internet," Nettime, March 22, 1999, online at www.nettime.org/nettime.w3archive/199903/msg00061.

19. Bill Gates, *The Road Ahead* (New York: Norton, 1995), 171.

20. Peter Schwartz and Peter Leyden, "The Long Boom: A History of the Future 1980–2020," *Wired* (July 1997); John Browning and Spencer Reiss, "Encyclopedia of the New Economy," *Wired* (April 1998), online at www.hotwired.com/special/ene/.

21. Network Wizards <www.isc.org/ds/>. There are difficulties in comparing results for this, the most reputable of domain name surveys, across time because of changes in the survey methodology. The figures here have been adjusted according to the procedures recommended by Network Wizards.

22. Mathew Gray, online at www.mit.edu/people/mkgray/net/web-growth-summary.html.

23. Cited in Patelis.

24. Steve Lawrence and Lee Giles, "Accessibility of Information on the Web," *Nature* 400 (1999): 107–9.

25. Sources for this section include Andrew Ross, "Hacking Away at the Counterculture," in *Technoculture,* ed. Constance Penley and Andrew Ross (Minneapolis: University of Minnesota, 1991), 107–34; B. Clough and P. Mungo, *Approaching Zero: Data Crime and the Computer Underworld* (London: Faber & Faber, 1992); K. Hafner and J. Markoff, *Cyberpunk: Outlaws and Hackers on the Computer Frontier* (London: Fourth Estate, 1991); Geoffrey Sauer Hackers, "Order and Control," *Bad Subjects* 24 (1996), online at www.eserver.org/bs/24/sauer.html; Paul A. Taylor, *Hackers: Crime in the Digital Sublime* (London: Routledge, 1999).

26. *The New Hackers Dictionary,* 1994, online at www.tuxedo.org/~esr/jargon/.

27. Stephen Levy, *Hackers: Unsung Heroes of the Computer Revolution* (Garden City, N.Y.: Anchor Press/Doubleday, 1984).

28. *The New Hackers Dictionary.*

29. Dorothy E. Denning, "Concerning Hackers Who Break into Computer Systems." Proceedings of the thirteenth National Computer Security Conference, Wash-

ington, D.C., October 1990, 653–64. Online at www.cs.georgetown.edu/~denning/hackers/Hackers-NCSC.txt.

30. Dorothy E. Denning, "Postscript to Concerning Hackers Who Break into Computer Systems," June 11, 1995, online at www.cs.georgetown.edu/~denning/hackers/Hackers-Postscript.txt.

31. Bruce Sterling, *The Hacker Crackdown: Law and Order on the Electronic Frontier* (New York: Bantam Books, 1993). For an account of comparable operations in Europe, see Peter Ludlow, "The Italian Hacker Crackdown," in *High Noon on the Electronic Frontier: Conceptual Issues in Cyberspace*, ed. Peter Ludlow (Cambridge, Mass.: MIT Press, 1996), 487–506.

32. Ernst and Young, "Information Week's Fourth Annual: Information Security Survey," October 21, 1996, online at www.info-sec.com/internet/infoseed.html-ssi.

33. CERT/CC Statistics 1988–2000. Online at www.cert.org/stats/. Accessed April 12, 2000.

34. Dorothy Denning, "Hacktivism: An Emerging Threat to Diplomacy," *American Foreign Service Association*, 1, online at www.afsa.org/fsj/sep00/Denning.html.

35. Linebaugh and Rediker, 162–72.

36. Quoted in Lesley Ellen Harris, *Digital Property: Currency of the Twenty-first Century* (Toronto: McGraw-Hill, Ryerson 1998), 162.

37. As Nicholas Garnham observes in *Capitalism and Communication*, there is a contradiction at the heart of the communication commodity, arising from media business's need to simultaneously maximize and restrict distribution. On the one hand, they want to sell as much as they can. Therefore they increase the speed and efficiency of communication methods to reach more people, more of the time, in more and more various ways. But on the other hand, media corporations want to *sell* as much as they can; they are interested not just in getting out messages, but in getting back money. So they confront a paradoxical requirement to expand and restrict communication at the same time—simultaneously creating plenty and imposing scarcity.

38. Software & Information Industry Association, online at www.siia.net/piracy/default.asp; Business Software Alliance online at www.bsa.org/.

39. David Tetzalf, "Yo-Ho-Ho and a Server of Warez: Internet Software Piracy and the New Global Information Economy," in *The World Wide Web and Contemporary Cultural Theory*, ed. Andrew Herman and Thomas Swiss (New York: Routledge, 2000), 77–99.

40. David McCandless, "Warez Wars," *Wired* 5.04 (1997): 134. Online at www.wirednews.com/wired/archive/5.04/ff_warez.html.

41. McCandless, 178.

42. McCandless, 177.

43. McCandless, 136.

44. McCandless, 175.

45. In the United States, pirate bulletin board became a target of the FBI. January of 1997 saw operation "Cyber Strike" in which FBI agents seized computers, hard drives, and modems in California and half a dozen other states. Corporations involved in the operation included Sega and Sony. McCandless, 178.

46. IDSA, 23.

47. *The Economist*, "Intellectual Property: Bazaar Software," March 8, 1997, available from www.economist.com/archive/view.cgi.

48. *The Economist*, March 8, 1997, available from www.economist.com/archive/view.cgi.

49. The UCLA Online Institute for Cyberspace Law and Policy, online at www.gseis.ucla.edu/iclp/hr2265.html.

50. UCLA Online Institute, online at www.gseis.ucla.edu/iclp/dmca1.htm.

51. Tetzalf, 111.

52. Tetzalf, 111.

53. Tetzalf, 122.

54. Herbert Schiller, "The Information Superhighway: Paving over the Public," *Z Magazine* (March 1994): 46–50. The classic work on this topic is Robert McChesney's study of how early days of populist radio experimentation in the United States were extinguished by commercial interests, *Telecommunications, Mass Media, and Democracy: The Battle for the Control of U.S. Broadcasting* (New York: Oxford University Press, 1993).

55. McKenzie Wark, *Virtual Geography: Living with Global Media Events* (Bloomington: Indiana University Press, 1994).

56. McCandless, 178.

57. For enunciations of this doctrine see K. Kelly, "New Rules for the New Economy: Twelve Dependable Principles for Thriving in a Turbulent World," *Wired* 5, no. 9 (September 1997): 140–44, 186–97; John Perry Barlow, "The Economy of Ideas," *Wired* 2, no. 3 (1994), online at www.wired.com/wired/archive/2.03/economy.ideas_pr.html.

58. Richard Barbrook, "Cyber-Communism: How the Americans are Superseding Capitalism in Cyberspace," Hypermedia Research Centre, University of Westminster, London, 1999, online at www.hrc.wmin.ac.uk.

59. Nathan Newman, "Storming the Gates," *American Prospect* 11, no. 10 (2000), online at www.prospect.org/archives/V11-10/newman-n.html. For in-depth examination of open source see Andrew Leonard's book in progress on the topic, at *Salon* <http://salon.com/tech/fsp/about/index.html>, and Eben Moglen, "Anarchism Triumphant: Free Software and the Death of Copyright," *First Monday* 4, no. 8 (1999) <http://firstmonday.org/issues/issue4_8/moglen/index.html#author>.

60. Free Software Foundation, "The GNU Manifesto," online at www.gnu.org/gnu/manifesto.html.

61. Free Software Foundation, "The GNU Manifesto."

62. Stephen Shankland, "Linux Sales Surge Past Competitors," CNET News.com, February 9, 2000, online at www.canada.cnet.com/news//0-1003-200-1546430.html.

63. Nathan Newman, "Storming the Gates."

64. Bryan Pfaffenberger, "In Seattle's Aftermath: Linux, Independent Media, and the Survival of Democracy," *Linux Journal*, December 13, 1999, online at www2.linuxjournal.com/articles/currents/013.html.

65. Eric S. Raymond, *The Cathedral and the Bazaar: Musings on Linux and Open Source by an Accidental Revolutionary* (Sebastapol, Calif.: O'Reilly, 1999), 37.

66. Garret Hardin, "The Tragedy of the Commons."

67. Jim Davis, e-mail to the author, June 11, 1994.

68. Jim Davis, e-mail to the author, June 11, 1994.

69. Computer Professionals for Social Responsibility, "A Public Interest Vision," October 13, 1997, online at www.cpsr.org/cpsr/nii_policy.

70. Computer Professionals for Social Responsibility, "A Public Interest Vision."

71. Pat Aufderheide, *Communications Policy and the Public Interest: The Telecommunications Policy of 1996* (New York: Guilford Press, 1999), 237–38.

72. U.S. Department of Commerce, National Telecommunications and Information Administration: "Falling through the Net: A Survey of the 'Have Nots' in Rural and Urban America," 1995; "Falling through the Net II: New Data on the Digital Divide," 1998; "Falling through the Net: Defining the Digital Divide," 1999. These reports are available online at www.ntia.doc.gov/ntiahome/digitaldivide/.

73. Jeff Chester, cited in Nicholas Confessore, "Boon or Boondoggle: The E-Rate Subsidy," *Salon*, December 16 1998, www.salonmag.com/21st/feature/1998/12/16feature.html. See also on the e-rate, Redmond K. Molz and Phyllis Dain, *Civic Space/Cyberspace: The American Public Library in the Information Age* (Cambridge, Mass.: MIT Press, 1999).

74. Dibya Sakar, "Communities Split Millions to Fight Divide," FW.Com, online at www.fwcom/print.asp. Accessed September 29, 2000.

75. See Todd Oppenheimer, "Greedy Clicks," *Salon*, February 2, 2000, online at www.salon.com/news/features/2000/02/02/digital, and the reply by Daryl Lindsey, "Opportunity Clicks," *Salon*, February 11, 2000, online at www.salon.com/news/feature/2000/02/11/clickstart.

76. U.S. Department of Commerce, National Telecommunications and Information Administration, "Falling through the Net: Toward Digital Inclusion," 2000, online at www.ntia.doc.gov/ntiahome/digitaldivide/.

77. NTIA, 2000. For some conflicting estimates of the current divide see Dibya Sakar, "More Low-income People Discover the Net," FCW.com, online at www.fcw.com/civic/articles/2000/oct> February 2, 2000, and CNN.com, "Consumer Groups Say 'Digital Divide' Puts Millions in US at Disadvantage," online at www.cn.com/2000/TECH/computing/10/11/digital.divide.

78. George Caffentzis and Silva Federici, "Modern Land Wars and the Myth of the High-Tech Economy," in *The World Transformed: Gender, Labour and International Solidarity in the Era of Free Trade, Structural Adjustment and GATT*, ed. Cindy Duffy and Craig Benjamin (Guelph, Ontario: RhiZone, 1994), 131–45.

79. Midnight Notes Collective, 321–24.

80. Peter Waterman, "International Labour Communication by Computer: The Fifth International?" Working Paper Series 129. The Hague: Institute of Social Studies, 1992, 47. Online at http://antenna.nl/~waterman/Pages/peters/fifth.htm.

81. Eric Lee, *The Labour Movement and the Internet: The New Internationalism* (London: Pluto Press, 1997); Jeremy Brecher and Tim Costello, *Global Village or Global Pillage* (Boston: South End, 1994); Tony Dowmunt, "An Alternative Globalization: Youthful Resistance to Electronic Empires," in *Electronic Empires: Global Media and Local Resistance,* ed. Daya Kishan Thussu (London: Arnold, 1998), 243–56; Nick Dyer-Witheford, *Cyber-Marx: Cycles and Circuits of Struggle in High-Technology Capitalism* (Urbana: University of Illinois Press, 1999).

82. Harry Cleaver, "The Chiapas Uprising," *Studies in Political Economy* 44 (1994): 15, online at www.eco.utexas.edu/faculty/Cleaver/zapsincyber.html.

83. See Harry Cleaver, "The Zapatistas and the International Circulation of Struggle: Lessons Suggested and Problems Raised," 1998. Online at www.eco.texas.edu/Homepages/Faculty/Cleaver/lessons.html; "Computer-linked Social Movements and

the Global Threat to Capitalism," 1999, online at www.eco.utexas.edu/Homepages/ Faculty/Cleaver/polnet.html; Lauren Langeman, Douglas Morris, Jackie Zalewski, Emily Ignacio, and Carl Davidson, "Globalization, Domination and Cyberactivism." Paper for Internet research 1.0. The State of the Interdisciplines. The First Conference Association of Internet researchers, September 14–17, 2000. University of Kansas, Lawrence; Naomi Kleine, "The Vision Thing," *The Nation*, June 27, 2000.

84. Mark Stevenson, "'Electrohippies' Trying to Jam WTO's Web Server," *National Post*, December 2, 1999, B2. Information in this section also from David Cassell, "Hacktivism: Taking It off the Streets, Protestors Are Acting up Online," *San Francisco Life*, April 12, 2000. Online at www.sfbg.com/SFLife/34/28/lead.html; and Dorothy Denning, "Activism, Hacktivism, and Cyberterrorism: The Internet as a Tool for Influencing Foreign Policy," Internet and International Systems: Information Technology and American Foreign Policy Decisionmaking Workshop <www.nautilis.org/info-policy/workshop/papers/denning.html>.

85. Stefan Wray, "The Electronic Disturbance Theater and Electronic Civil Disobedience," June 17, 1998, online at www.thing.net/~rdom/ecd/EDTECD.html.

86. The Electrohippies Collective. Occasional paper no. 1. "Client-Side Distributed Denial of Service: Valid Campaign or Terrorist Act?" February 2000, online at www.gn.apc.org/pmhp/ehippies/files/op1.htm; Stefan Wray, "Virtual Luddite Resistance: Weaving a World Wide Web of Electronic Civil Disobedience," April 7, 1998, online at www.gn.apc.org/pmhp/dc/activism/swray.htm.

87. Brendan I. Koerner, "To Heck with Hacktivism," *Salon,* July 20, 2000, online at http://salon.com/tech/feature/2000/07/20/hacktivism/index.html; Oxblood Ruffin, "The Cult of the Dead Cow's Response to Client-side Distributed Denial-of-Service: Valid Campaign Tactic or Terrorist Act?" online at www.gn.apc.org/pmhp/ehippies/files/op1-cdc.htm; Reinhold Grether, "How the Etoy Campaign Was Won," *Telepolis*, February 26, 2000, online at www.heise.de/tp/english/inhalt/te/5843/1.html.

88. For the claim that cyber-struggles displace street-level activism see Mark Poster, *The Mode of Information: Poststructuralism and Social Context* (Chicago: University of Chicago, 1990), 154.

89. Marita Moll and Leslie Reagan Shade, eds., *E-Commerce vs E-Commons: Communications in the Public Interest* (Ottawa: Canadian Centre for Policy Alternatives, 2001).

90. Paul Starr, "The Electronic Commons," *American Prospect* 11, no. 10 (2000). Online at www.prospect.org/archives/V11-10/starr-p.html.

91. Starr, "The Electronic Commons."

92. Edward Herman and Robert McChesney, *The Global Media: The New Missionaries of Corporate Capitalism* (London: Cassell, 1997). See also Dan Schiller, *Digital Capitalism*.

93. Herman and McChesney, 124–25.

94. Richard Barbrook, "Cyber-Communism: How the Americans Are Superseding Capitalism in Cyberspace," Hypermedia Research Centre, University of Westminster, London, online at www.hrc.wmin.ac.uk.

95. Barbrook, "Cyber-Communism."

96. Barbrook, "Cyber-Communism."

97. Computer Professionals, "One Planet, One Net: Principles for the Internet Era," December 8, 1999, online at www.cpsr.org/program/nii/onenet. On the right to communicate see Declaration of the New Delhi Symposium on New Technologies and the Democratisation of Audiovisual Communication, New Delhi, February 12, 1994, at www.videazimut.org/e/about/index.html; on the Bellagio Declaration see James Boyle, *Shamans, Software, and Spleens : Law and the Construction of the Information Society* (Cambridge, Mass.: Harvard University Press, 1996).

8

Convergence Policy: It's Not What You Dance, It's the Way You Dance It

Marcus Breen

Internet policy: oxymoron. Together the two words "internet policy" meet the terms of a definition of an oxymoron in contemporary societies where so much effort goes into claiming less government. "Internet policy: oxymoron" is especially the case at the nexus where new technology meets government and the government's stated objectives defined by the term "public interest." Indeed, in the bright new world of high technology, where human ingenuity and commerce collide, any suggestion that government has a role in the nature of things is tantamount to a declaration of war. Furthermore, any suggestion that intervention by government and its agencies should become part of what in the United States is known as public policy is given scant regard. People who argue this way believe strongly in keeping government and its policies out of private life and as far away from commerce as possible. The apparent threat of policy action by government is a significant part of a mythology that extends a well-established antigovernment political tradition. Not surprisingly, this tradition was reborn when the Internet arrived as a communications medium in the mid-1990s (Wills 1999).

Elsewhere, policy is considered the necessary first order responsibility of democratic organization and the public interest (Melody 1997). Ground rules must be set, frameworks constructed, laws and regulations must be made, written, legislated, altered, and discussed. Protagonists line up on either side of the policy battlefield, ready to argue for more or less policy, depending on any number of determinants. Confusing the matter is that unlike real, conventional warfare the battlefields are multiple, often differentiated by personal and professional interests and forces, legacies of technological expansion and associated economic growth and regulation.

In the resulting skirmishes, no Napoleon will be emerging to stand high above the battlefield to survey the troops and with one brilliant insight render the victory for his side. This war is a combination of the big meltdown and guerrilla fighters in the undergrowth, their AK-47s rat-a-tatting from unanticipated hiding places before they melt away leaving the dead and wounded behind. Big bombs may win the battle but not the war.

As if to add insult to injury, the Internet brings with it new economic opportunities that involve wealth-creating mechanisms that redefine the possibilities for democracy, while establishing new financial elites. Public policy operates here as well, in the struggle over resources in society: Who gets what? (Turow 1999). This is a battle as old as the dismal science (economics) itself. Adam Smith made it clear in his definitive eighteenth-century study *The Wealth of Nations* that the regulation of markets was the primary, disputed feature of the capitalist enterprise. Karl Marx argued somewhat later in his definitive study *Capital* that the struggle over who had the wealth in the first place went to the foundations of the structure of society and the realization of human ambition. Two different views, two traditions of thought that feed into current thinking on how public policy and the Internet are linked. The tradition arguing for a move away from government being involved in the freedom of individuals to seek rents at whatever cost to others (Smith) and the argument in favor of remaking society along lines that reflect egalitarian principles of freedom from the tyranny of the great monetary power and influence (Marx) are still being played out. Smithian principles in the Internet policy world argue for freedom from government regulation so that the market itself can determine the way resources are allocated in society, free from constraints.[1] Marxian principles argue for a world where the combination of capital creation with the release of human ingenuity generates wealth for all owing to shared societal goals, or what might be termed policy goals. In the latter case, from the market perspective, it is possible to see governmental policy settings as social and economic constraints on the market. However, they are best characterized as tools for use in directing the outcomes of the society towards meeting citizens' needs.

Attentive readers may hesitate to accept my assumptions about the role of Marxian construction in policy. Yet it is in the arguments over how policy comes about that issues such as the structure and order or social and economic relations in society are best understood. And traditions of thought, theory, and practice in the field of social reform and governance, for the purposes of this discussion, can be traced to progressive political traditions characterized as Marxian. In the U.S. tradition they can also be traced to institutional economics—particularly the work of Thorstein Veblen, who argued for a set of governmental institutions that would intervene in the biased activities of business interests (1958). From a critical perspective, policy making seeks to match a complex set of considerations about government and society with economic and social outcomes. This normative tradition begins with the high-level objective of enhancing participatory democratic institutions and processes within society. Of course, there is a struggle over agreeing on the normative approach: Is it more or less government? Is it bigger or smaller institutions that implement the government's political aims? Should more or less information be available to citizens, based on the assumption that all individuals can make correct and informed choices? Would such information help society achieve its objectives of helping citizens realize their economic and social potential? And so on.

These are political questions about which there is always a dialogue in society. In many cases the outcomes are more in line with the analogy used above—a state of "war," as the struggle over the ideas about the structure of society is fought over by different groups and their politicians[2] (Turow 1997).

How then can Internet policy be imagined? This chapter considers the forces that have been unleashed in this multisited "war" and reflects on the structure of industrial relations that telecommunications has ushered in with the Internet, identifying the vectors that make up the various forces that contest for the space of public and private life in advanced societies. As those forces contend, they shed light on differing philosophical traditions that are well entrenched in society but tend to become explicit in public discourses when political parties or movements speak and are identified. In other words, the Internet has made otherwise hidden political forces relevant to everyday people, giving them a voice—for good or ill—that were taken from the battlefields of the past. In this theory for a reinvention of political policy making, advanced world policy making has not changed so much as become more complex, potentially more responsive to diverse interests and reconstructed accordingly. It is not new, so much as reworked, which is a view that Internet boosters tend to reject. Boosters have tended towards the invention of public-policy instruments, rather than the reinvention or redirection of existing ones (Neuman, McKnight, and Solomon 1998, 7). In fact, policy making has not changed, so much as been transformed by unexpected, dormant intellectual traditions. The results of engaging in the politics of the Internet policy process will still produce normative results for society, in an unavoidable challenge for us all. Thus, it's not what you dance, it's the way that you dance it.

INTERNET POLICY—IS THAT YOUR FINAL ANSWER?

The breadth of the Internet policy issue stretches far beyond this discussion. Indeed, in borrowing from the restricted reality of television game shows like *Who Wants to Be a Millionaire*, the answer to the question, "Is that your final answer?" is never as easy as a one-word answer of the game show genre.

Remarkably however, we could imagine *Who Wants to Be a Millionaire* as a motif of the Internet generation (just as *The $64,000 Question* was for the emerging middle class of new consumerists in the affluent euphoria of post–World War II, 1950s Americana, including not just the United States, but also Canada, Western Europe, Australia, New Zealand). "Is that your final answer?" becomes a shortcut for the metaphor of the Internet in a speed dial world, where the image of highly concentrated information sets are mythologized into knowledge, when they are actually banks of unprocessed data (Breen 1997). There is no finality in the search for Internet policy, unlike the game show. Instead there is a requirement that the public interest be brokered by the government and its agencies in such a way that the complex new sets of relationships evolving within and around the Internet and telecommunications be given direction, in order to best influence and exploit society's resources.

How did we get here? Part of the answer lies in the culture where the Internet took root. Late capitalism, defined by its postindustrial and postmodern characteristics of communication diffusion, speed, and geographical uncertainty in a globalized world of consumption, is the confusing starting point (Volkmer 1997). In a word: complex. The characteristics of contemporary society have complicated all human relations. This is especially so in those advanced societies like the United States, Western Europe, Australia, and Japan, where already ubiquitous telephone services met with the 1990s rush of microprocessing in computerization. As these and their related industries converged they produced telecommunications, including the Internet and the Information Technology boom that accompanied it.

By the early 2000s, the boom had created new issues in the underdeveloped world, as the "digital divide" added to the woes of the have-nots. Rather than solving the world's problems, as the boosters had promised, the gap between the information haves and the have-nots widened, as various U.S. Government departments noted in *Falling through the Net: Towards Digital Inclusion. A Report on Americans' Access to Technology Tools* (October 2000). This was not only the case in the underdeveloped nations where this might be expected, but in the United States as well. The digital divide became a buzzword for the process whereby technologized elites with access to the Internet and related services, such as the World Wide Web and e-mail, embraced the Internet with such overwhelming enthusiasm that a "new economy" was created. Just as quickly the e-economy soured, becoming less like the speculative gold rushes of the nineteenth century and more like the refuge for a new class of fortunate super rich, who moved with speculators early to collect on the euphoria, but not the vision (Herman and McChesney 1997, 135). The elites soon gave way to something approximating more general use, but nothing as ubiquitous as the telephone—or the universal service policies that accompanied its gestation. In fact, there seemed to be little policy making as the Internet boomed.

Unsurprisingly, a policy gap exists with the Internet, promoted by advocates against public policy and regulation. Why? One answer has been offered by Lawrence Lessig, a law professor, whose insight has been to acknowledge that computer code together with its architecture regulate human activity. Lessig suggests that the range of control of the Internet has been determined by its architecture and that this deterministic characteristic defines its regulability, or "the ability to control behavior within a particular cyberspace" (1999, 30). The debate over the "regulability" of the architecture of the code mirrors in many ways the debate about the control over nature, with an important twist: The human-created code and its architecture is the result of human choices and actions, not a preexisting order of relationships, such as the ecoystem. Failure, inability, or direct choice not to realize and accept that distinction is a failure not just to regulate, but an abject failure of responsibility to civilize. While this is not an easy subject to broach, it is clear that any assumptions about how nature is managed and civilized is deeply contentious, philosophically challenging, and continually changing.

Furthermore, environmentalism as a movement has pushed many of the ideas about the civilizing rights of human beings into center stage, assisted by critical thinking stemming from training in the liberal arts—but also by the fact that the internal combustion engine and nuclear power contribute both benefits and appalling negative outcomes for our planet, on a par with other features of the debate over the control of nature (Singer 1993). Governments have a responsibility to manage—governance itself is defined as the responsibility of elected officials and their institutions to use and allocate societies resources for the benefit of citizens. The debate is over how the resources are distributed across the society, by whom, for whom, and to what effect.

Governments, especially those adopting the advanced capitalist model of lesser government, are, Lessig argues, in an especially difficult position with code, because code incorporates utopian possibilities for enhancing the public interest, while simultaneously providing the government and private interests with the ability to behave unjustly and inequitably. Code has become a reiteration of the Smithian principle of the invisible hand of the market, free to impose its own solutions on society, regardless of the consequences. Choices about how society is regulated will be made *for* the public, rather than by its representatives, or the public itself.

> If we let the invisible hand work unimpeded, these choices will be made according to the set of interests that are expressed by commerce on the Net. In some cases, certainly, those interests will be constrained by government. But now we must think specifically about how we could structure the choices we will confront and how we could resolve the conflicts of values these spaces present. (Lessig 1999, 83)

Seen from a legal perspective—which is where Lessig's work is primarily situated—a framework for the rhetoric associated with lawyerly practice becomes somewhat overpowering. How would an argument be sustained in favor of the unimpeded invisible hand of the free market? Conversely, how would an equally powerful argument be sustained that supports the public interest in its search to share in the information riches offered by the Internet? The answer turns on Lessig's use of "latent ambiguity"—the liberal political response to the possibility that all sides in a debate will freely have their say, as promised in the U.S. Constitution (Lessig 1999, 181). The slippage in the discourse presents the gray area in which most of us in the advanced Western world live out our lives (perhaps I should say this is the gray area in which political choices seem to be constrained by political realities—the appeal to the middle class and its own selfish interests). No extreme tends to claim the upper hand in any model of democracy, as divergent forces work to establish supremacy, but are reduced to inflections of a model that serves capital. No one goes to war over the injustice of the benefits of contemporary democracy to capitalism—because those with voices in society tend to benefit from the growth of the capitalist apparatus. Equally, nobody gets angry over the disproportionate distribution of the Internet to the same fragment of society that tends to enjoy the benefits of the flourishes of the economy. The imbalance in this distribution of resources is a site of competition. As Lessig notes: "Always there is a competition between the public interest and private; always the rights of the private must be balanced against the interests of the public. Always a choice must be made about how far each side will be allowed to reach. These questions are inherently questions of public law: How will a particular constellation of constitutional values be reckoned? How will a balance be struck in particular factual contexts?" (1999, 187).

Legal approaches are inevitably defined by the society in which the law operates, by those who make the law and their interests.[3] To expand the perspective, we must search for a way to make sense of the Internet policy challenge, where the convergence of technologies has pushed together a variety of different laws, interests, values, and economies, even while the contest over who wins is the central philosophical feature of the players. Now, more than ever, a multidisciplinary approach that is constituted by divergent yet connected disciplinary perspectives will help to identify the competing views.[4] Yet, in the mess of competing views, it is difficult to identify a winner. They have piled on top of each other—much like baseball players do in the crazy World Series postgame ritual of players diving onto a huge pile of fellow players, although at least in baseball they share the same team objectives. Remarkably, they compete in their coexistence. The pragmatics of this coexistence is an acceptance that the playing field of the converged domains must somehow be managed, but to the advantage of each position being argued. Strict instrumentalism plays itself out as private interests seek their own advantage, influencing policies that directly impact the financial benefits of Internet policy. Importantly therefore, the prevailing view from every stakeholder in the space filled by the Internet is that there is a place for policy: There is no consensus about what form it will take. Indeed, in some cases, there is a strong argument in favor of regulation, defined as the implementation and oversight of policies, which in their turn are the legal demands the public or their institutions put in legislative form.

Refusal to acknowledge this pragmatic feature of the policy landscape would lead to a type of policy vacuum, where some interests are not recognized. (I will return to this point later). In a normative setting, indeed, in any form of liberal democracy, this is considered untenable and against the public interest. As it is, there is every reason to acknowledge that the full range of interests in society are not taken into consideration in Internet policy issues, producing an asymmetrical set of policy forces that reflect the interests of those stakeholders best able to influence the development of Internet policy. Yet civilizing influences of governance have created and continue to construct their own renditions of policy. Communications policy making in the United States has a set of institutions that are extensive, relevant, and variously influential in Internet policy making, including Congress, the Senate, the White House, state legislatures, state governors, local governments, the Federal Communications Commission, the Department of Justice, the Federal Trade Commission, citizens' groups, state commissions, the courts, state consumer advocates, and industry organizations/lobbyists. Some of these institutions are much more influential than others, creating asymmetries. The next section will provide a model that describes how this asymmetrical power relation comes into being. I will conclude by describing four value categories that have been enlivened by the Internet policy debate.

PRIVATE INVESTMENT—PUBLIC ISSUES

If the public interest presents a standard by which policy is seen to rise or fall in a democracy, how would the public interest of the Internet be assessed? Certainly the principle of participation is key. In some cases it has been argued that the communications policy debate in the United States requires a new civil rights agenda, which includes rights to speak, rights to information, to service, to economic opportunity, privacy, and participation in the political process (Aufderheide 1999, 107). Unfortunately, the foundations of the political economy of the Internet do not open up to such dramatic calls for restructuring. Governments of all persuasions have become deeply involved in supporting the private interests of the telecommunications sector and, in so doing, skewing the distribution of financial resources towards those interests that are already well placed to take advantage of the Internet. Fortner suggested that in the United States, a process of "cultural excommunication" may be under way, where private interests have been promoted by government policy makers to the detriment of the civil society, "fragmenting [it] into fractious congeries of prejudice" (1995, 150). However, such is the domination by market economic forces in U.S. policy making that a critical blast such as Fortner's does little to shed light on the multiple forces actually at work in the policy making domain. Indeed, the way of the world marks a commitment by governments to advance the competitive advantage of their national industries to benefit their national firms and thereby create employment and wealth (Porter 1990).

We can see the complexity of this relationship in the United States in table 8.1.

These large sums of money go directly from the government to private business to assist the creation of competitive products. Many of the products are technology related. The importance of this illustration is that the history of the Internet itself is the result of government funding of an interwoven set of telecommunication network initiatives.

In fact, the Internet went from a university and defense/military government supported special research and communication network—the Advanced Research Projects Agency (ARPANET)—linked to the National Science Foundation's CSNET in the early 1980s—to a fully commercialized, yet mixed private-public system: arguably a "giveaway" by the U.S. Government (Kahn 1995). Not surprisingly, the principle of government "investing" in private research and development is a central feature of liberal government policy and action that creates a rock-hard nexus of the private-public interaction that directly impacts the policy process. The question is, how does the government reflect the public interest with this allocation of resources directly into private hands? What guarantees, if any, does the government and its policy makers make to the public interest, given this level of investment in the private national industrial base? These are central questions of economics. When applied in the communi-

Table 8.1. Summary of Federal Funds for Research and Development and for R&D Plant: Fiscal Years 1999, 2000, and 2001. Total Obligations.

R&D, performers	1999	2000	2001
Industrial firms	$31,901,700,000	$32,815,500,000	$33,026,200,000
Intramural[5]	$18,084,700,000	$32,815,000,000	$33,026,200,000
FFRDCs[6]	$1,328,000,000	$1,335,500,000	$1,385,500,000

Source: National Science Foundation/Division of Science Resources Studies, Survey of Federal Funds for Research and Development: Fiscal Years 1999, 2000, 2001.

cation/cultural studies domain, they demand multidisciplinary answers, too extensive to discuss in this context. However, an answer can be found in the relationship identified in figure 8.1: that the nexus of private innovation with public use is a central means of characterizing the initiation of the policy making relationship between government and the marketplace. Private innovation is largely the result of public use of the technology innovations that result from the capitalist enterprise. The entangled web of economy-technology interfaces means that private innovation is "hosted"

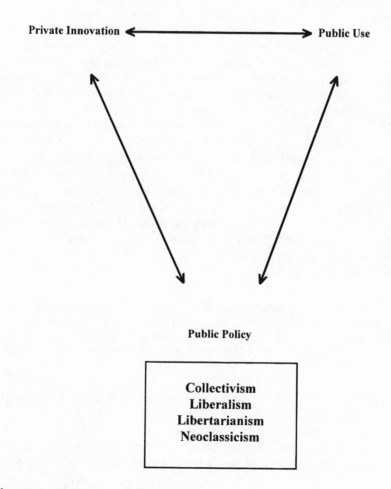

Figure 8.1.   Convergence Policy

if you will, by the state, whose policies, especially via direct government investment and through monetary policy as created by the Federal Reserve (interest rates as an engine to promote or restrain consumer spending and bank lending) to be realized by the utility of the product and the creation of demand, through the advertising industry. Taxation policy also plays a part.

Internet history suggests that these interests are articulated together (linked) by numerous historical agents, particularly funding systems, that include direct subsidies from high profit urban telecommunication centers, to loss-making rural locations. Such subsidies are necessary because the national telecommunications system could not exist without them. In the United States and many other nations, they are central policy features defined by the term "universal service," which is generally articulated to the creation of the Federal Communication Commission itself, following the Communications Act of 1934 (Wilson 2000, 59–63). Universal service recognizes the value of a telephone for all citizens at an affordable price, thereby marrying economic and social policy concerns. In more recent times, the idea of universal service has become a rallying point for Internet policy makers and the public, offering former vice president Al Gore a basis for arguing what can be seen as a trade policy in the guise of universal service.[7] Gore was especially prominent in the early 1990s, promoting the idea of a U.S.-based National Information Infrastructure (NII) and a related Global Information Infrastructure (GII), where government and private interests would work as partners. It is worth viewing some of the policy statements in this area as examples of the continuation of the universal service policy, while also shedding light on the private innovation–public use policy nexus.

The National Information Infrastructure: Agenda for Action, Executive Summary notes that the NII will:

> Extend the "universal service" concept to ensure that information resources are available to all at affordable prices. Because information means empowerment—and employment—the government has a duty to ensure that all Americans have access to the resources and job creation potential of the Information Age. (http://nii/NII-Executive-Summary.html)

The private sector was central to the advancement of the NII concept. Arguably, however, an imbalance in emphasis can be detected not in the rhetoric—which is finely crafted with public interest benefits in mind—but in the trade benefits that primarily reward corporations with economic advantage for their support of the NII, once corporations became engaged with the initiative:

> These changes promise substantial benefits for the American people, but only if government understands fully their implications and begins working with the

private sector and other interested parties to shape the evolution of the communications infrastructure. . . .

The benefits of the NII for the nation are immense. *An advanced information infrastructure will enable U.S. firms to compete and win in the global economy*, generating good jobs for the American people and economic growth for the nation. (Executive Summary, emphasis added)

The challenge in all of this was and still is to draw attention to the relationship between government, industry, and progressive political interests in expanding the scope of democratic opportunities across society through the agency of Internet (Kahin and Wilson 1997). Termed "instrumental progressivism" by Robbins and Webster, the volatile and expanding set of interests associated with the Internet is nuanced by the terms and conditions of contemporary capitalism's advance across all sectors of advanced postindustrial societies (1999, 195–99).[8]

As the interest groups or stakeholders express their views, the "old" policy concerns such as universal service, conflate with emerging issues of social and economic opportunity to become a new set of more complex ones, defined by "the digital divide." Here, digital technology in its Internet manifestations is identified as deeply schismatic—that is, the technology itself tends to either generate or reinforce existing or new lines of social and economic power and access to knowledge. Those who are left behind become examples of continuing political realities: the poor—the vast majority of the world's population has little or no chance of joining the digital revolution—become the focus of government action in reviews such as the U.S. government's *Falling through the Net* (1999). In this instance the policy shortfall precipitates in state and federal governments a reaction to their failure to promote opportunity for all. In a reactive move, the state begins the necessary task of documenting its own inability to initiate a level playing field for citizens, which began when it constructed the Internet as a vehicle that commercial trade interests would benefit most from (as noted above in relation to the NII). *Falling through the Net* is a postfactum attempt to resolve the policy blindspots of the original policy, which was a creation of U.S. political culture in the first place. As such the NII involved a set of political choices that provided government sponsored benefits for commercial operators. The "failure" of a policy initiative such as the NII (and many similar ones around the world) is that is has been characterized as a democratic tool for citizen advancement through access to information (and all the associated tools of social and economic growth) when in effect the initiatives have almost always featured the rhetoric of official, top-down electronic democracy. As Roza Tsagarousianou suggests, electronic democracy

is a very particular version of publicness, arranged around ordered forms of dissemination of information, in which official political channels decide on the definition of the problem and the content of the message and thus strongly influence the direction of the outcome. (1998, 174)

According to this approach, "the people" get what has been decided for them by political interests.

VALUES ARE NOT SCHMALUES

Continuing the struggle over who decides what becomes of the Internet is a discourse over values. What values are inherent in the Internet? Whose values are dominating? There are few clear answers to these questions, in part because of the contemporary complexity conundrum that magnifies each of the stakeholder positions within the Internet domain. For example, Al Gore's government-brokered boosterism for the NII became the dominant stakeholder position in the early 1990s that faded as research centers and commercial interests took hold. Microsoft's disinterest in the World Wide Web in 1993 was transformed in just two years into a frenzied set of initiatives, culminating in the launch of the Microsoft Internet Explorer and associated anticompetitive practices that, in turn, invoked federal antitrust laws and thus the Department of Justice case against the company. By 2001, dot.coms were known as dot.bombs, as the speculative bubble of unworkable financial ideas for making the Internet a business-transforming initiative went off like so much unsold dog food at pets.com. Yesterday's stakeholder is today's has-been is tomorrow's historical footnote.

As the Internet grows into adolescence in the 2000s, the context in which each of the stakeholders operates changes—in some cases dramatically. Late in the 1990s and early in the 2000s, the Internet dot.coms were in an apparently policy-free zone. In this remaking of the California/Australia gold rushes of the mid-nineteenth century (perhaps the Spanish conquistador gold frenzies in Latin America are also relevant, but do not fit so well with the analogy) fantastic speculation was rewarded with large fortunes, created out of extraordinary-venture capital promotion of business opportunities. Where government-sponsored visions of information wealth gave way to venture capitalism visions of money wealth, values flew and sank in and around the Internet, apparently free of government policy involvement.

The Internet and the public policies reflected in figure 8.1 can be defined by the four philosophical traditions that coexist within contemporary capitalism: collectivism, libertarianism, liberalism, neoclassicism. Without revisiting each of these political philosophies in any detail, suffice to say that the slippage in meaning and interpretation across and into each other occurs with disarming regularity.

To illustrate: Libertarianism can be seen as the quest for personal freedom—arguably a tenet of American society, following Thomas Paine's essay on freedom, *The Rights of Man*. As the American Libertarian Party proclaims:

> The Libertarian Party is committed to America's heritage of freedom: Individual liberty and personal responsibility; free-market economy of abundance and prosperity a foreign policy of non-intervention, peace, and free trade. We welcome your participation and support. (Libertarian Party Web Page, 2001)

Of course, it is not this simple—the slippage from broad appeals to liberty from tyranny and the practice of everyday choices associated with claims for personal freedom are another thing altogether.

We live in a society where personal freedom from any sort of domination or authority manifests itself in circa 2000 pax-Americana-capitalism. Here the greed of everyday consumption produces a "leisure class" of wage and salary earners who use economy as a means of advancing material well-being often to the detriment of all else: their families, their communities, their environment, their humanity. To most people this is the stuff of paying the bills while working for a living. It is the stuff of daily decisions about what we do with our income, our behavior as consumers, our behavior as sentient beings seeking pleasure and gratification, and so on. This domain is largely constructed out of a set of private/public ideas and expectations that in turn are defined by social values and ultimately the reach of government to control personal behavior. In the end, the way the values are played out by individuals and groups is a discourse (about values) that makes a society a highly charged political environment. The laws that define personal freedom (say, free speech) are in some cases absurd—the reason Nazis have speech rights is because their rights equal the rights of feminists to speak and to deny one set of interests the right to speak in the United States is to deny all speech.[9]

At the other end of the libertarian spectrum are those people who bombed the Alfred P. Murrah Federal Building in Oklahoma City on April 19, 1995, and the numerous extremist militias who President Bill Clinton suggested believed that "the greatest threat to freedom comes from the government . . . I say to you, all of you . . . there is nothing patriotic about hating your country, or pretending that you can love your country but despise your government" (cited in Klein 2000, 210). Hatred and distrust of government is a uniquely U.S.-based syndrome, created by the founding folk in their quest to be free of the demands of the ruling classes of Britain. And the consequence of this tradition, as in many if not all nations, is that a state of internal warfare against the government exists in the United States.

Perhaps the most extraordinary example of such warfare was the Contract with America led by Newt Gingrich in 1994. It is not too far removed from the libertarian tradition of "get the government off our backs" conservatism, within the traditions of let business be free to do business ("The business of America is business") that libertarianism is highly charged by capitalist values. This tradition suggests the freedom to make and keep one's wealth, rather than using that personally generated benefit to create a common-wealth, as the philosopher John Locke suggested.

In the many details of a discussion about libertarianism, and for every category of theoretical libertarianism and its associated value systems, there is an equivalent set of ideas mirrored in the Internet.

When Microsoft chief Bill Gates wrote *The Road Ahead* in 1995, he wrote that the Internet would have multiple permutations: "The network will draw us together, if that's what we choose, or let us scatter ourselves into a million mediated communities" (1995, 273). In this sort of statement we can see the main marketing rhetoric of libertarian values expressed as business opportunities (knowing Gates and his aim of selling higher volumes of computer software) *and* human ambition, freedom, and achievement for users of the Internet. Moreover, what Gates projects as a collective vision of "community" incorporates the entire set of values at play in the Convergence Policy schema.

Simply put, a Microsoft perspective views unconstrained opportunity to exploit markets for profit through innovation and selling new products as a "right." The fact that Microsoft did not follow the conventions of competitive behavior was merely an act—according to the Microsoft libertarian philosophy of competitive market behavior—of total freedom. This market libertarianism is described by neoclassical economics. Here, the market is the final arbiter and will perform best without any government-sponsored limitations—laws or regulations.

The more pressing example of this political movement associated with the Internet is the Internet Tax Freedom Act. Premised on the libertarian idea that all government taxation is a burden and as such counterproductive to the contemporary capitalist enterprise of the freedom to trade, the act gained widespread support and opposition in the late 1990s and into the 2000s. A well-organized group orchestrated the Advisory Commission on Electronic Commerce and submitted a report to Congress on April 12, 2000, much of the sponsorship coming from California Republican Christopher Cox (2000). The point to the debate put by this side of the case was that no taxation should be associated with Internet commerce innovation. The other side argued that taxation loss directly affects the role of government in society—the absence of taxation actually removes the legitimacy of government, and the need for citizens to vote. Public policy can only struggle to exist in such an environment.

And what of collectivism? Bill Gates made the point that the Internet will bring many communities together. That has been the case. In fact, the formal nature of the collectivist approach can be observed in federal and state government policy initiatives to use the Internet to create community networks (Harrison and Stephen 1999). Many informal communities of interest also came together before that and continue to find mutual concerns that are shared on the Internet, through Web sites and chat rooms and so on. The very nature of this virtual communication is the result of telecommunication networks that reach those who are empowered by access to computer mediated communication. By definition the people in that network make up a community of users, even if they are not talking to each other. Governments have been keen to identify the opportunities for using the networks for public policy initiatives such as education and information dissemination. The collective sensibility becomes part of the texture of the Internet.

Much of the debate about Internet values incorporates the normative proposition that human beings will be enriched by increasingly ubiquitous networked communications. At its most basic, the NII and associated policy proposals incorporate the idea of the benefits of human communication. Where extreme libertarianism, as practiced by extremists using terror against the state, is a perversion of this community of humanity, the innocence quotient fades very quickly. For all those people using the Internet for beneficial outcomes, there are many promoting and practicing violence and race hatred. The tolerance that liberalism promotes for every type of human activity obviously is stretched and constantly in need of review in this new communication world: Internet policy has yet to find a way of working in this twilight zone of values.

CONCLUSION

The bottom line in all this is that the values in the Internet are shades of a complex capitalist system played out on private keyboards and monitors. It is the private reaction that tends to promote the idea that Internet policy is an oxymoron. Nothing is quite that easy. While almost everyone would like more freedom, government is not going away—even if a well-funded argument to that effect is promulgated. Furthermore, the Internet offers government a way of growing the economy and opportunities within it: a role that can be seen as one of the fundamentals of government—job creation leading to a rising standard of living and improved human dignity for all, which can be seen as the basic tenets of any claim by a government to practice democracy.

The issues mapped out here are not minor. They are not issues that only apply to the Internet—in fact the Internet has magnified them, bringing some of them into greater relief in the policy debates that make society what it is: a place where the contest over what values prevail really matters. The continuing challenge is in making the Internet a site where the policy discourse can continue, producing real and concrete improvements for all human kind. The dancers will just have to improve their steps.

NOTES

1. Except in those curious instances where issues like technical standards must be put in place to assist the "free market" to succeed, or where anticompetitive behavior is such that competition regulators must intervene. But in many instances the policy ground rules to be applied in the new domain are unclear, in transition, and—in cases involving networked communications—unstable and poorly suited to modernist legal interpretations. The most suitable example being the U.S. Department of Justice antitrust case against the Microsoft Corporation.

2. In some cases the struggles do in fact become the basis for war—although thankfully, in most Western nations, that is not the case. Sadly, in many other places around the world, real wars, with real death and destruction is common, and increasingly so!

3. In 2000–2001, the Libyan Government insisted that the trial of the defendants in the Lockerbie bombing of the Pan Am jet over Scotland be held according to Scottish criminal law, because it was over Scottish skies that the explosion took place and also because the Libyans considered Scottish law the most appropriate system for trying their defendants.

4. Robert Lock has made the following astute observation on the study of universal service policy: "It is critical to understand the multidisciplinary approach to the analysis of universal service, given that the concept is a veritable monument to the influences of a multitude of disciplines over the past 90 years. Law, economics, corporate strategy, as well as the social and political sciences, have all contributed to the patchwork evolution of the concept. Only by undertaking an analysis that examines principles from all these relevant disciplines can a rational universal service policy, which reflects the characteristics of individual jurisdictions, be defined and constructed. Restricting analysis to less than the entire menu of perspectives risks the development of myopic and mismatched policies that could ultimately do more harm than good" (1999, 240).

5. Intramural funds are those the federal government pays itself, funding of internal federal agencies.

6. Federally funded research and development centers.

7. This is not the place to argue the case in detail, but an examination of the NII, the GII, indeed the Internet itself, can be seen as thinly veiled U.S. trade policy initiatives, whose objective was to leverage U.S. technology innovation into a supercompetitive first mover advantage in the early 1990s. When viewed in the context of the World Trade Organization's Basic Telecommunications treaty—a tool to open world markets for companies seeking offshore expansion—the Gore policy succeeded beyond the Clinton administration's wildest dreams.

8. Robbins and Webster use this term to describe the remaking of university education as a "conjunction of employers' and governments' desires to change the university, with that of progressives' campaigns for reform within higher education" (1999, 197).

9. In France, they don't pretend otherwise, and in 2000 Yahoo accepted a French government request to remove Nazi hate speech from Yahoo Web sites.

BIBLIOGRAPHY

Aufderheide, Patricia. 1999. *Communications Policy and the Public Interest: The Telecommunications Act of 1996.* New York: Guilford Press.

Breen, Marcus. 1997. "Information Does Not = Knowledge: Theorizing the Political Economy of Virtuality." *Journal of Computer Mediated Communication,* December, online at www.ascusc.org/jcmc/vol3/issue3/.

Closing the Digital Divide, online at www.digitaldivide.gov.

Commission on Electronic Commerce, online at http://cox.house.gov/nettax/.

Falling through the Net: Toward Digital Inclusion. A Report on Americans' Access to Technology Tools (October 2000). Department of Commerce, NTIA, Economics and Statistics Administration, Washington, D.C. Online at www.ntia.doc.gov/ntiahome/fttn00/contents00.html.

Fortner, Robert. 1995. "Excommunication in the Information Society." *Critical Studies in Mass Communication* 12, 133–54.

Gates, Bill. 1995. *The Road Ahead.* London: Viking.

Harrison, Teresa, and Timothy Stephen. 1999. "Researching and Creating Community Networks." Pp. 221–42 in *Doing Internet Research: Critical Issues and Methods for Examining the Net,* ed. Steve Jones. Thousand Oaks, Calif.: Sage Publications.

Herman, Edward, and Robert McChesney. 1997. *The Global Media: The New Missionaries of Corporate Capitalism.* London: Cassell.

Kahin, Brian, and Ernest Wilson. 1997. Introduction. Pp. 1–23 in *National Information Infrastructure Initiatives: Vision and Policy Design.* Cambridge, Mass.: MIT Press.

Kahn, R. E. 1995. "The Role of Government in the Evolution of the Internet." Pp. 13-24 in *Revolution in the U.S. Information Infrastructure.* Washington, D.C.: National Academy Press.

Klein, Joe. 2000. "Eight Years: Bill Clinton Looks Back on His Presidency." *New Yorker* (October 16 and 23), 188–217.

Lessig, Lawrence. 1999. *Code and Other Laws of Cyberspace.* New York: Basic Books.

Libertarian Party of America, see, for example, www.lp.org.

Lock, Robert. 1999. "Breaking the Bottleneck and Sharing the Wealth: A Perspective on Universal Service Policy in an Era of Local Competition." Pp. 237–49 in *Making Universal Service Policy: Enhancing the Process through Multidisciplinary Evaluation,* ed. Barbara Cherry, Steven Wildman, and Allen Hammond. Mahwah, N.J.: Lawrence Erlbaum Associates, Publishers.

Marx, Karl, *Capital.* Moscow: Progress Press, 1978.

Melody, William H. 1997. "Policy Objectives and Models of Regulation." Pp. 11–24 in *Telecom Reform: Principles, Policies, and Regulatory Practices,* ed. William H. Melody. Den Private ingeniorfond, Technical University of Denmark, Lyngby. (Reprinted 2001.)

Neuman, Russell W., Lee McKnight, and Richard Jay Solomon. 1998. *The Gordian Knot: Political Gridlock on the Information Highway.* Cambridge, Mass.: MIT Press.

Porter, Michael. 1990. *The Competitive Advantage of Nations*. New York: Free Press.

Robbins, Kevin, and Frank Webster. 1999. *Times of Technoculture: From the Information Society to the Virtual Life*. New York: Routledge.

Singer, Peter. 1993. *How Are We to Live? Ethics in an Age of Self-Interest*. Melbourne, Australia: Text Publishing Company.

Smith, Adam. 1994. *The Wealth of Nations*. New York: Modern Library.

Tsagarousianou, Roza. 1998. "Electronic Democracy and the Public Sphere: Opportunities and Challenges." Pp. 167–78 in *Cyberdemocracy: Technology, Cities, and Civic Networks*, ed. R. Tsagarousianou, D. Tambini, and C. Bryan. London: Routledge.

Turow, Joseph. 1997. *Media Systems in Society: Understanding Industries, Strategies, and Power*. New York: Longman.

Turow, Lester. 1999. *Building Wealth: The New Rules for Individuals, Companies, and Nations in a Knowledge-based Economy*. New York: HarperCollins.

Veblen, Thorstein. 1958. *The Theory of Business Enterprise*. New York: Mentor Books.

Volkmer, Ingrid. 1997. "Universalism and Particularism: The Problem of Cultural Sovereignty and Global Information Flow." Pp. 48–83 in *Borders in Cyberspace: Information Policy and the Global Information Infrastructure*, ed. Brian Kahin and Charles Neeson. Cambridge, Mass.: MIT Press.

Weinhaus, C., T. Pitts, R. McMillin, et al. 1994. *Abort, Retry, Fail? The Need for New Communications Policies*. Boston: Telecommunications Industries Analysis Project.

Wills, Gary. 1999. *A Necessary Evil: A History of American Distrust of Government*. New York: Simon and Schuster.

Wilson, Kevin. 2000. *Deregulating Telecommunications: U.S. and Canadian Telecommunications 1840–1997*. Lanham, Md.: Rowman & Littlefield.

9

Internet Globalization and the Political Economy of Infrastructure

Bram Dov Abramson

At the millennium's turn, scarcely a half decade into the emergence of the World Wide Web, the adjective "global" had already become a pervasive prefix to discussions of the Internet. Indeed, globalization has become a meta-narrative organizing how the Internet's ongoing evolution is made sense of and described. "The Internet today is vastly different from that of only a few years ago," explained a former Internet Society (ISOC) president,[1] "if for no other reason than that it has grown so dramatically geographically" (Heath 1998). And, indeed, by providing connectivity across national borders, the Internet enables network participants to exchange e-mail, download one another's Web pages, and generally engage in an extensible set of communicative acts across great distances.

Yet the globalization of media and communications is an ongoing process with a long history indeed.[2] Transactions between physical spaces and across political borders—human migration; trade in goods and services; financial and investment capital; audiovisual, oral, print, and electronic communication—have always been key vectors in the process through which social spaces and human identities are configured.

Transactions require infrastructures. Infrastructures help shape what can and cannot be done, and how: It is easier to send e-mail via a narrowband dial-up connection than hold a video conference. Infrastructures are always sociotechnical artifacts, the embodied translations of a series of economic, political, and social negotiations. Yet they come in various guises. Some infrastructures appear to us as technologies—trains, cargo containers, or communication satellites, for instance. Some appear juridical—like the treaties that govern transborder movement of goods, services, and people. Some are straight out of a political philosophy textbook, such as the nation-states that

183

became the building blocks for a panoply of linked systems that, together, define globalization as a series of relationships between countries—an international order which, "[f]ar from being a set of secondary interactions among preexisting and self-constituting national entities . . . serves to reproduce, naturalize, legitimate, and even generate the 'nation form' all over the world" (Malkki 1994, 41, 42).

The Internet is sometimes written into the long history of media globalization as the infrastructure that renders the nation-state extinct. There is a grain of truth to this perceived disjuncture between packet geography and political geography: although the nation-state is a key vector for the Internet's diffusion, the micromovements of packets inside Internet infrastructure show little concern for political territory. But to pin the nation-state's supposed extinction on the Internet is to make several category errors, not least of which is the separation of Internet infrastructure from the economic, political, and social negotiations that lead to its ongoing manufacture. Nor are the movements of network packets oblivious to this set of negotiations. The political economy of Internet infrastructure is not an island.

Still, set alongside the media which precede it, something has changed with Internet globalization. Consider the Canadian North. In 1972, a piece of space hardware named Anik A1 was launched as the world's first geostationary satellite deployed for domestic communications. Pressed into service by the Canadian government, Anik was to ensure the Canadian Broadcasting Corporation's congruence with Canadian territory. Blanketing the North with Canadian programming, it would "open the North to cultural integration" (Raboy 1990, 161).

This urge on the part of state planners was unrequited. Inuit and other northerners manifested little immediate desire for these technologies, and when satellite reception dishes were dispatched a number of communities refused to accept them, in some cases preventing the technology-bearing airplanes from landing. "Concern among satellite planners about the lack of native access to broadcasting technologies, or the impact southern television programming might have on native languages and cultures" was, as Roth and Valaskakis have explained (1989, 222), lacking.

Now compare this episode to *Wired* magazine's tale, a quarter century later, of the hunt for entrepreneurial individuals to lead Inuit across a "digital ice bridge to the 21st century," building a "new, digital Arctic now taking shape" amidst caricatures of Canadian hosers, *coureurs de bois,* and noble natives (Teitelbaum 1997, 262, 286). In *Wired*'s updating of the story, the mobilization of communications infrastructure to imbue mapped territory with national culture—a practice dubbed "technological nationalism" by Charland (1986)—fades into the background, ceding nationalist rhetoric to capitalist heroics.

Rendering of the Arctic as another exciting episode in the forward march of frontier capitalism characterizes a genre of travel writing that helps readers track the becoming-wired of exotic locales, tut-tutting the foolhardiness of clueless politicians who have not yet adopted the market libertarianism apparently welded to Internet culture. No longer a matter of national identity, the spread of communication infrastructure across geographic space is in cybertourist writing linked to an infrastructure of political and economic policies basic both to the network's expansion and to its destiny. How else could a single *Wired* article manage at once to acknowledge the lack of interest many Inuit express toward a technology they judge inappropriate, marvel that "even die-hard [Inuit] technophiles . . . view the North's impending digitalization unromantically," and conclude that the "northern future" can meaningfully be discussed as an extension of its Internet connectivity?

The distance between the policy narrative wrapped around Anik and the travel writing printed in *Wired* captures a difference in rhetorics of communication globalization then and now. Then, as now, the extended reach of a single network excited proponents because of what it stood for, waystation toward the production of an imagined place that was larger than life. Then, however, that place was the space of nationhood. Now it is a global cyberspace, the annexing of new territories a prerequisite for their abolition as distinct and unwired places. Instead of technological nationalism, technological globalism?

In a way cyberspace's spread would become iconized through displays such as the country-by-country Internet world connectivity[3] maps which, published by computer science professor and Internet pioneer Larry Landweber, adopted the visual language of geopolitics in framing cyberspace's spread as national question.[4] Rather than the globalization of Internet infrastructure per se, however, inquiry's endpoint lay rather in mapping access to a sphere of action separate from physical geography, emblematized by the cartoon insisting that "on the Internet, nobody knows you're a dog," and characterized by studies that at their crudest celebrated cyberspace's liberatory potential as staging ground for new identities unencumbered by historic or geographical baggage (Steiner 1993).

A decade earlier, science fiction author William Gibson (1984, 51) had famously defined cyberspace as a "consensual hallucination experienced daily by billions of legitimate operators, in every nation. . . . A graphic representation of data abstracted from the banks of every computer in the human system. Unthinkable complexity." As cognitive map and, indeed, organizing principle for computer-mediated communication, the users-without-bodies version of cyberspace posited a plane far more ethereal than had Gibson: As Bukatman argues cogently (1993, 146–56), the physical/virtual overlay at work in Gibson's elaborate exploration of cyberspace's bodily interface is what lends the notion its thickness and complexity. By staking out an imagined cyberspace autonomous from the physical world, on the other hand, advocates could take things in a different direction. If cyber and material worlds are separate, then cyberspace—and, by extension, the Internet—can be declared exempt from the physical world's institutional configuration.[5]

This "cyberlibertarian" stance held that the national state should not and could not regulate the Internet—that globalization of the Internet was the same thing as the death of the nation-state. Boyle (1997) has called this position the "Internet trinity," a group of clichés holding that "the Net interprets censorship as damage and routes around it," that "in cyberspace, the [U.S.] First Amendment is a local ordinance," and that "information wants to be free." Perhaps at its peak when, in 1996, a vast online "Blue Ribbon" campaign denounced a piece of proposed American legislation known as the Communications Decency Act, the cyberlibertarian position was exemplified by political activist groups such as the Electronic Frontier Foundation (EFF; Eudes 1996) and manifestos like EFF co-founder John Perry Barlow's Declaration of the Independence of Cyberspace (1995) or the Progress and Freedom Foundation's Magna Carta for the Information Age (1994). In this context, designating Canadian media theorist Marshall McLuhan as the object of *Wired* hagiography—he was thought to have forecast the coming of a "global village"—seemed only appropriate, so long as one did not delve too deeply into the context of McLuhan's pronouncement.

As financial investment in Internet infrastructure and applications overtook even inflated rhetoric, however—from $5 billion in 1996, the capital raised by venture-backed companies in the information technology sector rose to $41 billion by 2000, achieving a 153 percent compound annual growth rate (VentureOne 2001)—the cyberlibertarian conceit began to wane. Increasingly integrated into the real world of markets, institutions, and the social formations of popular cultures, the Internet grew increasingly ordinary, a quotidian technological system whose roots cannot easily be yanked free from the applications, uses, and features of everyday life that assume its presence (Agre 1998). Claims of a separate cyberworld came to seem outlandish; even the trade press began to focus on cyberspace's institutional embeddedness, developing an avid interest in the "click-and-mortar" hybrids of physical and virtual storefronts suddenly trumpeted as key to Internet success.

Echoes of the cyberlibertarian conceit continued to echo, of course. But if cultural identity is the narrative that helps organize the production and promotion of large-scale investment in communication infrastructure, it is rarely what motivates said investment, regardless of whether that identity is national, as in the Anik narrative, or cyberlibertarian, as with *Wired*: "with a complex technological system in place, you search for applications and thus reverse the conventional relationship of means and ends," as Jody Berland has put it (1996, 130), following Winner (1977). For a case in point, we need look no further than the one-world vocabulary adopted by advertising agencies to transform the narrowly focused specifications of Cisco routers,

Alcatel fiber, and other pieces of Internet infrastructure, into visions of a planetary future that investors everywhere could believe in.

Take an IBM television ad campaign from the late 1990s, featuring representatives of apparently non-modern societies chattering away in what subtitles revealed to be the hip cyberjargon of computerese. The campaign's impact drew from the imagined temporal fissure between backward-looking tradition and forward-looking technology, unifying the opposites under the sign of IBM and, more broadly, of an idyllic global village. "I read about it in *Wired*," murmured one Czech nun to the other in one such commercial, the urge to reach out to a networked world contrasting with the visual language of the nunnery setting. The slogan: "Solutions for a small planet." Equipment makers and service providers are interested in revenues from corporations who, in turn, hope to reach markets and execute tasks more efficiently, but a connected global culture is the image injected into the cultural economy. International Internet infrastructure and transnational corporate activity are pieces of a larger itinerary, yet it is the "Internet" that comes to stand for the whole, metonym for a larger process of globalization.

That is why, even after oversimple models of the Internet as separate realm give way to a more sophisticated understanding of overlaid virtual and physical spaces with limited autonomies and multiple points of intersection, it is difficult to abandon the image of a world shrunk and connected thanks to a liberatory Internet. "Internet" at once signifies a system of media infrastructure, a body of content and applications that makes use of this infrastructure, and a process of globalization that has seized upon this infrastructure as one of its key channels. The Internet domain name system is a case in point, mixing global top level domains (gTLDs) like com, org, and net with country code top level domains (ccTLDs) that provide users with ways to signify political territoriality[6] while leaving open other uses for the markers—as attests the use of Tuvalu's tv or Moldova's md to stand for television and medical doctor, respectively. Even the technical drawings that engineers create tend to represent the Internet as a cloud. In the strictest sense, there is no Internet—only networking standards like TCP (Transmission Control Protocol) and IP (Internet Protocol) that allow an ever-increasing number of private data networks across the world to exchange digital information. These networks and the traffic they carry give the Internet its form; that they interconnect gives the Internet its substance.

Look inside the cloud, however, and distinct structures begin to emerge. Traditionally, the Internet's basic transmission facilities have been centered on the United States, the hub whose backbone spokes connected the rest of the world. Some spokes were quite thick, like those linking the United Kingdom, Canada, and Japan. Others were quite thin—Russia's and Brazil's, for example. Thus far we have examined Internet globalization as spatial model and metonym for a larger process of realignment, suggesting that the understanding and promotion of Internet diffusion as gateway to a universal cyberspace—

the "technological globalism" that marks the Internet's entry into the history of media globalization—must accommodate an infrastructure-focused analysis. If so, however, then what are the geopolitics of this underlying infrastructure? How did a U.S.-centric infrastructure come into place, and what has happened to it? Indeed, why does it matter at all?

THE INTERNET GOES ABROAD

Most Internet histories begin with ARPANET, a research network whose initial build was in large part contracted to Bolt Beranek Newman (BBN, now Genuity), funded by the U.S. military's Advanced Research Projects Agency (ARPA), and online from 1969. Non-U.S. research institutions would later follow the lead of University College London—in 1973, UCL provisioned the Internet's first international segment—by leasing facilities to the U.S. backbone. In a sense, then, the Internet was international within five years of its start, with roots in academic and research facilities.

As the early years passed and milestones were achieved—standardization of TCP/IP, the Internet's basic operating system (1983); introduction of the modern method of mapping domain names to numbers (1984), establishment of NSFNET (1985) to run the research ARPANET split off from MILNET two years earlier—academic interest in the network grew. From 4 percent and three countries in mid-1988, by mid-1994 over 40 percent of networks connecting to the NSFNET were linking from outside the United States, representing eighty-two different countries (NSFNET 1995). Yet, while the historical continuity that traces the modern Internet back to the ARPANET and through later incarnations as DARPANET and NSFNET is well established, until the 1990s the Internet was just one section among the many computer networks that together constituted what John Quarterman has called a networked "Matrix" (Quarterman and Carl-Mitchell 1994). Until 1997, UUCP—Unix-to-Unix Copy Protocol, a peer-to-peer store-and-forward protocol distributed with the Unix operating system—reached more countries than did the Internet; until 1996, so did FidoNet, a hobbyist network that had existed only since 1983; until 1993, so did BITNET (Because It's Time Network), which had once been the academic world's major computer networking facility (Zakon 2000).

The Internet's initial diffusion across geography was in this sense cobbled together through the absorption of university-linked and research-linked networks with their own institutional histories. UUNET (laterWorldCom), the Internet's largest backbone provider, came into the world to facilitate UUCP networking with funding from a user group called the USENIX Association; EUnet (later KPNQwest), one of Europe's largest backbone providers, originated as the European Unix Network. Other networking efforts, meanwhile, had alternate relationships to the Internet, or, more often, lack thereof. Some, like France's Cyclades, were similar but lacked the Internet's critical mass. Others were treated as outright competitors: For years the world's telecom carriers rejected IP-based networks in favor of the centralized Open Systems Interconnect (OSI) model promulgated by the CCITT[7] through its X.25 standard, successful in France as Minitel but a short-lived experiment elsewhere.

Yet, by the late 1990s, the Internet's rise to prominence was complete, and most non-IP networks had either ported themselves over to the Internet or moved to ensure their interoperability with it. Where academic or research institutes had been most countries' first link to the Internet, now those countries that remained unconnected were being hooked up by the monopoly telecom providers that had for so long ignored or rejected the Internet. Such hookups usually amounted to a bid to get there before an enterprising citizen set up a clandestine satellite or other connection, true, but the shift was a basic step in the Internet's globalization, marking a logical conclusion to the growth in critical mass that had made it a key resource and, by extension, a network with which it was worth connecting. How did the Internet get there—and why the U.S.'s Internet altogether? The process would cluster around three nodal points.

The first involved the move from designated backbone to private network interconnections. From 1985, the U.S. National Science Foundation had funded the NSFNET, an IP network that became the Internet's main transport infrastructure, or backbone.[8] As more and more institutions secured connectivity to this network, an increasing number of uses and applications were developed for it. The NSF had a mandate to address, however, and in 1989 it implemented an Acceptable Use Policy (AUP) to govern its backbone's utilization: "NSFNET backbone services are provided to support open research and education in and between U.S. research and instructional institutions, plus research arms of non-profit firms when engaged in open scholarly communications and research. Use for other purposes is not acceptable."

For the small but growing group of network providers selling access to the Internet as a commercial proposition, this posed a problem. On the one hand, they could hardly tell their clients what to do with their Internet access; on the other, it was hardly feasible to filter client traffic based on the nature of its content. In 1991, three commercial IP network service providers—General Atomic (CERFnet, later absorbed by AT&T), Performance Systems International (PSINet), and UUNET—therefore made an end run around the AUP by creating the Commercial Internet eXchange (CIX), an open peering point for the exchange of network traffic. By interconnecting their networks directly, each CIX member could bypass the NSFNET backbone altogether, securing separate connectivity to their commercial counterparts and to the NSFNET backbone and, hence, granting users access to the whole Internet without recourse to the NSFNET AUP.

The idea caught on. By 1992, the U.S. government was calling for privatization of the Internet infrastructure, and the NSFNET's backbone transmission network would by 1995 revert to research network status in favor of four new CIX-like exchange points on the East and West Coasts of the United States. From hierarchical network with a well-defined core, the Internet would be converted to a more diffuse topology of private data networks for whom seamless traffic exchange was simply a good idea. This shift to commercial backbones to provide the Internet's long-haul infrastructure signalled both the emergence of an industrial sector with a strong interest in encouraging widespread Internet use, and a private market framework for its development; Internet backbone interconnection became the focal point for a nonuniform negotiating process in which each provider attempts to extract maximal benefits from its counterpart.

Alongside this evolving technical infrastructure was an ongoing shift in the Internet's policy infrastructure. Initiatives undertaken through a variety of formal and informal international forums began to trace the beginnings of a global policy regime for telecommunication infrastructure marked by territorial fluidity. A 1995 Brussels meeting of the G-7 group of countries proved the key moment in this process. Then U.S. vice president Al Gore proposed a blueprint for telecommunications policy known as the Global Information Infrastructure (GII), a follow-up to the U.S. National Information Infrastructure (NII) plan. The GII's adoption by member countries—the opinion leaders of the nation-state set—is properly understood, not as mythologized origin for a new era of transnational information brokerage, but as essential moment in a longer process, already ensconced in the international policy coordination rallied around converting digitized information into a new source of financial transaction (G-7 1995).

Brussels was the second nodal point in the Internet's conversion from research network to international communications infrastructure.[9] It is where a set of rules about the state's role in the governance of information infrastructure was hammered out to be coordinated across national boundaries, helping set the stage for the 1997 General Agreement on Trade in Services (GATS) which, negotiated through the World Trade Organization (WTO), carried these commitments through by binding sixty-nine countries representing 95 percent of the world's telecom revenues to schedules for liberalizing telecom services competition—including the bandwidth and leased lines necessary for Internet provision.[10]

As the blueprint for a multilateral communications framework, this policy infrastructure was a high profile endeavor. It anticipated both greasing the wheels of existing economic activity through fast-flowing data ("friction-free capitalism"), and making data itself the object of exchange, promoting it from the role of accessory to other groups of transaction. The similarity of such an information transaction infrastructure to the "free flow" principle, which had been a basic U.S. policy objective for more than seventy years, is striking. Frustrated time and again in the effort to make free flow the de facto international communication policy via multilateral forums, the emerging global infrastructure was instead part of a trajectory which, Hollifield and Samarajiva have demonstrated (1994), saw the call to let markets regulate information flows slide from political argumentation (as democratic necessity) to economic argument (as commercially indispensable). The economic argument worked; the policy infrastructure it put into place went beyond the Internet to impact upon the entire field of communications—just as the Internet was snaking across world territory. For a network whose technical infrastructure was built around a liberalized market and whose penetration was high enough to matter but not high enough to regulate as a public service, the timing could not have been better.

A comparison with international voice telephony is instructive. Where the geography of competition had since the NSFNET backbone's decommissioning provided the basic map for the Internet service provider (ISP) sector's evolution, the world of telephony had for years been a so-called "carrier's club" aligned with countries. The telecom providers that constituted this regime—usually called PTTs in reference to the common grouping of post, telegraph, and telecommunication services in a single administration—traced the roots of their relationship to the International Telecommunications Union (ITU, previously the International Telegraphic Union), founded in 1865 as a multilateral mechanism for the negotiation of interconnection fees for cross-border communications, and a part of the United Nations since 1947.

By agreeing multilaterally on common charging arrangements for international PSTN interconnection, PTTs could reduce the number of individual agreements they had to negotiate even as they ensured that providers would not attempt to outdo one another by negotiating advantageous terms with one another on a case-by-case basis. This would change, however. As regulatory reform and technological innovation put pressure on the carrier's club regime, transforming monopoly territories into competitive markets and enabling newly licensed or clandestine competitors to route around the ITU settlements regime, the ancien régime began to give way to a new environment. Rather than the collegial at-home monopolies who came together annually to renegotiate the per-minute payments they provided one another in return for completing their counterparts' phone calls, everyone was everyone else's competitor everywhere, no one's territory insulated from global markets.

As the new policy infrastructure came online, PSTN geography began to look much like the Internet's. The playing field grew increasingly cluttered; from 367 international phone carriers in 1995, 586 existed worldwide in 1997; 1,042 in 1998; and 2,085 by 2000, a compound annual growth rate of

134 percent over five years (TeleGeography 2000a, 12). But the boom in international voice carriers was not simply the result of a topology based on competition and a policy infrastructure that permitted it: voice telephony was a well-established, widely used application. The Internet would require its application, too, and found it in the World Wide Web, the media system that would provide the Internet with a home page and the third key conjuncture in its transition to widely used network. The Web's hypertext markup language had been outlined at the European Nuclear Research Centre (CERN) in 1989; its first prominent browser, Mosaic, launched in 1993 at the University of Illinois National Center for Supercomputing Applications (NCSA); and Web use had achieved enough volume to constitute the Internet's heaviest traffic load by the time NSFNET gave way to private backbone interconnection in mid-1995. Technically, the Web gave the Internet an extensible multimedia interface created through the interaction of client-side browser with server-side provision of HTML-encoded files. Functionally, the Web was the first Internet platform amenable to already-existing business plans, in the form of the print and electronic broadcasting model of aggregating audiences (in the new media version, "eyeballs") to sell to advertisers.[11] Conceptually, the Web provided a powerful way of imagining the Internet, granting it an interface whose form, structure, and metaphoric vocabulary would frame its vendors' approach to market.

With infrastructure in place, a critical user base online, an easy-to-understand media platform to start from, and capital markets abuzz, incentive for Internet services could only grow. Between 1994 and 1999, the worldwide Internet user population leapt from just under 4 million to over 250 million; its routing table—the constantly updated road map that guides traffic between Internet nodes—quadrupled to 70,000 routes; and the venerable USENET feed that distributes public discussion groups around the world grew from 25 to 70 gigabytes during 1999 alone, a far cry from the 700-odd megabytes (under 0.7 GB) that a full news feed had demanded in 1994 (TeleGeography 2000b, B3).

Unlike the PSTN whose years of carefully negotiated globalization had provided it with a set of ground rules to help shape the transition to a competitive market, however, the Internet had little to prepare it for this extreme growth. Its diffusion internationally would depend on the economic, political, and social conditions that it encountered. Income level, democratic governance, and mastery of the English language all play roles in this process: the United States first-mover advantage lent English-language content an overwhelming presence, while rough estimates put Anglophones at nearly half the Internet's population compared with just 8 percent of world population (Global Reach 2001). Economic development is a basic factor; so are connectivity measures, not least of which is a regulatory environment that permits both affordable access pricing and flourishing network connectivity (Hargittai 1999). Among the Internet's key uses has been in connecting dispersed cultural communities and diasporic populations across boundaries but, suddenly on the other side of unplanned and uncoordinated international growth, the Internet's underlying infrastructure more resembled a network gone abroad, based in America but with tentacles extending far afield.

Not too far, however. In October 2000, a report from the Organization for Economic Cooperation and Development noted, 95.6 percent of the Internet's hosts remained in the wealthy OECD countries, of which 89 percent were in North America and Europe (OECD 2001, 13). This rate of growth put connected countries even further ahead of the unconnected: "[i]n October 1997, the digital divide in Internet host penetration between Africa and North America was a multiple of 267. By October 2000, this has grown to a multiple of 540." A U.S.-centric Internet indeed.

BEYOND U.S.-CENTRIC

Still, at first a U.S.-centric Internet made sense. Nodes and networks leased bandwidth to the U.S. Internet, where they exchanged traffic with other networks. As a critical mass developed, the Internet's traffic topology began to benefit from network effects: the more bandwidth that runs to the hub, the more economies of scope and scale make the hub a key destination for more bandwidth, because everyone else is already there. Nor did it hurt to have organizational ties rendered both through explicit efforts like the International Connections Program, an NSFNET-funded effort to help other countries connect to the U.S. backbone, and informal relationships, such as the many engineers who attended U.S. schools and then provisioned research connections once back home, dealing with the folks that they already knew to help make things happen.

But network effects have limits. When enough Internet-connected networks are distant from U.S. shores but physically close to one another, it should be more efficient for those networks to build out their regional infrastructure, allowing more traffic to be exchanged locally, and cutting down on the route kilometers that providers must provision. Once geographical diversity makes this kind of regional hubbing a regular feature, Internet topology should enter a third stage characterized by a distributed global presence; ongoing proliferation of hubs should place users ever nearer to network centers and prevent a center-periphery model from emerging.

And, indeed, large-scale network planners have begun to explore such a model. They call it a grid—a highly meshed network that lets users deploy distributed, peer-to-peer applications regardless of their position on the network. A highly equitable cybergeography that spreads access to network resources across its topology, in other words. In practice, however, things are less simple. The ad hoc and uncoordinated push of the Internet outward from the United States into the rest of the world, combined with monopoly pricing on intercountry bandwidth within world regions, enabled the United States to play the ongoing role of hub to the global Internet's spokes. Traffic between two neighboring countries often trombones through American Internet facilities, going halfway around the world before arriving back at its final destination. This, some argued, is unfair to non-U.S. ISPs. Unlike the telephony regime where circuit costs are shared through bilateral agreements coordinated under multilateral auspices, went the reasoning, U.S. backbones can sit back and allow their foreign counterparts to pay the full cost of capacity into the United States, secure in the knowledge that no alternative exists. This lets U.S. providers "free ride" on correspondents' international backbones without having to pay for the privilege.

Some of this criticism was directed by European parties: a January 1998 paper published by the European Internet Service Providers Association (EuroISPA) laid the blame at regulators' feet, pointing to "over-regulation and monopolistic prices for national telecom circuits" that "force European ISPs to pay American telcos to buy up the European Internet." European provider complaints have lessened as growing competition has made West Europe a secondary Internet hub, however, with in-region connectivity exceeding 75 percent of total European international Internet bandwidth as of mid-2000. More vocal was the Asia-Pacific Economic Cooperation (APEC) forum's TEL working group which, between 1998 and 2000, convened a task group to investigate "compatible and sustainable international charging arrangements for Internet services" (APEC TEL 1998). APEC members tabled a similar proposal at the International Telecommunications Union, recommending in September 2000 that "administrations involved in the provision of international Internet connection negotiate and agree on bilateral commercial arrangements applying to direct international Internet connections whereby each administration will be compensated for the cost that it incurs in carrying traffic that is generated by the other administration" (TAS 2000).

Regions with limited local infrastructure and high bandwidth pricing are indeed characterized by a U.S.-centric Internet topology. Asia's international Internet connectivity was in mid-2000 hubbed more often through the West Coast of the United States than through any Asian city: Of the top ten hub cities for international Asian Internet bandwidth, of top three were San Francisco (14.1 Gbps of Asian international Internet connectivity), Tokyo (10.8 Gbps), and Los Angeles (3.3 Gbps).[12] Yet the growth of a well-connected regional Internet infrastructure may have much to do with creating a framework for multiple providers of international telecom services: Between 1999 and 2000 Internet bandwidth connecting Asia's countries grew faster than any other region-to-region route in the world. Thirteen-and-a-half percent of Asia's international Internet capacity remained in-region as of mid-2000, up from 6.2 percent the previous year.

This should not be unsurprising. As long as regulatory barriers allowed monopoly providers of international private lines to impose prohibitive costs on cross-border capacity, there was little incentive to connect to a neighboring country when it was no cheaper (often, more expensive) than a transoceanic connection to the United States. Other factors provided an incentive, of course: from 55 to 85 percent of Web pages are hosted in the United States, depending on who you ask (OCLC 2000; Cyveillance 2000), while various estimates made the United States home to somewhere between one-third and one-half of all Internet users in 2000. Make bandwidth cheaper, however, and regional infrastructure develops; bandwidth pricing has been the key factor in keeping the Internet U.S.-centric.

As suggested, that pricing has started to drop, U.S.-centric cybergeography to change, and Internet topology to diffuse. Enormous differences remain from country to country and, within each country, between commercial, residential and rural zones. The U.S.-centric pattern wanes only with substantial and sustained infrastructure builds of the sort that have swept Europe, rolled into Asia, announced themselves in Latin America, and stalled in most of Africa. Yet the wealthy regions of Western Europe and East Asia have become secondary hubs; enormous connectivity differences remain from country to country and, within countries, between commercial zones and elsewhere, but those differences have been transposed onto an emerging three-axis topology. Instead of a lonely hub-and-spoke, the Internet's international infrastructure map has come to look more like a tricycle.

Bandwidth geography may be less U.S.-centric. But Internet globalization is also a question of network ownership—of the bandwidth economy. The global backbone service provider sector has traditionally been dominated by players with strong U.S. roots, and through the late 1990s they moved beyond the U.S. Internet, acquiring counterparts and continuing to invest in infrastructure abroad. As Western Europe and East Asia established themselves as global axes, much of the building and acquiring was done by hungry U.S. providers extending the American provider industry outwards.

Why? Consider: In May 1998 the Australian Competition and Consumer Commission (ACCC) issued—though later revoked—a competition notice requiring dominant backbone provider Telstra to sign reciprocal interconnection agreements with other Australian backbones, making a regulatory issue of Internet backbone market power (ACCC 1998). From September 1998 through late 2000, the issue would be revisited on a larger scale as European Commission and U.S. Department of Justice officials intervened in World-Com's successive bids to acquire major Internet backbone providers MCI and Sprint as well as American provider Intermedia, forcing the divestment of MCI's and Intermedia's Internet backbones and witnessing an abandonment of the Sprint acquisition altogether. Genuity, the Internet backbone provider formerly known as BBN, had in the meantime filed papers with the

U.S. Securities and Exchange Commission noting (2000) that "loss of market share for our services could cause the loss of our status as a Tier 1 provider . . . [which] would adversely affect our ability to maintain our free private peering relationships with other Tier 1 Internet backbone providers."

Genuity's filing underscored the critical role—and uncertain terms— played by interprovider relationships in constituting the international Internet. Because the Internet backbone consists of a series of private network operators who interconnect at various points, providers who sell Internet access are—unlike their regulated PSTN counterparts—in a position to define which operational information they choose to reveal and which is to remain proprietary. Interconnect agreements favor the ISP that operates a more extensive network, generates more traffic, or can offer better connectivity than the other, making a provider's disclosure of information on network activity, topology, or capacity a highly strategic activity. The result is a lack of baseline statistical data, providing negotiating providers with incentive to exaggerate their network characteristics in order to portray access to their network as a tangible and, therefore, valuable service. And that lack of baseline information creates incentive to make a splash—through mergers and acquisitions. Telstra Internet official Geoff Huston has famously described this negotiating process as Internet service providers blinking at each other in the dark. As Huston argues (1999), acquiring other providers is in a data-poor environment rendered doubly advantageous, affording benefits both at a technical level—retention of more traffic within one's own network, adding heft in interconnect negotiations—and for its bluster, by appearing larger to competitors and therefore commanding their respect.

More typical than consolidation under one roof, however, is some mixture of four interprovider arrangements. Two are straightforward: Under the classic Sender-Keep-All (SKA) arrangement, usually referred to as "peering," some form of historic or perceived parity leads each negotiating party to agree that it is easier not to count and not to charge for traffic exchange— though this unmonetized relationship is rarely extended to traffic destined for the negotiating parties' other interconnection partners. Under unilateral supplier-client settlement, on the other hand (usually referred to as "transit"), the downstream provider simply pays the upstream network to carry its traffic, often including traffic to be exchanged with the upstream's own interconnect partners.

The other two models are less simple. Telephony-style bilateral settlement is a refinement of Sender-Keep-All, in that two providers replace perceived parity with an agreement to track actual traffic exchanged, measure the imbalance on a recurring interval—the key variable is how this is to be measured—and pay for the difference. Under multilateral settlement, several providers construct shared facilities, such as an Internet exchange point, and agree to share the costs involved. This makes multilateral settlement hard to follow: Inevitably, it encompasses secondary arrangements that may range from simple SKA among all providers present at the facility to a more complex series of nested bilateral relationships—or some combination thereof.

A review of the four models confirms Huston's "blinking in the dark" theory. In each case, horizontal concentration in the Internet backbone segment translates to significant negotiating leverage; any provider responsible for routing a large portion of Internet traffic is difficult for others to avoid or bypass if they are to ensure connectivity to the whole Internet. A dominant provider is in a position to leverage its market power via both discriminatory pricing for interconnection and nonprice discrimination, which degrades quality or denies service to potential competitors. By building across borders, a global Internet infrastructure sector reminiscent of the global media empires that trip across the content sector would seem to represent a threat.

From a network standpoint, commonly accepted Internet industry lore posits no more than six so-called "Tier One" backbones who have rich interconnection relationships with all other significant providers. From a geographic standpoint, ten backbones controlled three-quarters of the world's international Internet capacity, slightly up from the 70 percent they had operated a year earlier (TeleGeography 2000a, 102–5). Yet nonregulatory strategies are available to providers seeking to avoid an oligopolized environment. They can minimize indirect traffic exchange by actively promoting use of traffic exchanges and content caching. They can pool traffic via a multilateral settlement model, creating formal or informal joint backbone ventures whose aggregated traffic commands more market power than the sum of the parts. And they can increase network value by specializing in a subset of Internet services, such as data hosting or multicast media streaming, thereby differentiating or boosting their on-net traffic. That widespread synchronization of this type has not occurred parallel to regional appeals for far-reaching regulatory forbearance is often pointed to as evidence of IP network provisioning markets that lack either the maturity or the external stimuli that would promote effective coordinating mechanisms. Consolidation continues apace. While the Internet's bandwidth geography has become less U.S.-centric, a highly centralized bandwidth economy persists.

REDRAWING INTERNET GLOBALIZATION

When is Internet topology global? As this chapter suggests, it is getting there—slowly. Yet something else may be going on. Connectivity indicators for metropolitan areas show that the U.S.-centric Internet's diffusion is giving way to a globalized core of meshed connectivity between world cities. The Internet's five largest international hub cities—London, Amsterdam, Paris,

New York, and Frankfurt—were endpoints for thirty-four of the Internet's fifty busiest routes; combined, the international connectivity of the top ten cities was greater than that of the next forty.

This chapter began by posing the apparent disjuncture between physical and network geography. Ironically, that disjuncture may be intensifying. Network geography is wrought, as we have seen, of material infrastructure. Yet the effect of that infrastructure may be to strew the division between upper-tier and lower-tier places across the globe. Take the U.S.-oriented bent of the global backbone provider sector: by 2000, non-U.S. providers had begun to make major strides in holding their own on the global Internet, a combination of newcomers and PTTs hailing from Europe and Asia beginning not only to play important regional roles at home, but also to build out their networks on the U.S. players' home turf, even to acquire major providers themselves. Take the domain name system's character set, which maps Internet geography as English-language territory: At this writing, multiple efforts toward a multilingual name space were well under way. In each case, an apparent regional gap is closed—and an international digital divide respatialized as a set of global conditions, geographic distance replaced by economic difference.

In an oft-cited passage, Doreen Massey (1993, 155) has suggested that "we need to conceptualize space as constructed out of interrelations, as the simultaneous coexistence of social interrelations and interactions at all spatial scales, from the most local level to the most global." Understanding Internet globalization is not simply a matter of tracking linear geographical diffusion. The geographies of infrastructures are networked spaces atop physical places; in the interplay between these, territory is configured and inequalities remapped. At the same time, however, the Internet itself is at a crossroads. Convergences that from a technical standpoint might once have seemed unlikely have been latched onto and pursued enthusiastically, spurred on by the network effects inherent in promoting single-standard interoperability between media applications that can then be "processed and exchanged as part of a social system" (Nass and Mason 1990, 53).

How will this so-called new public network accommodate very different types of traffic inside the same links? Some want to solve the problem by bestowing Quality of Service (QoS) provisions upon the Internet Protocol so that networks can distinguish between what needs to be delivered immediately and what needs to be delivered with care. Some, pressed for time, prefer to forego fancy traffic engineering by throwing more bandwidth at the problem, hoping to give every packet the room it needs to get to its destination in style. And some are abandoning the general Internet altogether: Distinct backbones have emerged for self-similar traffic generators like VoIP or the USENET's text- and photo-oriented discussion groups. The so-called Internet, in other words, may be on its way to disappearing altogether, fractured into an increasing number of interoperable but largely separate sections optimized for particular application types. Who will chart this process to ensure that unprofitable portions are not dropped off entirely? For which applications do networks need to be optimized when their starting points are the nooks, crannies, and spokes wedged between physical and virtual spaces and omitted from the technological globalism that animates the marketing of future Internets? To respond to these questions is to replace Internet globalization with what it has been all along: Internet localization writ large.

NOTES

1. ISOC is a U.S.-based professional membership society created in 1992 to act as a nongovernmental institutional and fund-raising umbrella group for the Internet. A self-described "international organization for global coordination and cooperation on the Internet," ISOC's creation marked the Internet's first nongovernmental coordinating body, and as the formal legal entity responsible for the Internet Engineering Task Force (IETF) and Internet Engineering Steering Group (IESG), it is the seat for the Internet's technical standards-setting process. Though its initial intent was to move into other areas of Internet governance, too, ultimately its influence was limited to an informal role that the ISOC's annual INET conferences help promulgate.

2. See, for instance, Innis's work on the biases (1950) and empires (1951) of communications.

3. The maps colored countries according to the volume of deployed, operational bandwidth running the Internet Protocol and connected at one end to Internet facilities within the country in question. Similar country-to-country data sets were at this writing maintained by IDATE (2000) and by TeleGeography, Inc. (2000a, 2000b, 2001).

4. See Dodge (2000) and www.cs.wisc.edu/~lhl/maps/.

5. See, for instance, Johnson and Post's suggestion that the Internet be considered a separate legal domain (1997), or Reidenberg's discussion (1997, 88) of the "emergence of network sovereignty" wherein "infrastructure organizations acquire attributes of traditional territorial sovereignties."

6. In some cases, the names of physically separated dependent territories of other countries.

7. CCITT: Conseil consultatif internationale de télégraphie et de téléphonie, the international telecom standards organization that in the early 1990s was absorbed by the ITU as its "T" division.

8. The NSFNET was contracted out in 1987 to the Merit, Inc., based at the University of Michigan, working with partners at IBM and MCI; the three incorporated Advanced Networking Systems (ANS, later absorbed by WorldCom's UUNET) to handle the operation in 1990. Other backbones were provided by U.S. federal agencies, including NSI (NASA Science Internet), the ESnet (Energy Sciences Network), MILNET (U.S. military network), and an experimental network by dARPA, the Defence Advanced Research Projects Agency (formerly ARPA) which had first funded the

Internet. The Federal Internet eXchange (FIX) points near San Francisco and Washington, D.C., provided traffic exchange between agency networks and NSFNET, binding the networks into a logical system. See Huston (1999, 14, 15) and Salus (1995).

9. A theme paper prepared for a global communication and trade policy conference held two years later (EC 1997) ascribes similar import to the Brussels meeting: "Market opening is central to the rapid growth in the use of new services and of the take-up of innovative technologies, in accordance with the eight core principles agreed to at the G-7 Brussels conference in February 1995. . . . These Principles have become guiding principles for the leading nations in their national strategies and action programmes."

10. "Increasingly," as Colin Scott has noted (1998, 245), "there is pressure to treat telecommunications for regulatory purposes as part of the broader information society apparatus, attempting to develop common regimes for the economic and content regulation aspects of broadcasting, computing and telecommunications."

11. A classic rendering of this business model is outlined in Dallas Smythe's "On the Audience Commodity and Its Work" (1981, 22–51).

12. Rounding out the ten were (in order) Hong Kong, Seoul, Sydney, Singapore, Taipei, New York, and Osaka.

BIBLIOGRAPHY

Agre, Philip E. 1998. "Communities and Institutions: The Internet and the Structuring of Human Relationships." Essay circulated on Red Rock Eater mailing list, 3 May.

ACCC (Australian Competition and Consumer Commission). 1998. "ACCC Issues Internet Competition Notice to Telstra, 28 May." Press release, 28 May. Online at www.accc.gov.au/media/mr1998/mr92-98.html.

APEC TEL. 1998. "A Study of Compatible and Sustainable International Charging Arrangements for Internet Services (ICAIS): Terms of Reference." Online at www2.apii.or.kr/telwg/ICAIS/tor.html.

Berland, Jody. 1996. "Mapping Space: Imaging Technologies and the Planetary Body." Pp. 123–38 in *Technoscience and Cyberculture,* ed. S. Aronowitz, B. Martinsons, and M. Menser. New York: Routledge.

Boyle, James. 1997. "Foucault in Cyberspace: Surveillance, Sovereignty, and Hardwired Censors." *Cincinatti Law Review* 66. Online at www.law.duke.edu/boylesite/foucault.htm.

Bukatman, Scott. 1993. *Terminal Identity: The Virtual Subject in Postmodern Science Fiction.* Durham, N.C.: Duke University Press.

Charland, Maurice. 1986. "Technological Nationalism." *Canadian Journal of Political and Social Theory* 10, nos. 1–2: 196–220.

Cyveillance. 2000. "Cyveillance Web Study." Online at www.cyveillance.com/us/contact/form_whitepapers.asp?sc=13.

Dodge, Martin. 2000. "Mapping the Global Spread of the Net." *Mappa Mundi.* Online at http://mappi.mundi.net/maps/maps_011.

Eudes, Yves. 1996. "Bataille pour la liberté sur les réseaux." *Manières de voir,* hors série. October: 37–41.

EuroISPA (European Internet Service Providers Association). 1998. "Good Intentions: The Effects of Telecoms Pricing Policies on the European Internet." Online at www.euroispa.org/telecoms1.html.

G-7. 1995. "A Shared Vision of Human Enrichment." Chair's conclusions to the G-7 Ministerial Conference on the Information Society, Brussels.

Genuity. 2000. S-1 filing to the U.S. Securities and Exchange Commission, 7 April.

Gibson, William. 1984. *Neuromancer.* New York: Ace Books.

Global Reach. 2001. "Global Internet Statistics (by language)." Online at www.glreach.com/globstats/index.php3.

Hargittai, Eszter. 1999. "Weaving the Western Web: Explaining Differences in Internet Connectivity among OECD Countries." *Telecommunications Policy* 23, nos. 10/11: 701–18.

Heath, Donald. 1998. "The Globalization of the Internet." *Telecommunications Magazine,* June. Online at www.teleconferencemag.com/html/issues/issues1998/jun_1998/698global.html.

Hollifield, Ann, and Rohan Samarajiva. 1994. "The Rise of the Trade Paradigm in International Communication Policy: Implications of the National Information Infrastructure." Paper presented to the International Association for Mass Communication Research, Seoul.

Huston, Geoff. 1999. *ISP Survival Guide: Strategies for Running a Competitive ISP.* New York: John Wiley & Sons.

IDATE. 2000. *The World Atlas of the Internet.* Montpellier: IDATE.

Innis, Harold Adams. 1951. *The Bias of Communication.* Toronto: University of Toronto Press.

———. 1950. *Empire and Communications.* Toronto: University of Toronto Press.

Johnson, David R., and David G. Post. 1997. "The Rise of Law on the Global Network." Pp. 3–47 in *Borders in Cyberspace,* ed. Brian Kahin and Charles Nesson. Cambridge, Mass: MIT Press.

Malkki, Liisa. 1994. "Citizens of Humanity: Internationalism and the Imagined Community of Nations." *Diaspora* 3, no. 1: 41–68.

Massey, Doreen. 1993. "Politics and Space/Time." Pp. 141–61 in *Place, and the Politics of Identity,* ed. M. Keith and S. Pile. New York: Routledge.

Nass, Clifford, and Laurie Mason. 1990. "On the Study of Technology and Task: A Variable-based Approach." Pp. 46–67 in *Organizations and Communication Technology,* ed. J. Fulk and C. Steinfeld. Newbury Park, Calif.: Sage.

NSFNET. 1995. "History of NSFNET Growth by Networks." Online at FTP <nic.merit.edu/nsfnet/statistics/history.netcount>.

OCLC. 2000. "Web Characterization Project." Online at http://wcp.oclc.org.

OECD (Organization for Economic Cooperation and Development). 2001. *Understanding the Digital Divide.* Paris: OECD. Online at www.oecd.org/dsti/sti/prod/Digital_divide.pdf.

Quarterman, John S., and Smoot Carl-Mitchell. 1994. *The Matrix: Computer Networks and Conferencing Systems Worldwide.* Reading, Mass.: Addison-Wesley.

Raboy, Marc. 1990. *Missed Opportunities*. Kingston, Ont.: McGill-Queen's University Press.

Reidenberg, Joel R. 1997. "Governing Networks and Rule-making in Cyberspace." Pp. 84–105 in *Borders in Cyberspace,* ed. B. Kahin and C. Nesson. Cambridge, Mass.: MIT Press.

Roth, L., and Gail Guthrie Valaskakis. 1989. "Aboriginal Broadcasting in Canada: A Case Study in Democratization." Pp. 221–34 in *Communication For and Against Democracy,* ed. M. Raboy and Peter Bruck. Montreal: Black Rose.

Salus, Peter. 1995. *Casting the Net: From ARPANET to INTERNET and Beyond . . . .* Reading, Mass.: Addison-Wesley.

Scott, Colin. 1998. "The Proceduralization of Telecommunications Law." *Telecommunication Policy* 22, no. 3: 243–54.

Smythe, Dallas W. 1981. *Dependency Road: Communications, Capitalism, Consciousness, and Canada*. Norwood, N.J.: Ablex.

Steiner, Peter. 1993. "On the Internet, Nobody Knows You're a Dog" [cartoon]. *The New Yorker* 69, no. 20 (5 July): 61.

TAS Group. 2000. "Proposed Draft Recommendation on International Internet Connection." Online at www.wia.org/ITU/ITU-T-SG3/120_ww9.htm.

Teitelbaum, Sheldon. 1997. "The Call of the Wired." *Wired* 5, no. 11: 238–43, 278–86.

TeleGeography. 2000a. *TeleGeography 2001*. Washington, D.C.: TeleGeography, Inc.

———. 2000b. *Hubs + Spokes: A TeleGeography Internet Reader*. Washington, D.C.: TeleGeography, Inc.

———. 2001. *Packet Geography 2002*. Washington, D.C.: TeleGeography, Inc.

VentureOne. 2001. "Q4 Financing Data." Online at www.ventureone.com/Netscape/ii/quarter.html.

Winner, Langdon. 1977. *Autonomous Technology*. Cambridge, Mass.: MIT Press.

Zakon, Robert H. 2000. "Hobbes's Internet Timeline v5.2." Online at www.zakon.org/robert/internet/timeline/.

Index

Abramson, Bram Dov, xi
acceptable use policy (AUP), 30–31, 189; and FreeNets, 37; and Valletri Agreement, 39
access: as domain of privileged, 147–48, 168, 175; to Internet technology and decision making, 91; movements regarding, 147–48; and "open access" requirements, 149–50; politics of, 146–50
activism: and Fidonet, 34; and future of Net, 156; international groundroots, and Zapatista movement, 105; and networking, 37–41; and "open access," 149–50; working through movements, 38. *See also* cyberactivism
Adams, Charles Francis, Jr., 9
Advanced Research Projects Agency (ARPA), 172, 188
Advanced Technology Program (ATP), 31
Advisory Commission on Electronic Commerce, 178
A-Infos, 151
AltaVista, 68, 70–71, 78
Amazon.com, 59–60
American Libertarian Party, 177
America Online, 33, 50, 58
Anik A1, 184, 185, 186

antiglobalization movements, 151
anthropology of Web, 67–70
Apache, 145
ARPANET, 188
Asia-Pacific Economic Cooperation (APEC), 194
Association for Progressive Communications, 40–41, 152
associative reasoning: and entering issue networks, 71–73; as hit-or-miss technique in locating issue networks, 79; as method to evaluate entry point, 68, 69. *See also* issue networks
Aufderheide, Pat, 148
Austin, J. L., 96–97
Australian Competition and Consumer Commission (ACCC), 195
automobile, 6, 11, 14, 16–17
autonomous tradition of civil society, 36–37

backbone service, global, 195–97; and interprovider arrangements, 196–97; for self-similar traffic generators, 198
bandwidth and U.S.-centric Internet, 195
Barad, Bob, 34
Barbrook, Richard, 155
Barglow, Raymond, 11, 16–17

Barlow, John Perry, 102n1
Baudrillard, Jean, 17
Bell, Daniel, 20
Bellagio Declaration, 156
Bellman, B., 100
Berland, Jody, 186
Best Buy, 50
BITNET, 188
Bolt Beranek Newman (BBN) or Genuity, 188, 195–96
Bourdieu, Pierre: and critique of idealist linguistics, 92, 93; and *habitus,* 99, 100, 101; linguistic capital and, 101; and performative utterances, 97; and social and political life, 98, 102; social origin and use of language and, 93–96
Boyle, James, 21, 186
Breen, Marcus, xi
Brussels meeting and Global Information Infrastructure (GII), 190, 200n9
Bukatman, Scott, 185–86
bulletin board system, 33–34
Bush, Vannevar, 86n26
Business Software Alliance, 139, 142

Canada: and activist groups and "Third World," 38–39; and FreeNets, 35, 36, 39; and media and Internet in North, 104–5
Canadian Broadcasting Corporation, 184
Canadian International Development Agency (CIDA), 38–39
Capital (Marx), 166
capitalism: beginning of and enclosures and private accumulation, 130–31; benefits of democracy to, 170; and collectivism, 178–79; four philosophical traditions that coexist within, 176–77; "friction free," 18, 20, 49, 134–35, 143; global financial trading system and, 32; libertarianism and, 177–78; and marginalization of indigenous peoples, 112; and Smith and Marx, 166; social values of, 23–24. *See also* e-capital
Carnegie Mellon University, 137
CERT. *See* Computer Emergency Response Team (CERT)

Certeau, Michel de, 29
Chiapas peoples, 105, 106, 111–12, 120, 121; and television, 109–10. *See also* Zapatista movement
Childers, Peter, 132
China, 89, 101, 153; and piracy, 141
civil society, 36–37
Clandestine Revolutionary Indigenous Committee-General Command (CCRI-GC), 112, 117
Clarke, Roger, 51
Cleaver, Harry, 105, 112, 119, 151
Cleveland FreeNet, 35
"click start" program, 148, 149
climate change debate, 65, 66, 69
Clinton, Bill, 89, 101, 132, 141, 148
"code, technical," 7, 14, 169
collaborative filtering, 82
collectivism, 178–79
Collier, George, 111–12
.com: as entry point into Web, 65; and higher authority thresholds, 82; rise in numbers of, 135
Commercial Internet eXchange (CIX), 189–90
commercialization. *See* e-capital
commodity, information as, 21–24
common carriage, 149
common lands, 130, 131–32
commons, 129; continued existence of in Net, 154, 156; as metaphor for Net, 147, 154
Communications Decency Act, 186
community: creation of new form of, 90; of democracy, 16; and disembodied/despatialized interface, 90–91; homogenous speech and Internet, 93, 94; Internet creating and bringing together, 178–79; technologically enabled, 91. *See also* indigenous communities
community networking, 35–36
Comprehensive Crime Control Act of 1984, 137
CompuServe, 33, 133
Computer Emergency Response Team (CERT), 137, 138

Computer Fraud and Abuse Act of 1986, 137

Computer Professionals for Social Responsibility, 156

Comte, August, 93, 94

consciousness, computers as extension of human, 11–12

consumer product development, 32

Contract with America, 177–78

control: of human behavior, 12; and information in business, 21, 23–24; and internal structure of computer, 13; and microprocessor, 18–19; technology as, 4

convergence of technology and public policy, 170

cookies. *See* Web browser cookies

"copyleft," 145

corporate colonization of Net, 148–50

corporate monopolies, public assistance for development of, 32

counterpublics, 119, 120

Course in General Linguistics (Saussure), 92

Cox, Christopher, 178

"cracker," 136

Crawford, Alice, ix–x

cross-domain participation, 64

Cult of the Dead Cow, 153

cyberactivism, 150–53, 154; independent networks and, 152; and making visible and linking struggles, 153; "new internationalism" or "alternative globalization" and, 151. *See also* activism

"cyber-communism," 155

cyberlibertarian stance, 185–86

cyberspace as separate world, 185–86

cybter-utopians. *See* utopianism, techno-

Cyclades, 189

data processing, 20

Davis, Jim, 147

Davos network, 82

debate, 63–64; and debate geography, 64; globalizing, 70; and "issue networks," 64; mapping spaces of on Web, 66–67; preferred paths for navi-

gators of, 67; similar or different and entry points, 66; topography of, 64–65

Declaration of Independence of Cyberspace, 89, 102n1, 186

Delany, Paul, 132

democracy, participatory, 90, 175; Internet as creating, x, 16–17, 166; skewed brand of created by Internet, 175–76; technological empowerment as only part of, 101

democratic communication technology, Internet as, 105

democratic struggle, new, 122n12

denial of service attacks, 138–39, 152, 153

Denning, Dorothy, 137

Department of Commerce, 31

development workers and Fidonet, 34–35

Diamond, Sara, 43–44n35

digital divide, 147–49, 168, 175; international, and domain names, 198

digitalization, 10, 17; and convergence of distinct industries and social labor, 147; and information as commodity, 22

digital knowledge, development of, 32

Digital Millennium Copyright Act of 1998, 142

discursivity, 64, 65, 66, 82

discussion lists: and entering issue networks, 76, 78; and findings regarding efficacy in locating issue networks, 79; as method to evaluate entry point, 68, 69. *See also* issue networks

disembodied nature of Internet, xi, 90–91. *See also* space

domain names, 132, 198

Doubleclick, 58

Dyer-Witheford, Nick, x, xi, 7, 21

dystopianism, 4, 5

e-advertising, 133

easier life, 49

East Timor, 152, 153

e-capital: and access, 146–50; and activist-influenced future of Net, 156; advance of on digital territories of Net, 129; and commercialization menacing more inclusive Net, 147; and commercial sale of domain names, 132; cyberactivism and hacktivism and, 150–53; doctrine of market supremacy and, 134–35; and eventual business domination, 154–55; free software and, 144–46; and future movement toward cyber-communism, 155; and generating social control within virtual space, 142; and globalization linked to communication, 150; and growth of .coms, 135, 158n21; hackers and, 135–39, 152–53; and liberal coexistence, 154; and ownership of high-level networks by telecommunications companies, 132; pirates and, 139–44; predictions of future regarding, 154–56; subverters of, 135–53; and triad of oligopolistic Interest controlling Internet, 134. *See also* access; capitalism

economic development, 192

economic meltdown of Internet of 2000/2001, 155, 168, 176

economy: information as commodity and, 21–24; and labor and information, 18–20; reduction of uncertainty and, 20–21

Ejército Zapatista de la Liberación (EZLN, or Zapatista National Liberation Army), 107; background of, 111; *encuentros* gatherings and, 117–18; and negotiations with Mexican government, 120; radio and, 107; and resistance to all authoritarian hierarchical structures, 117; television and, 109–10; use of arms in 1994, 111–12; Web page of, 112–19, 123n17. *See also* Zapatista movement

electricity, 29

Electronic Disturbance Theatre, 152

Electronic Frontier Foundation, 137, 186

Ellul, Jacques, 4, 5

enclosure, 129, 130; versus disclosure, 155; and hacking, 136; and Internet, 132–35; old and private accumulation, 130–31

Encuentro (Encounter) for Humanity and Against Neo-Liberalism, 117–18

English as global language, 95, 103n11, 192

entry points into Web, 65; and demarcating issue network, 68–69; and differing or similar networks, 66–67; evaluating, 67; methods by which to evaluate choice of, 67–68

environmentalism, 169

e-rate, 148, 149

e-selling, 133

e-tailers and use of cookies, 52

EU-net, 188

European Internet Service Providers Association (EuroISPA), 194

European Nuclear Research Centre (CERN), 192

EZLN. *See* Ejército Zapatista de la Liberación

Falling through the Net: Towards Digital Inclusion. A Report on Americans' Access to Technology Tools, 168, 175

Federal Communication Commission, 174

Feenberg, Andrew, 6–7, 13–14, 24–25n9

felicitous language, 97–99, 102

Fidonet, 33–35, 36–37, 188

fire, 5

Ford, Tamara, 113

Fortner, Robert, 172

Foucault, Michel, 14

Fox, Vincente, 119, 122n11

Fraser, Nancy, 119

freedom: and disorganizing information technology, 23–24; enhancement of, 12

FreeNets, 35, 36, 37, 142

Freeport, 35

Free Software Foundation (FSF), 144, 145

French language, 95

freshness, 69–70, 85n13

Froehling, Oliver, 111, 120

FSF. *See* Free Software Foundation

future for e-capital, 154–56

Gandy, Oscar, 21
Garnham, Nicholas, 159n37
Gates, Bill: and cyber-hype, ix; "friction free capitalism" and, 18, 20, 49, 134–35; and *The Road Ahead* and collectivism, 178
General Agreement on Trade in Services (GATS), 190
Genetically Modified (GM) food debate, 65, 68–69; and entering issue networks by surfer preferences, 70–78; findings regarding routes through issues networks and, 78–82; freshness of debate on, 69–70; why chosen for study, 69
GenTech, 78
Genuity (Bolt Beranek Newman), 188, 195–96
GeoNet, 40
Gibson, William, 185
GII (Global Information Infrastructure), 174, 180n7, 190
Gil, Genève, 113
Gingrich, Newt, 177
Global Information Infrastructure (GII), 174, 180n7, 190
globalization, 33; and activism, 106; "alternative," 151; and backbone service providing, 195–97; communication and, 150; debate regarding, 70; as description of Internet, 183; expansion of worldwide markets and, 150; factors in process of Internet, 192–93; of media and communications, 183; and meshed connectivity between world cities, 197–98; seizing on infrastructure of Internet and, 187; spread of Internet nation by nation and, 185; telephones and, 192–93; and world as shrunk and connected, 187
"GM Experiment Will Continue" media story, 74–76
GNU, 144–45
Golden Shopping Centre in Shamshuipo, 141
Gore, Al, ix, 132, 180n7; and Global Information Infrastructure, 190; and

HPCA, 31; and universal Internet service, 35, 174, 176
.gov: and higher authority thresholds, 82; as entry point into Web, 65; as highly intranetworked, 66
government, hating and distrust of, 177–78
government intervention, 165. *See also* policy, Internet public
Graham, Gordon, 9
Gramsci, Antonio, 37
GreeNet, 40
Greenpeace, 65–66, 69, 73, 110
Grundner, Tom, 35

habitus, 99, 100, 101
hackers, 135–39; denial of service attacks and, 138–39, 152, 153; ethic of, 136–37; and hacktivism, 152–53; mass, 138; and use of cookies, 58
Hall, Stuart, 29, 115
H & R Block company, 33
Hardin, Garret, 129, 145
Hegelian/materialist tradition of civil society, 37
Herman, Edward, 154
High Performance Computer Act (HPCA), 31, 32
history of Internet, 27–41, 154; academic and research institutions and, 189; activist systems and, 37–41; and competing social forces creating range of networks, 28–29; consumer product development and, 32; and convergence of private innovation and public use, 173–76, *173;* diffusion and, 30; Fidonet and, 33–35; first wave of networks, 35, 132; funding of by government, 32, 172; global orientation of, 33; and infrastructure, 188–89; origin of World Wide Web, 192; period of ideation and prototype development, 29–30; and privatization of Internet structure, 31, 189–90; public networking in early 1990s, 31–32; resistance activities and, 37; and shift to commercial backbones, 189–90; and

TCP/IP, 30, 187, 188, 189; theoretical perspectives on, 29; and unitary technocorporate origin hypothesis, 27–28
Hollifield, Ann, 191
human body, and analogies of technology, 11
Huston, Geoff, 196, 197
hydra, many-headed, origin of metaphor, 129
hyperlinking, 64, 66
hypertextual availability of information, x, 17, 192

indigenous communities, 106–11; and access to audiences through media, 106–7; and Internet, 110–11, 120–21; marginalization of by capitalism, 112; radio and, 107–8; television and video and, 108–10
individual interface, 49
individuality, 11
information: as commodity, 21–22; disorganizing technology of, 23–24; and global economy, 18–20; "perfect," 21; and reduction of uncertainty, 20–21; selling of, 159n37; "wants to be free" and cannot be owned, 136–37, 186
"information age," 8
information explosion, 17
information highway model, 17, 25–26n34
Information Infrastructure Task Force (ITTF), 31
information society, disorganizing of, 23–24
Information Technology boom, 168
infrastructure, Internet: and backbone providers, 195–97; beyond U.S.-centric, 193–95; compared to international voice telephony, 191–92; financial investment in, 186; geographies of, 198; history of regarding policy, 190–91; history of technical development of, 188–89; and hookup by monopoly telecom providers, 189
infrastructures, variety of, 183–84

Institute for Global Communications (IGC), 40
Intel, 61n6
intellectual property rights, 156; and enclosure, 129, 133; and Internet service providers, 142
Interdoc, 39–40
Intergovernmental Panel on Climate Change (IPCC), 69
International Connections Program, 193
International Documentation Centre (IDOC), 39
International Monetary Fund (IMF), 106, 110
International Telecommunications Union (ITU), 191
Internet: and ambivalence as communications medium, 13–14; institutional embeddedness of, 186; meltdown of stock prices in e-commerce of 2000/2001, 155, 168, 176; as Network of Networks, 10, 29; potential fracturing of, 199; price of versus benefits of, 110; statistics of growth in usership, 192
Internet Explorer browser and cookies, 53
Internet Service Providers, x, 191; and anarchic use of Web, xi; arising of, 133; intellectual property rights and, 142
Internet Society (ISOC), 183, 199n1
Internet Tax Freedom Act, 178
interprovider arrangements among backbones, 196–97
Intuit, 115, 120–21, 184; bringing of Internet to, 184–85
Intuit Broadcasting Corporation (IBC), 109, 115, 120–21
Inuvik community, 111
issue networks, xi, 64, 65, 84n3; determination via hyperlinking of relevant players in, 64; entering by surfer-researcher preferences, 70–78; findings of study regarding routes through, 78–82; location of, 67–70; method to demarcate, 68; sampling method, 68–69; similar and different and starting points, 66; transdiscursivity in, 64, 65. See also public trust; search engine

Jennings, Tom, 33–34

Kidd, Dorothy, 107
"Knight Lightning," 137
Kolko, Beth, 118
Kowal, Donna, x
Krammner, Ray, 138

labor, 18–20
Lamberton, Donald, 20
language: coding of and cultural and class positions, 98, 99; existing independently of particular instances of its use, 92–93; "felicitous" and "in/felicitous," 97–99, 102; and *habitus,* 99, 100, 101; individual use of, 96; and linguistic competence, 96; and performative utterances, 97; politics and English as international language, 95; resources of unevenly distributed, 94; and social conditions determining establishment and use, 93–96; social nature of internal to language itself, 93; as sociohistorical phenomenon, 93–94; viewed as functioning "outside" or "above" the physical, 91–92
Language and Symbolic Power (Bourdieu), 93
Lanier, Jaron, 99
"latent ambiguity," 170
League for Programming Freedom, 145
legal approaches to public policy, 170, 171, 180n3
Lessig, Lawrence, 169–70
"level playing field," 89, 90, 91, 99
libertarianism, 177–78; and cyberlibertarian stance, 185–86
Linebaugh, Peter, 129, 131, 139
linguistic capital, 101
linguistic idealism: and homogeneous speech community, 92–93, 94; individual use of language and, 96; and language functioning "outside" or "above" the physical, 91–92. *See also* language
link. *See* hyperlinking
Linux, 145, 146

Lock, Robert, 180n4
Locke, John, 178
Ludd, Ned, 131
Luddites, 24n6

Macintosh computer: and emulating everyday life, 15; and Netscape browsers, 53
Magna Carta for the Information Age, 186
Maori, 107
Marcos, Subcomandante, 109, 122n10; and black ski masks, 116–17; communications to Web site of, 112, 113–14; and *encuentros,* 118; idealization of, 111, 112, 113; as *mestizo,* 115
Marx, Karl, 37, 166
Marxist point of view on Internet, 154–55
Massachusetts Institute of Technology, 29–30
Massey, Doreen, 198
mass hacking, 138
materialist tradition of civil society, 36, 37
Mayan Indians in Chiapas region of Southern Mexico. *See* Chiapas peoples
McChesney, Robert, 154
McDonnell Douglas Corporation, 32
MCI, 89
McLuhan, Marshall, 4, 12–13, 17, 186; and technology forming and affecting human consciousness, 5, 12
McSpotlight, 151
media: alternative producers of, 38; grassroots, and indigenous voices, 106–11; print, 13, 16; visual, 13
media stories, 68, 69; "Depiction of a potential 'story path,'" *80;* "Depiction of the overlay" of media and public trust maps, *81;* and digital journalism versus online news stories, 80–81; entering issue networks and, 74–76, *76, 77;* and findings regarding effectiveness in locating issue networks, 79–81. *See also* issue networks
media technology, theoretical models of, 19, 29

Mexican government: effort in cyberspace of, 119; and indigenous peoples, 120, 199; and negotiation with EZLN, 120
Michaels, Eric, 108–9
microprocessing, 10, 13; and control of other processes, 18–19; magic power of, 15
Microsoft: antitrust case against, 176, 180n1; and commercialization of software, 144; and coupons for commitment to Internet service provider, 50; lack of publicity regarding cookies and, 52; market libertarianism and, 178; monopolistic control of, 134; Network, 133; "open source" software movement in reaction to, 145; preferences of, 62n11
Midnight Notes Collective, 150–51
milk, 72
Millennium Digital Copyright Act, 133
Mitchell, William J., 91, 98
"mobile privatization," 6
modems, 33, 43n22
Mohawk community, 108
Monsanto.com, 65–66, 69, 73
Morris-Suzuki, Tessa, 22
Mosaic, 192
Mouffe, Chantal, 122n12
Multilateral Agreement on Investment (MAI), 105
Murphy, Brian Martin, x, xi
music pirating, 142–43, 155

Nakamura, Lisa, 118
Napster, x, 142–43
National Capital FreeNet, 35, 36
National Commission for Democracy in Mexico, 113
National Information Infrastructure (NII), 31, 35, 132, 174–75, 176, 179, 180n7, 190
National Public Telecomputing Network (NPTN), 35–36
National Science Foundation (NSF), 30, 132, 172, 189
National Telecommunications and Information Administration, 31, 148

nation-state, extinction of and Internet, 184, 186
natural organism, cyberspace as, 18
Negri, Antonio, 23
neoliberal institutions: organized resistance to, 105, 106; and Zapatistas, 115–16, 177. See also antiglobalization movements
Neo-Luddism, 5, 24n6
NetGuide magazine, 27
Netscape, 144, 145–46
Netscape Navigator and Communicator Web browsers: and America Online, 58; and cookie files on user's own hard drive, 61; definition of cookies and, 60–61; and effects of choosing cookie control preferences, 52; and lack of publicity regarding cookies, 52; study of, 50–51; version 3.0, 56–57, 57; version 4.01, 57–58, 59; version 6.01, 58–60, 60; versions 1.12 and 2.02, 55–56
networks, 10; community, 35–36; and control versus freedom, 13; and creation of communities and participatory democracy, 16; cyberactivism and independent, 152; and time and space, 17–18. See also issue networks
new, the, 8–9, 10
New Hackers Dictionary, The, 136
Newman, Nathan, 144, 146
NII. See National Information Infrastructure
nodes: in issue network, 65; and route findings, 80–81
"No Electronic Theft Act," 141
nongovernmental organizations (NGOs), 39, 40; Fidonet and, 34–35; Interdoc and, 39–40; and putting viewpoints online, 63; and symbiotic relationship with media, 38
nonlinearity of new media, 17
North American Free Trade Agreement (NAFTA), 105, 109, 111, 112
NPTN. See National Public Telecomputing Network

NSFNet, 30–31, 188, 189–90, 193, 199–200n8
Nunavut, 115, 121

Oklahoma City bombings, 177
online news stories, 80–81
"open access," 149–50
"open source" programming movement, 144
Open Systems Interconnect model, 189
Operation Sun Devil, 137
oppressed peoples, Internet as forum for, 105
.org: as entry point into Web, 65; as highly networked, 66
Organization for Economic Cooperation and Development (OECD), 32, 33, 193

Paine, Thomas, 177
Palczewski, Catherine, 119
Patelis, Korinna, 50
"perfect information," 21
performative utterances, 97
personal computer, 14, 32, 33
piracy: commercial, 141–43; eighteenth-century, 139; extent and costs of, 139–40; Internet, 139–44; mass, 142; music, 142–43; peer-to-peer, 142–43; and "warez" groups, 140–41, 142
pluralistic definition of Net, x
policy, Internet public: and assistance for development of American corporate monopolies, 32, 172; and code as both utopian and for government private interests, 169; and convergence of public innovation with public use, 173–74, *173*, 178; failure of NII initiative and, 175; lack of during "gold rush" days, 176; legal approaches to, 170, 171; and Marxian view of wealth, 166; no final answer in, 167–68; normative approach to, 166–67, 171; and private interests taking financial advantage of Internet, 170–74; public interests and, 165, 171, 172–74; regulation and, 165, 169, 171, 179; and resources in society, 166; and Smith-

like view of free markets, 166, 169, 178, 180n1; and society meeting citizen needs, 166; table summarizing federal funding of research and development, 172, *172;* values and, 176–79; and Veblen, 166
political discourse, broad participation in, 90
Poptel, 40
portalization, x, 133
Poster, Mark, 90
preference locations, 53, *54*, 55, 56, 58
"preferred placement," 81–82
print media, 13, 16
privacy control options, *54*, 55, 56, 58–59
privacy rights and Web browser cookies, 50, 57
private accumulation, 130–31
privatization of public networking, 31, 189–90
Prodigy, 33
Progress and Freedom Foundation, 186
PSTN globalization, 191–92, 196
public debate. *See* debate
public interest, 165, 171; and funding of research and development, 172–73
public network, new, 198
public policy. *See* policy, Internet public
public service content online, 148, 149
public trust: and "Depiction of overlay" of story and public trust maps, *81;* and "Depiction of the Organizations (and their interlinkings) in the GM food issue network," *74, 75;* entering issue networks and, 73–74; as method to evaluate entry choice, 68, 69; as round table network, 83; and transdiscursivity, 82. *See also* issue networks

Quarterman, John, 188
Questioning Technology (Feenberg), 7

radio, 107–8
railroad, 9
Rash, Wayne, 110
Ravetz, Jerome, 10

Raymond, Eric, 145, 146
Red Hat, 146
Rediker, Marcus, 129, 131, 139
regulation. *See* policy, Internet public
researcher. *See* surfer-researcher
Road Ahead, The (Gates), 178
Robbins, Kevin, 6, 16, 175
Rodman, Gilbert, 118
Rogers, Richard, x, xi
Rosseto, Louis, 4, 5
Roth, Lorna, 107–8
rules that structure uses of technology, 30

Samarajiva, Rohan, 181
sampling method and demarcating issue
    network, 68–69
San Andres Accords on Indigenous
    Rights and Culture, 120
Sassen, Saskia, 66
Saussure, Ferdinand de, 92–93
Scott, Colin, 200n10
search engines: and entering issue net-
    works, 70–71, *71;* findings regarding
    effectiveness in locating issue net-
    works, 78–79; industry of, 50; as
    method of evaluating entry points,
    68–69. *See also* issue networks
selfhood, 11, 15–16
Shannon's formulation, 20
Shell, 66, 84n7
Sholle, David, x
60 Minutes, 109
Smith, Adam, 134–35, 166, 169
Smith, Arthur, 114
social construction of technology, 5–7
social movements, activist, 35–36, 38,
    43–44n35
society and technology, 8–9
software: control over, 134; free, 144–46;
    and piracy, 139–44
Software & Information Industry Associ-
    ation, 139
Software Publishers Association, 139,
    142
space: abolishment of, 13, 90–91, 185;
    capitalism's mapping of, 24; con-
    structed out of interrelations, 198;

eradication of as human constraint,
    13, 17–18
"speech-act theory," 96–97
speech on Internet: and disembodied/
    despatialized community, 90–91; em-
    bodied inequities appearing as shad-
    ows on, 99–101; and overcoming bar-
    riers of embodied difference, 100. *See
    also* language
Spencer, George, 18, 19
Stallman, Richard, 144–45, 146
Stamps, Judith, 20
Starr, Paul, 154
starting points into Web. *See* entry points
    into Web
Strano Network, 152
structuralist linguistics, 92–93, 96; Bour-
    dieu's critique of, 93–96
subjectless activities, 11
surfer-researcher: entering issue net-
    works by preferences of, 70–78; pref-
    erences of, 67–70; recommendations
    of and finding relevant Web informa-
    tion, 66

"Tactical Media," xiin3
taxation, 178
"technical code," 7, 14, 169
technological determinism, 4
technology: contradictory potentialities
    of, 7–8; as control, 4; critical theory
    of, 6–8; definition of, 3–4, 8; design of
    and certain results, 14; as determinant
    of society, 8; digital as deeply schis-
    matic, 175; and evolution of new me-
    dia, 29; giving names to historical
    ages, 8, 9; linked to biological, 5;
    "meta," 19; and "newness," 8–9, 10; as
    simply inevitable, 4; social construc-
    tion of, 5–8; "as tool kit" approach, 6;
    as underdetermined, 7; and utopians
    and dystopians, 4; wireless, 20
Technology Council of Pittsburgh, Penn-
    sylvania, 89–90
"techno-populist rhetoric," ix, x, 89; and
    homogenous speech community, 93,
    94; and linguistic idealism, 92

telecommunications, 168, 190, 200n12
Telecommunications Act of 1996, 132
Telecommunications and Information Infrastructures, 148
Telecommunications Authorization Act of 1992, 31
Telecommunications Control Protocol/ Internet Protocol (TCP/IP), 30, 187, 188, 189; and proposed Quality of Service (QoS) provisions, 198
Telecommunications Policy Roundtable (TPR), 147–48
telephony, international voice, 191–92
television and video, 108–10
Telstra International, 195, 196
Tetzalf, David, 142
Thurow, Lester, 129
time: capitalism's mapping of, 24; eradication of as human constraint, 13, 17
Time Warner/AOL, 134
Torvald, Linus, 145
TPR. *See* Telecommunications Policy Roundtable
"Tragedy of the Commons, The" (Hardin), 129
transdiscursivity, 64, 65, 82
transnational nature of Internet, 90
transparency, 14–15
Tribal Flood Network (TFN), 138
Tsagarousianou, Roza, 175–76

uncertainty, reduction of, 20–21
United Nations and IDOC, 39
universal service, 35, 174, 175, 180n4
University College London, 188
Unix-to-Unix Copy Protocol, 188
"unmarked" communication, 90
URL, and all sites nineteen clicks away from each other, 67. *See also* entry points into Web
U.S.-centric Internet, 193; and bandwidth, 195; versus equitable cyber-geography, 193–94; giving way to globalized connectivity between world cities, 197–98; and in-region connectivity, 194; percentage of Web pages and users in United States, 195

U.S. Defense Department, 29–30
use values, dominant and resistant, 29
utopianism, techno-, 4, 24n6
UUCP, 188
UUNET, 188, 189

Valletri Agreement, 39
values, 176–79
Veblen, Thorstein, 166
Verzola, Robert, 134
video and television, 108–10
virtual/physical overlay, 185–86
visual media, 13

"warez" piracy groups, 140–41, 142
Warlpiri Media Association, 109
Warlpiri of Australia, 108–9
Wasch, Ken, 139
Waterman, Peter, 151
Wealth of Nations, The (Smith), 166
Web browser cookies, 50–61, 133; and changes in cookie preferences, 53–60; and default as not accepting, 59; definitions of, 60–61; hackers and, 58; information on cookies, 54, 55, 56; lack of publicity regarding, 52; and options to limit or disable, 61; and percentage of users changing, 62n12; preferences locations for, 53, 54, 55, 56, 58; privacy control options, 54, 55, 56, 58–59; as public relations challenge, 52, 56; and "Show an Alert before Accepting a Cookie," 57; technology of, 51–52
Webster, Frank, 6, 16, 175
Weston, Jay, 35
White, Wendy, 34
Who Wants to Be a Millionaire, 167–68
Williams, Raymond, 6, 29, 129
Winner, Langdon, 186
Winston, Brian, 29
Wired (magazine), 5, 27; and Canadian North, 184–85
wireless technology, 20
women: and participation as speakers on Internet, 99–100; and Zapatista movement, 123n20

WorldCom, 188, 195

World Trade Organization, 101; and General Agreement on Trade in Services (GATS), 190; Internet activism versus, 152; organized resistance to, 106; Seattle demonstrations of 1999, 28, 110, 152

WTO Civil society site, 152

Yahoo, 59, 85n21

Zapata, Emiliano, 111, 114, 122n11

Zapatista movement, 105–6, 111–21; and activist use of Internet, 106, 111, 118, 119, 120; creation of counterpublics and, 118–19; and flooding of Mexican government's Web sites, 152; focal points of struggle of, 112; mythification and, 114–15; as postmodern revolution, 105; as stimulus for international grassroots activism, 105; symbol of black ski mask and, 116–17; and term "Zapatista," 115; use of television and, 109–10; variety of Web sites, 115; wide agenda of, 115–16; and women, 123n20. *See also* Ejército Zapatista de la Liberación (EZLN)

"Zapatistas in Cyberspace" Web page directory, 105, 116

Zelman, Andrés, x, xi

Zizek, Slavoj, 15, 16, 17

Z-Net, 151

About the Contributors

Bram Dov Abramson (bda@bazu.org) has worked as director of Internet research at TeleGeography, Inc.; as virtual conference director at Videazimut, an international NGO; and, in the 1980s, as SysOp of baudNet Communications, a Toronto-based FidoNet node. He is currently a senior financial analyst at the Canadian Radio-Television and Telecommunications Commission, where his work involves measuring the state of competition in Canada's telecommunications markets.

Marcus Breen has worked as a music and film journalist for *Billboard, The Hollywood Reporter, Music Business International*, and numerous other publications. In the early 1990s he was director of the cultural industries program at the Center for International Research on Communication and Information Technologies (CIRCIT) in Melbourne, Australia, where he coauthored the state's 1994 multimedia policy. Dr. Breen worked as a consultant for the state government of Victoria until 1996 when he moved to the Department of Communication Studies at the University of North Carolina at Chapel Hill. He has worked for Gartner Inc. consulting on telecommunications public policy and regulatory matters. He is currently consulting on telecommunications public policy and regulatory matters for Gartner. His most recent book is *Rock Dogs: Politics and the Australian Music Industry* (1999).

Alice Crawford worked in Interface Design before being lured into a graduate program by the siren call of the academy. She is now a Ph.D. candidate in the Department of Communication at the University of Pittsburgh. Her dissertation research concerns the multiform ways in which information technologies impact the experience and use of urban and domestic spaces. Her ongoing interests are in the cognitive and cultural outcomes of design decisions, particularly in communication media. She currently teaches courses in media and design at Chatham College.

Nick Dyer-Witheford teaches in the Faculty of Information and Media Studies at the University of Western Ontario. He is the author of *Cyber-Marx: Cycles and Circuits of Struggle in High-Technology Capitalism* (1999) and is currently completing a collaborative study of the video and computer game industry.

Greg Elmer is assistant professor of communication at Boston College. Elmer's research focuses on critical and cultural approaches to communication and information technologies, media globalization, and Canadian cultural studies. Elmer recently edited a special issue of the journal *Space and Culture* on the topic of "Archives." He is in the process of completing a book on computer profiling for MIT Press. (elmergr@bc.edu)

Donna M. Kowal (Ph.D., University of Pittsburgh, 1996) is an assistant professor in the Department of Communication at the State University of New York, College at Brockport. Her area of research expertise is the rhetoric of social movements and other forms of political discourse.

Brian Martin Murphy is assistant professor of communication studies at Niagara University. He is author of numerous articles on the international history and political economy of "new" media. His first book in this area was *The World Wired Up: Unscrambling the New Communications Puzzle* (1983) and his forthcoming book is *The Hidden History of the Internet*. He has coauthored an academic Web page on the political economy of global communications corporations (www.mediaspace.org) and currently conducts research at the intersections of African information and communications technologies, media history, independent/alternative journalism, social movements, and cyberspace.

Richard Rogers (rogers@chem.uva.nl) is visiting professor in the philosophy of science and the social study of science at the University of Vienna, assistant professor in new media at the University of Amsterdam, and adviser to Infodrome, the Dutch governmental think tank on the information society. He recently was design and media research fellow at the Jan van Eyck Akademie, Maastricht, Netherlands, and lecturer in computer related design at the Royal College of Art, London. Dr. Rogers may be reached at New Media, University of Amsterdam, Nieuwe Doelenstraat 16, 1012 CP Amsterdam, the Netherlands.

David Sholle is associate professor in the Department of Communication at Miami University (Ohio). He is the author of *Media Education and the Reproduction of Culture* and is currently working on a book on cultural studies approaches to the information society.

Andrés Zelman (zelman@onebox.com) is currently completing his Ph.D. dissertation entitled "Mediated Communication and the Evolving Science System: Mapping the Network Architecture of Knowledge Production in Science and Technology Dynamics" at the University of Amsterdam. He may be reached at the Amsterdam School of Communications Research (ASCoR), University of Amsterdam, Oude Hoogstraat 24, 1012 CE Amsterdam, the Netherlands.